Compositions Book 6

Music for Chorus: Holiday Music

by

Ken Langer

Compositions Book 6

Original Music
for Chorus:
Holiday Music

by
Ken Langer

Compositions Book 6
Music for Chorus: Holiday Music
by Ken Langer

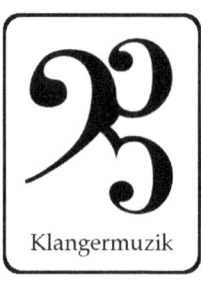

Klangermuzik

Klangermuzik
http://www.klangermuzik.com

First Edition (Softcover)

ISBN: 978-1-300-74829-8

Produced in the United States of America

The author may be contacted at ken@kenlanger.com.

Table of Contents

Introduction

This is a collection of choral works that can be used on special days or holidays. The term "holiday" is used in a broad sense. The music can be used to help celebrate a variety of special days. The first two works could be used for celebrating Thanksgiving. The next two honor holidays celebrated around the Winter Solstice and Christmas. The next piece was written for the new year and that is followed by a celebration of Easter, Spring, or the Spring Equinox. Finally, there is a collection of spiritual songs that use words from the sacred texts of eight different world religions. Each of these can be used to celebrate special days associated with that particular religion.

Works marked with an asterisk (*) in any of the Tables of Contents are published by Yelton Rhodes. Single copies should be purchased from them.. All other works can be obtained through me.

For more information and to hear recordings and transcriptions of music in this and all the other collections please visit http://klangermuzik.com.

Be Thankful

Ken Langer

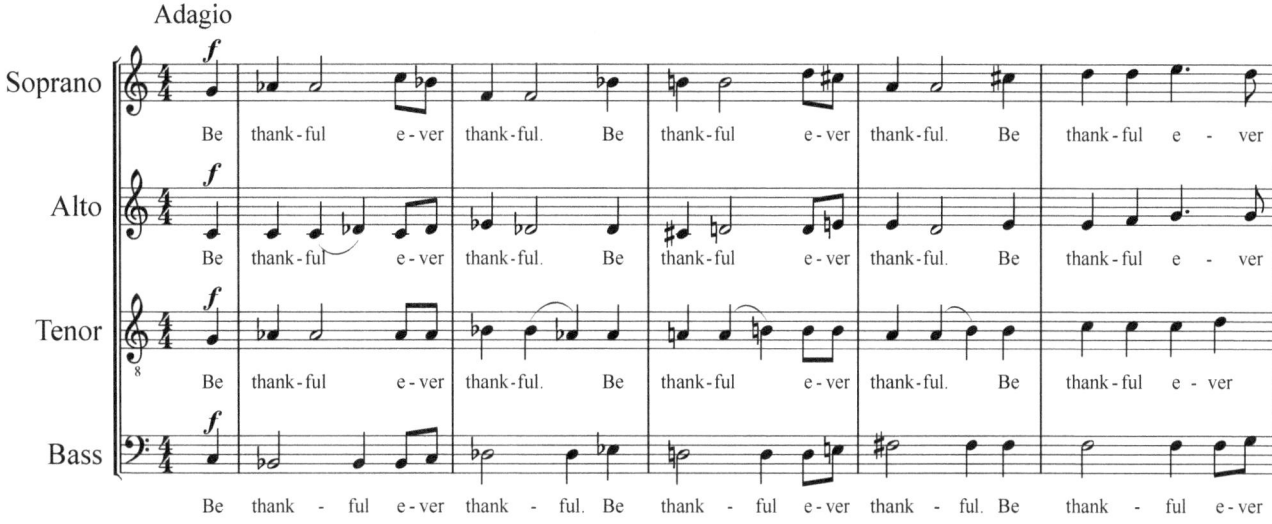

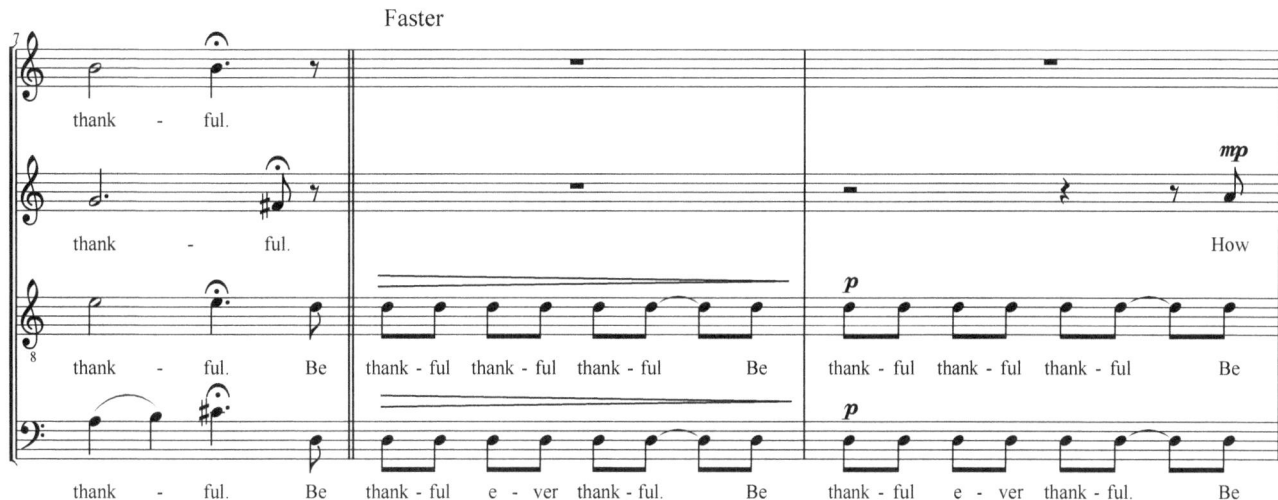

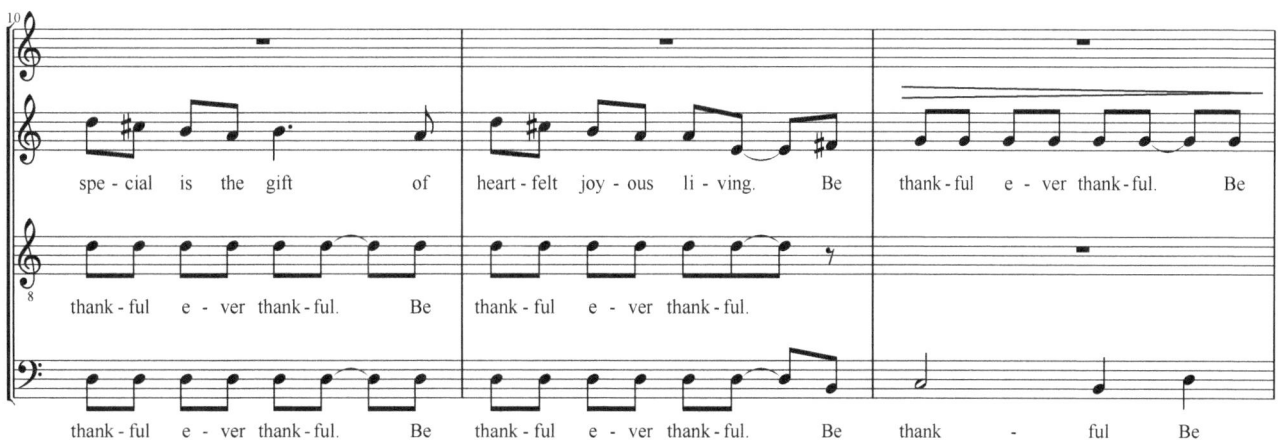

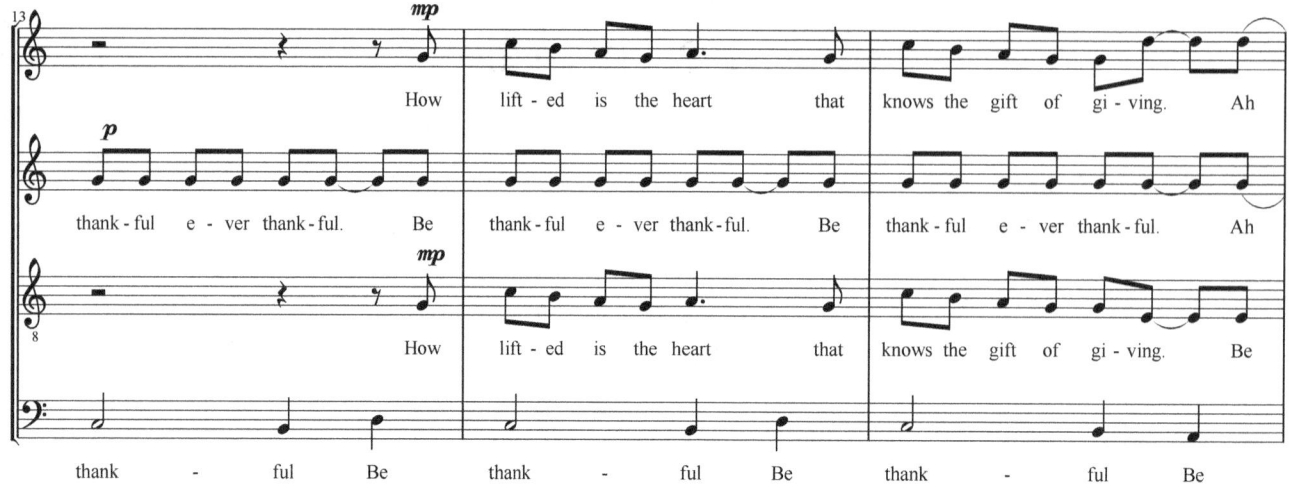

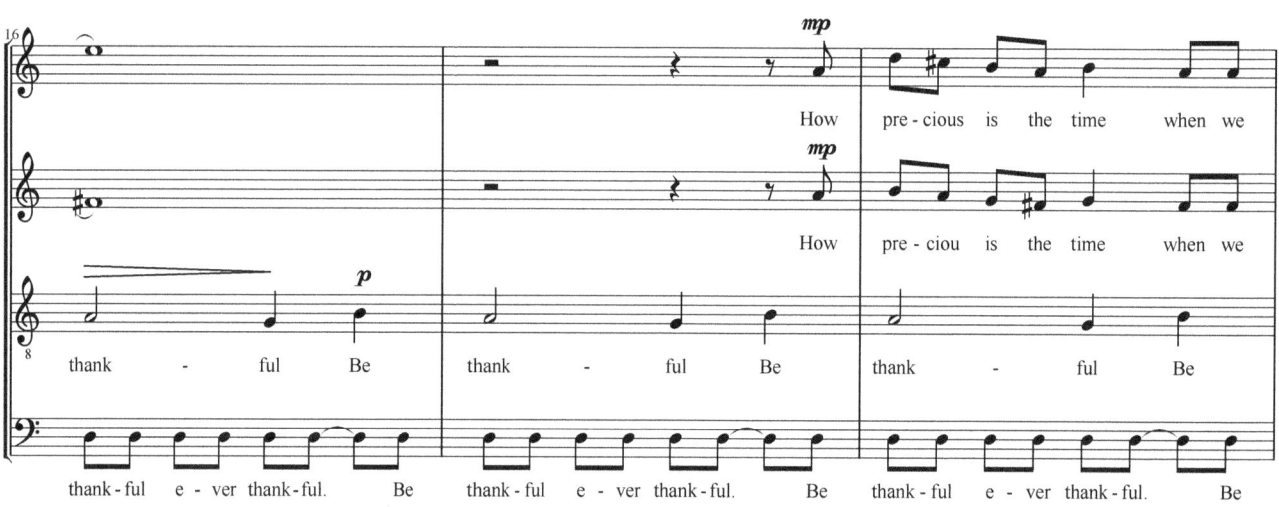

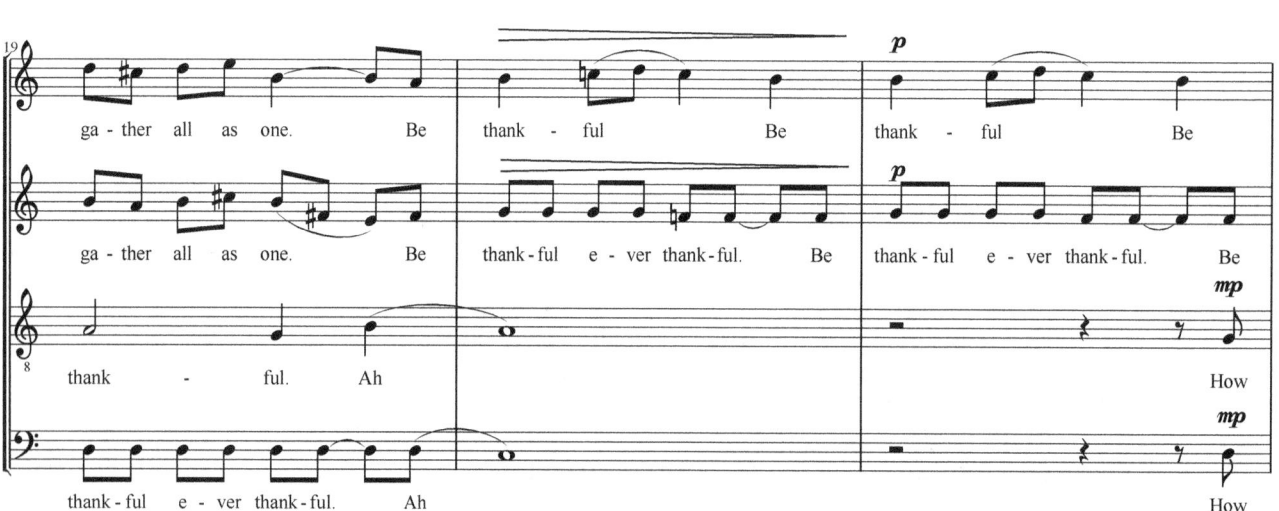

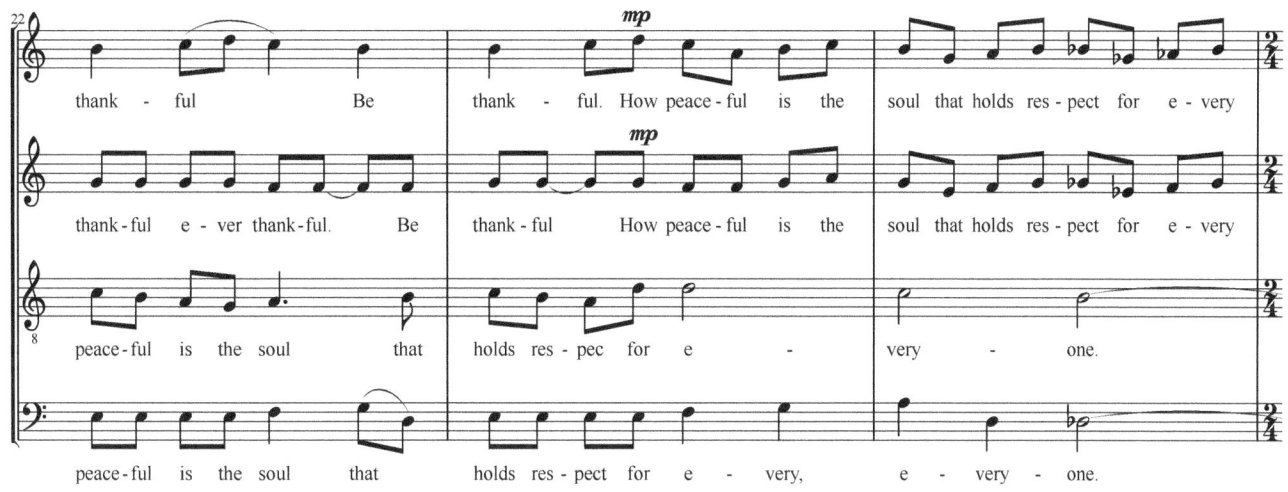

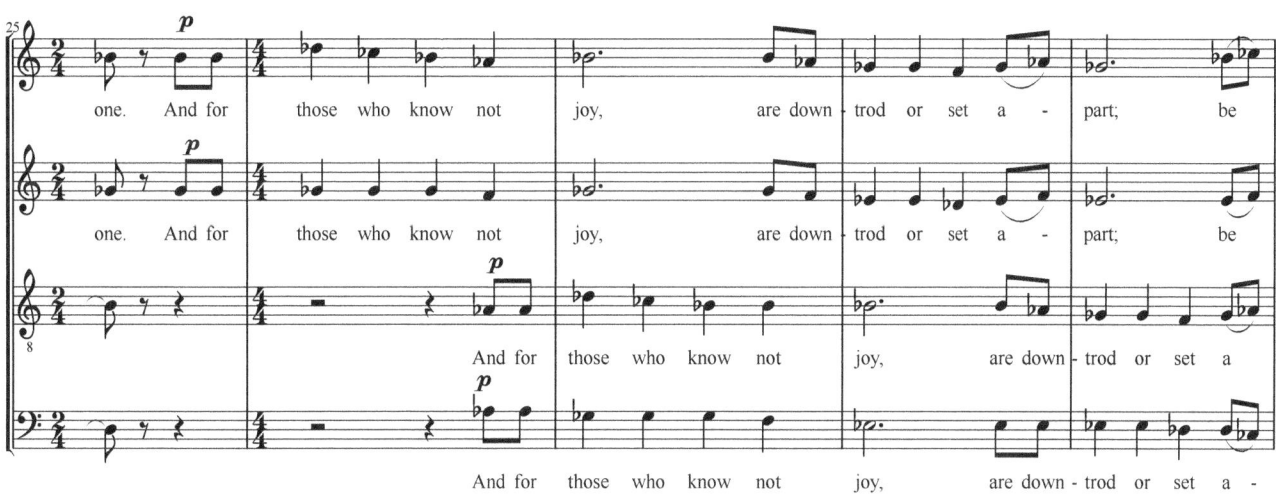

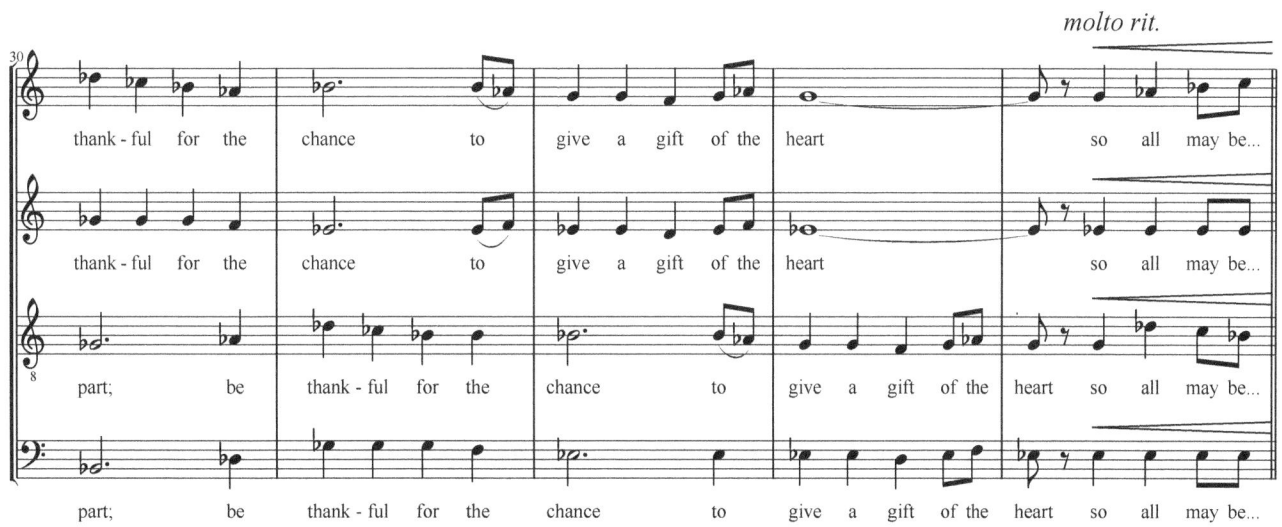

A Tempo

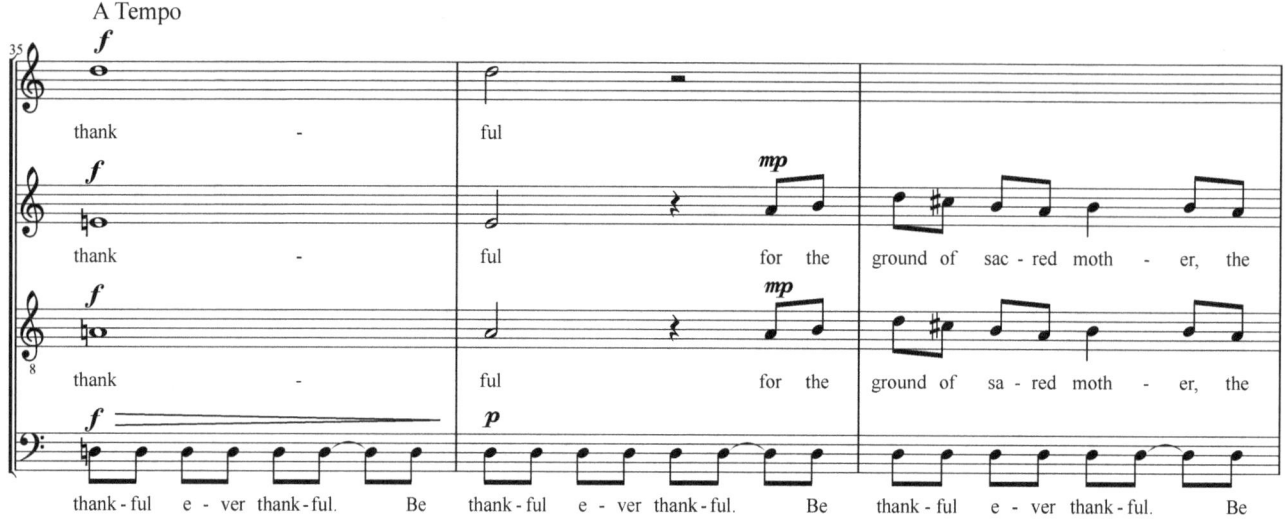

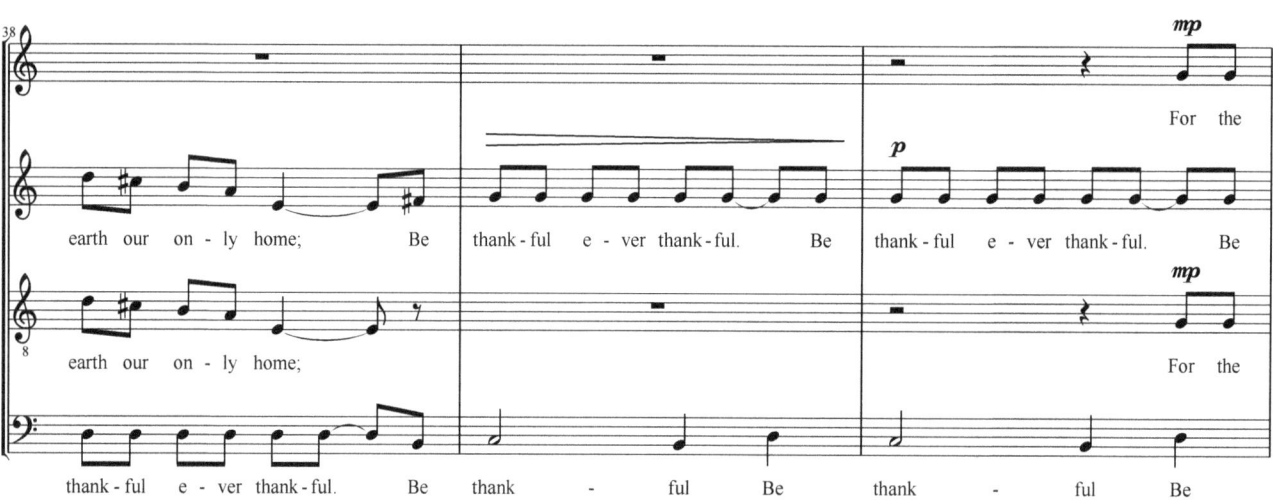

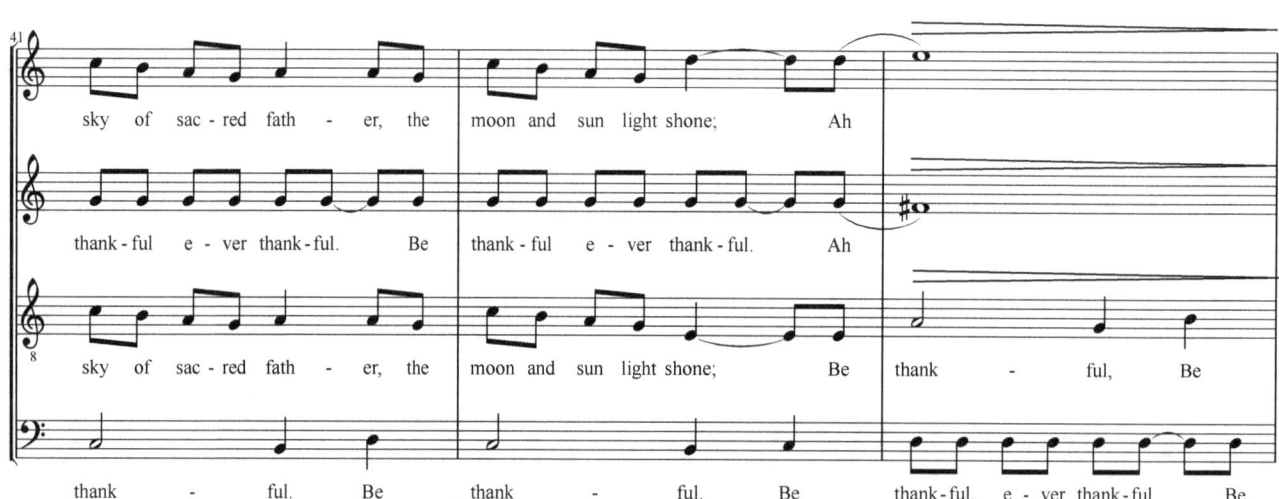

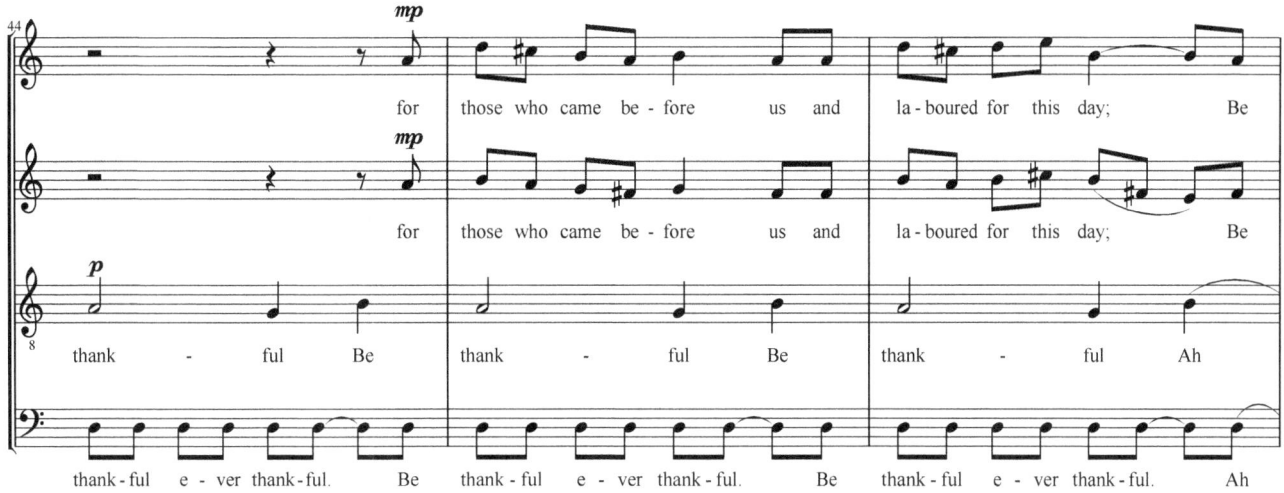

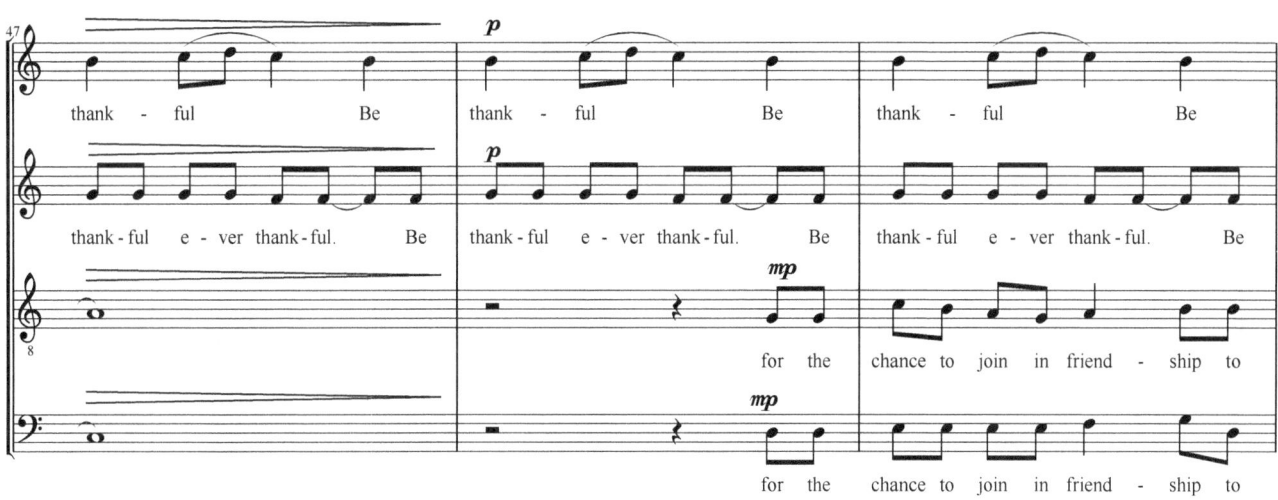

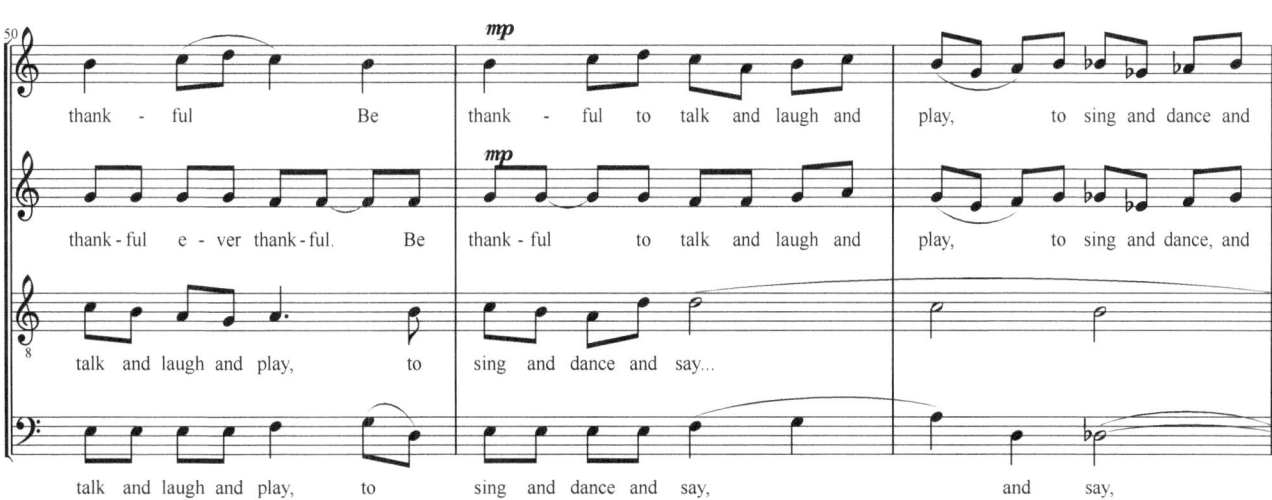

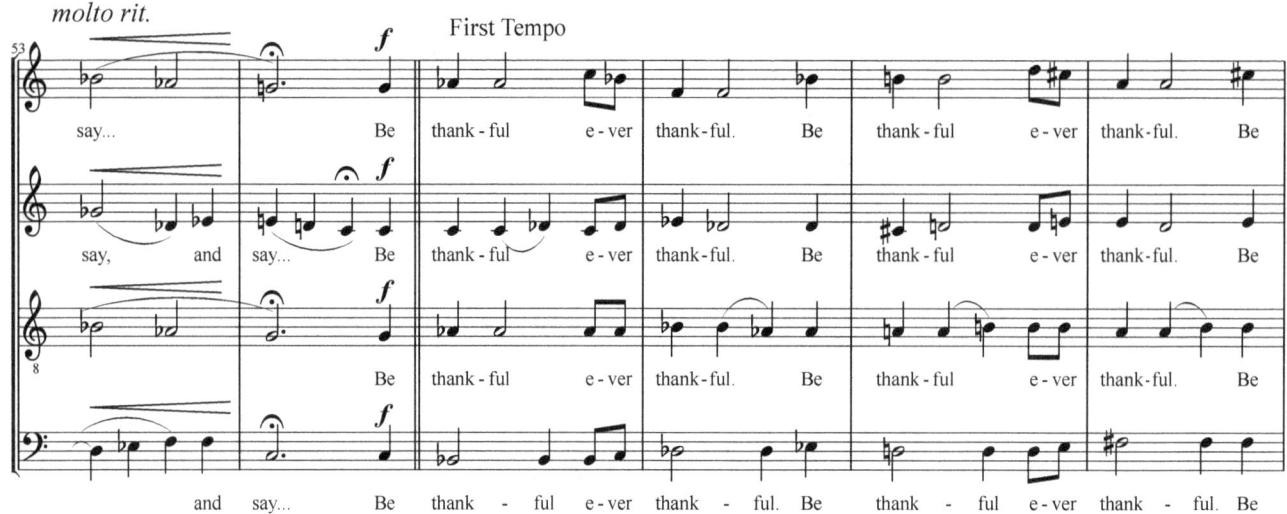

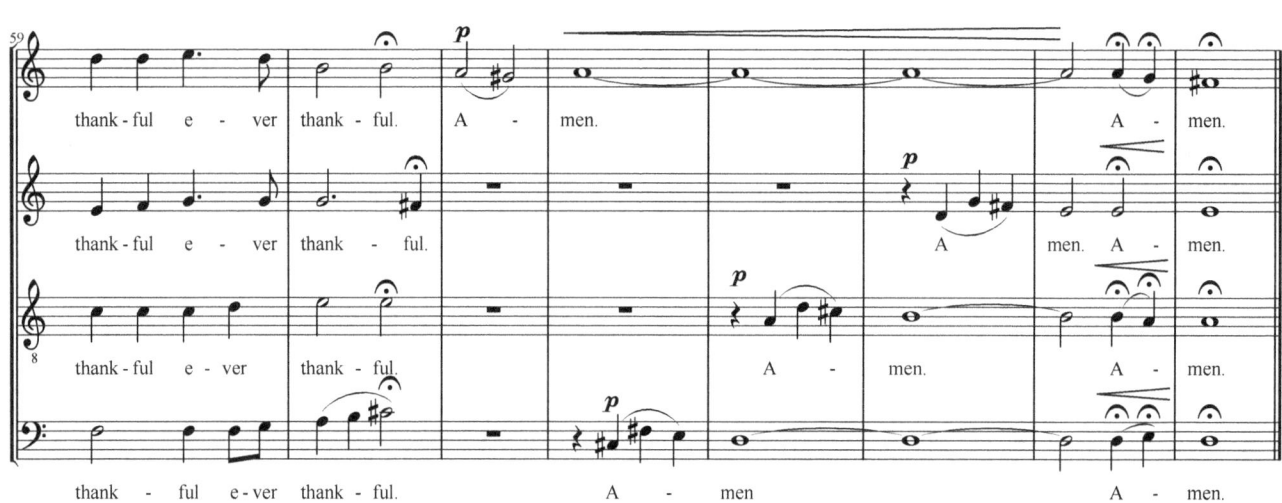

14

A Song of Thanksgiving

(a three part round)

Ken Langer

Moderate

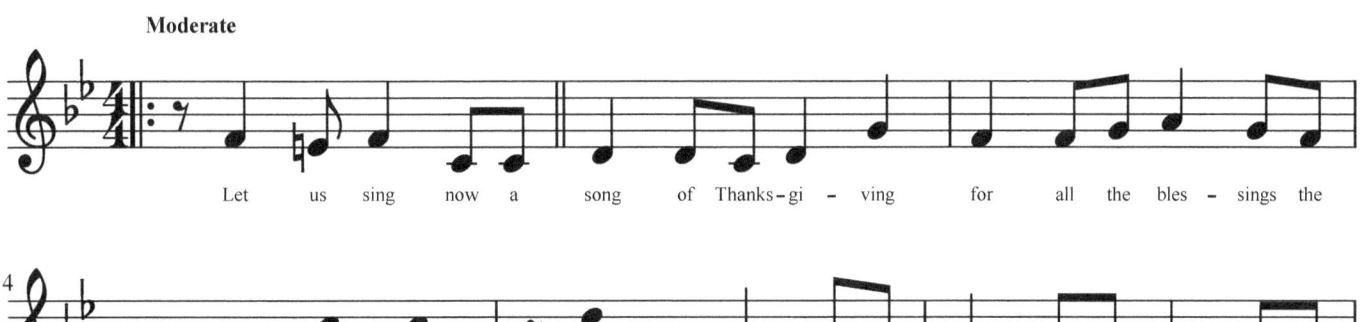

Let us sing now a song of Thanks-gi-ving for all the bles-sings the

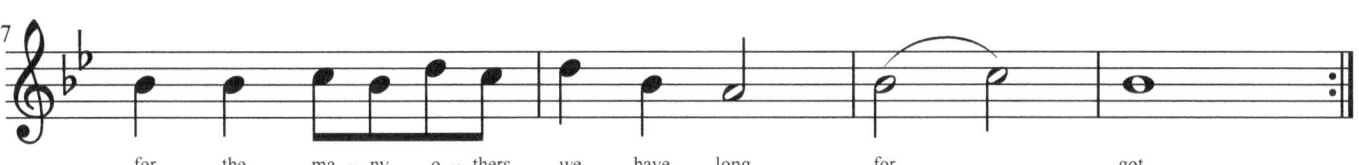

year has wrought and let us sing for those joys we re-mem-ber and

for the ma-ny o-thers we have long for-got.

This Is The Night

Ken Langer

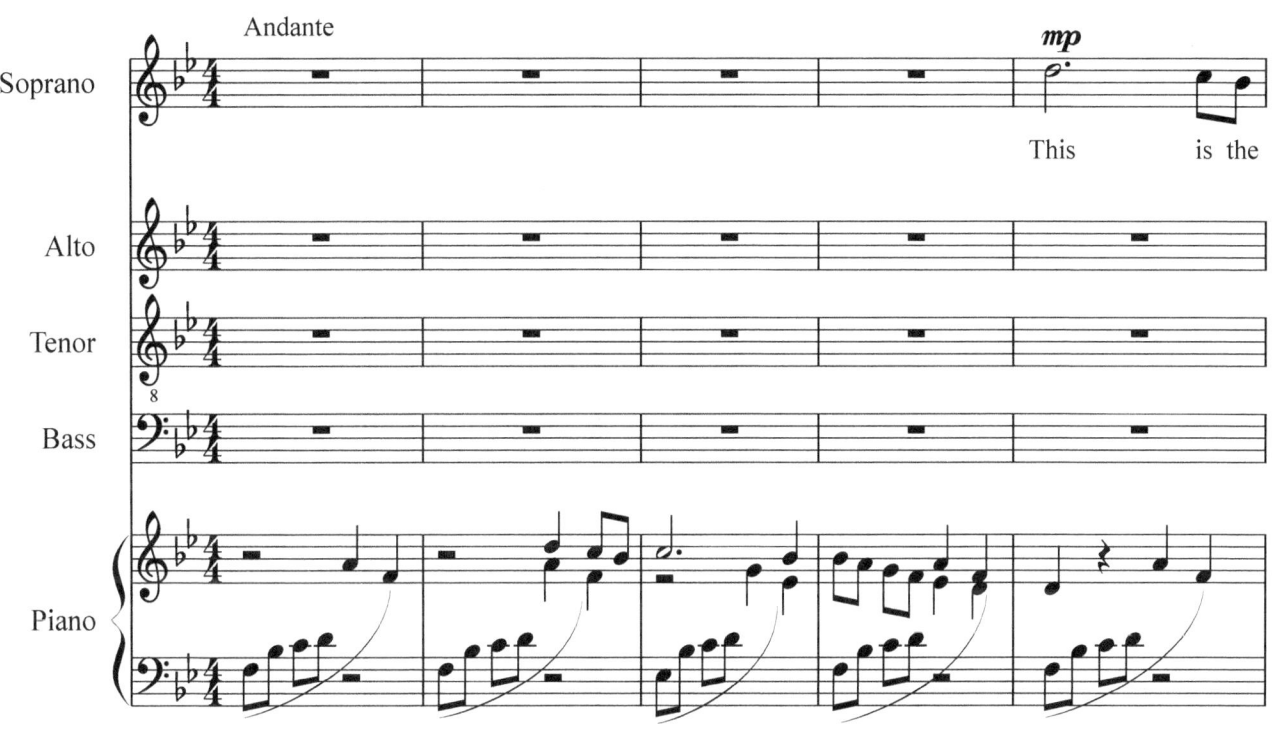

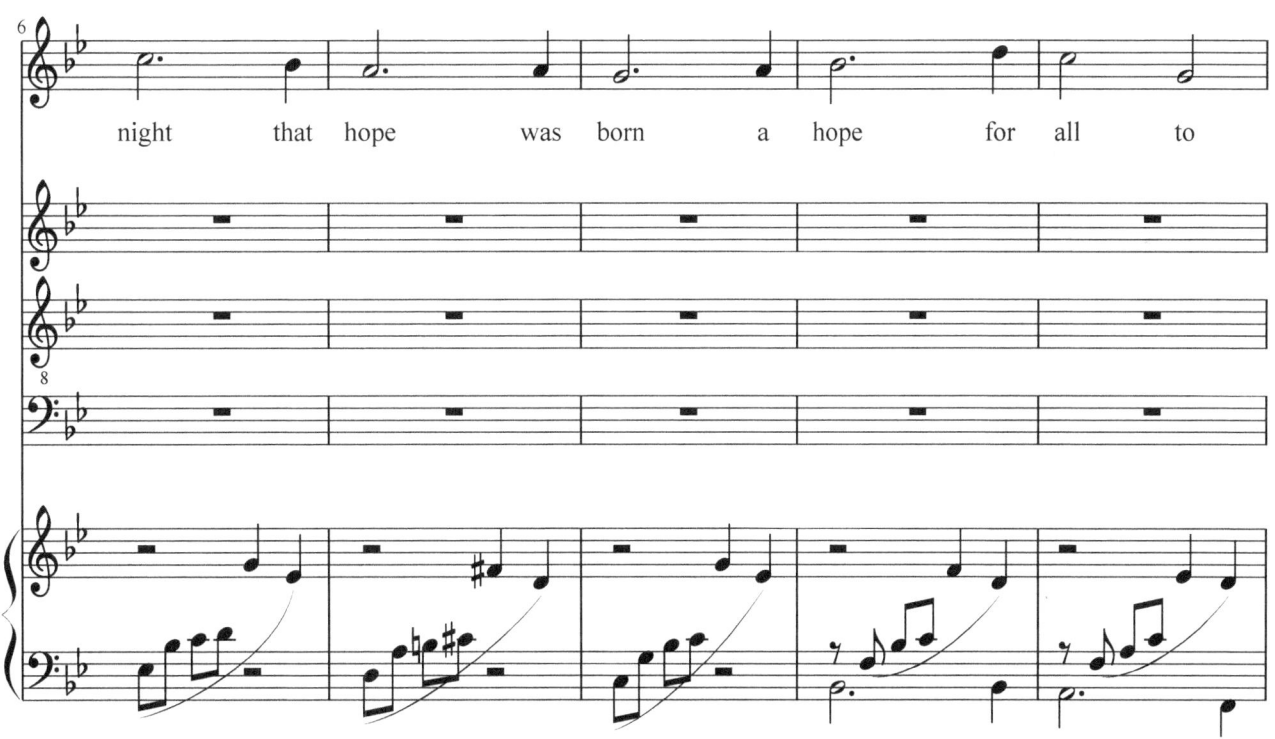

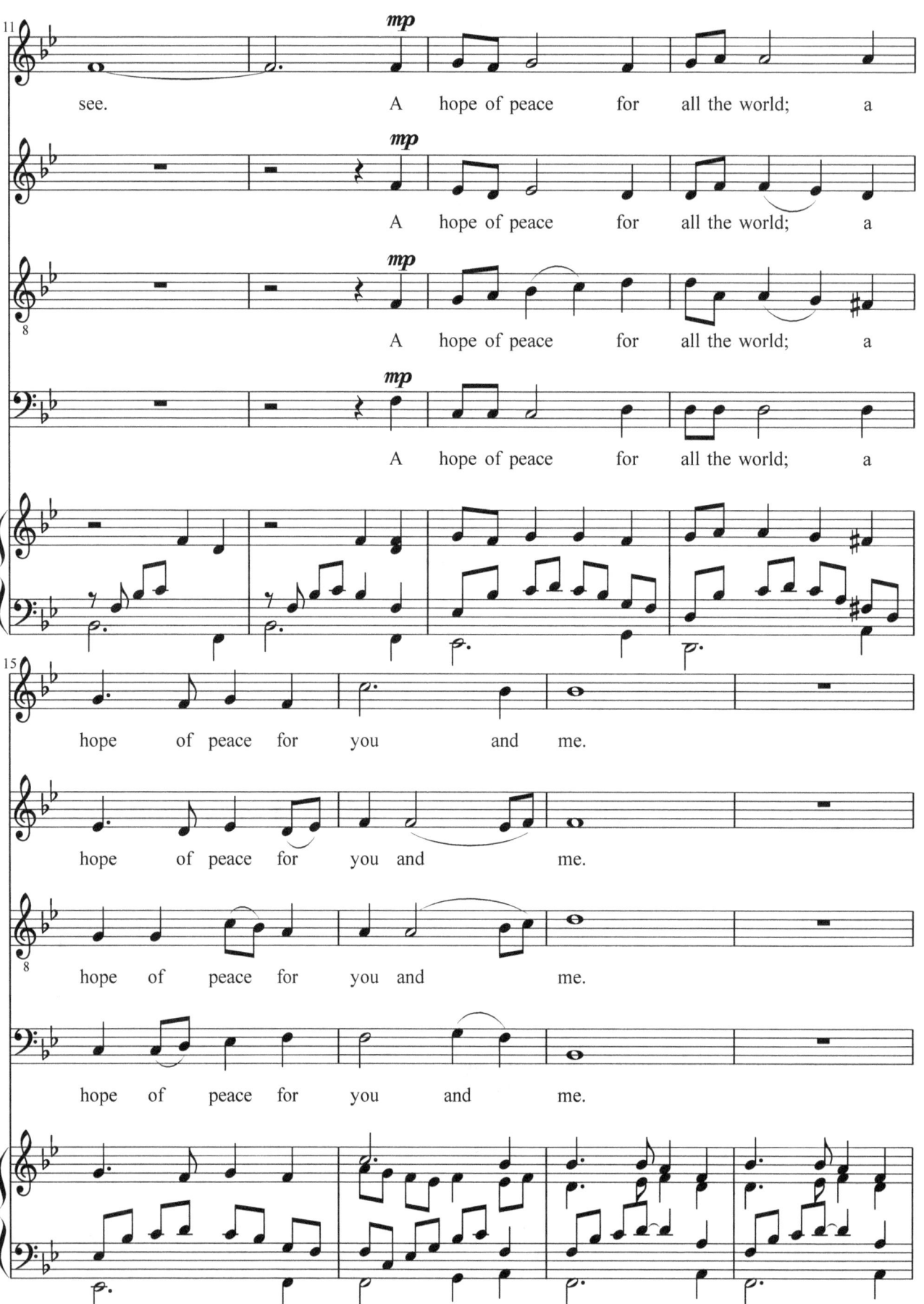

see.
A hope of peace for all the world; a

A hope of peace for all the world; a

A hope of peace for all the world; a

A hope of peace for all the world; a

hope of peace for you and me.

hope of peace for you and me.

hope of peace for you and me.

hope of peace for you and me.

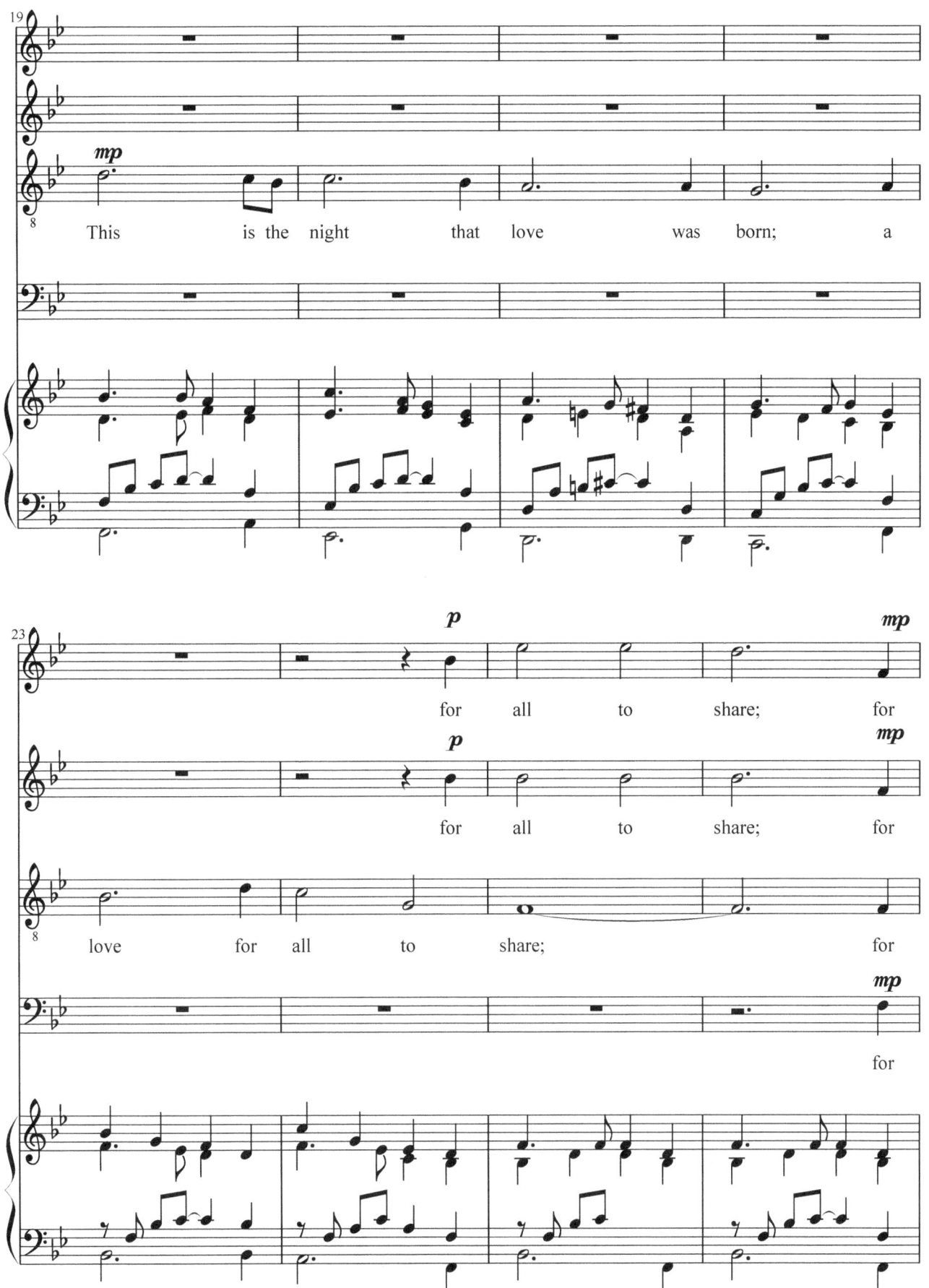

This is the night that love was born; a
for all to share; for
for all to share; for
love for all to share; for
for

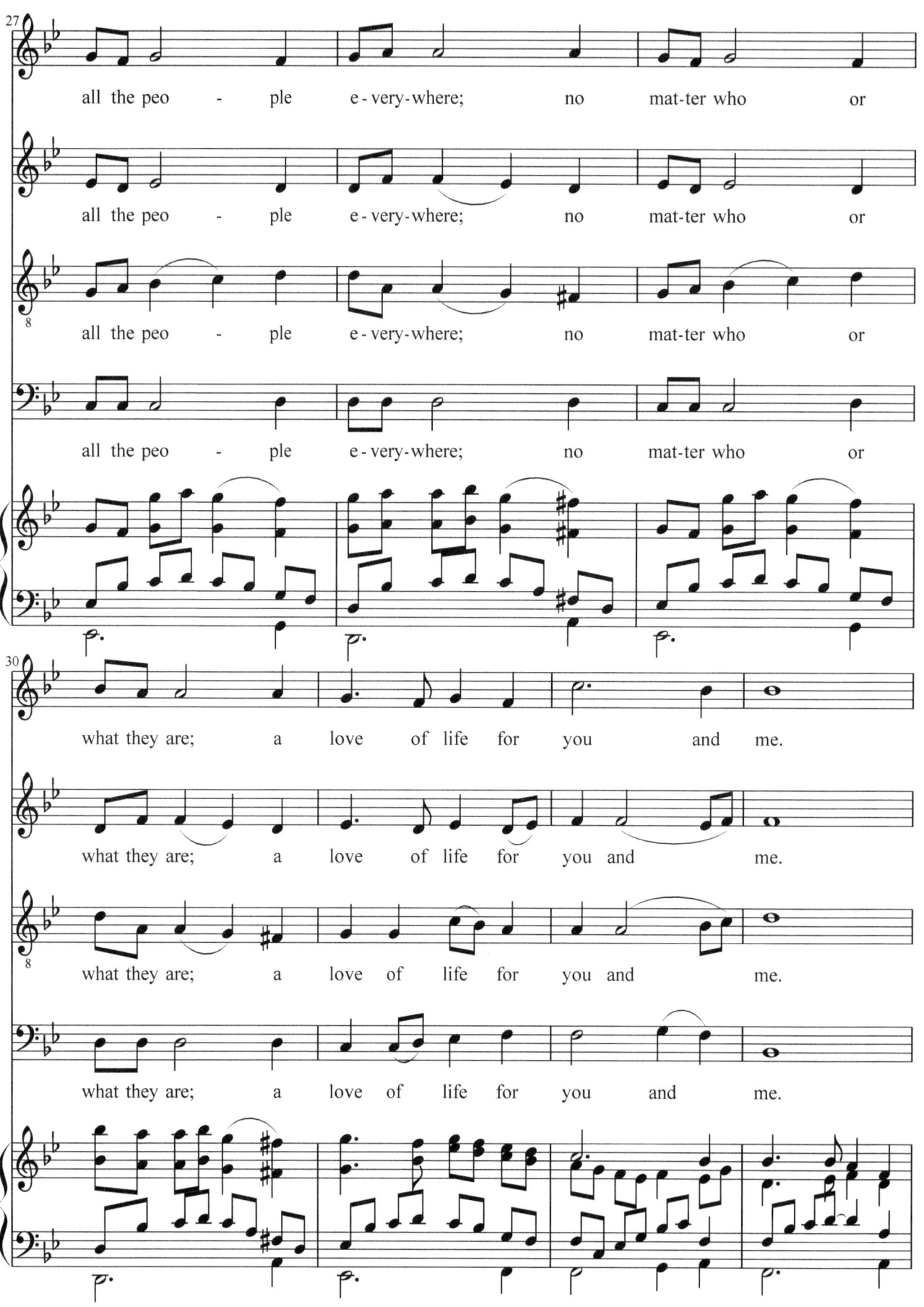

all the peo - ple e - very-where; no mat-ter who or

all the peo - ple e - very-where; no mat-ter who or

all the peo - ple e - very-where; no mat-ter who or

all the peo - ple e - very-where; no mat-ter who or

what they are; a love of life for you and me.

what they are; a love of life for you and me.

what they are; a love of life for you and me.

what they are; a love of life for you and me.

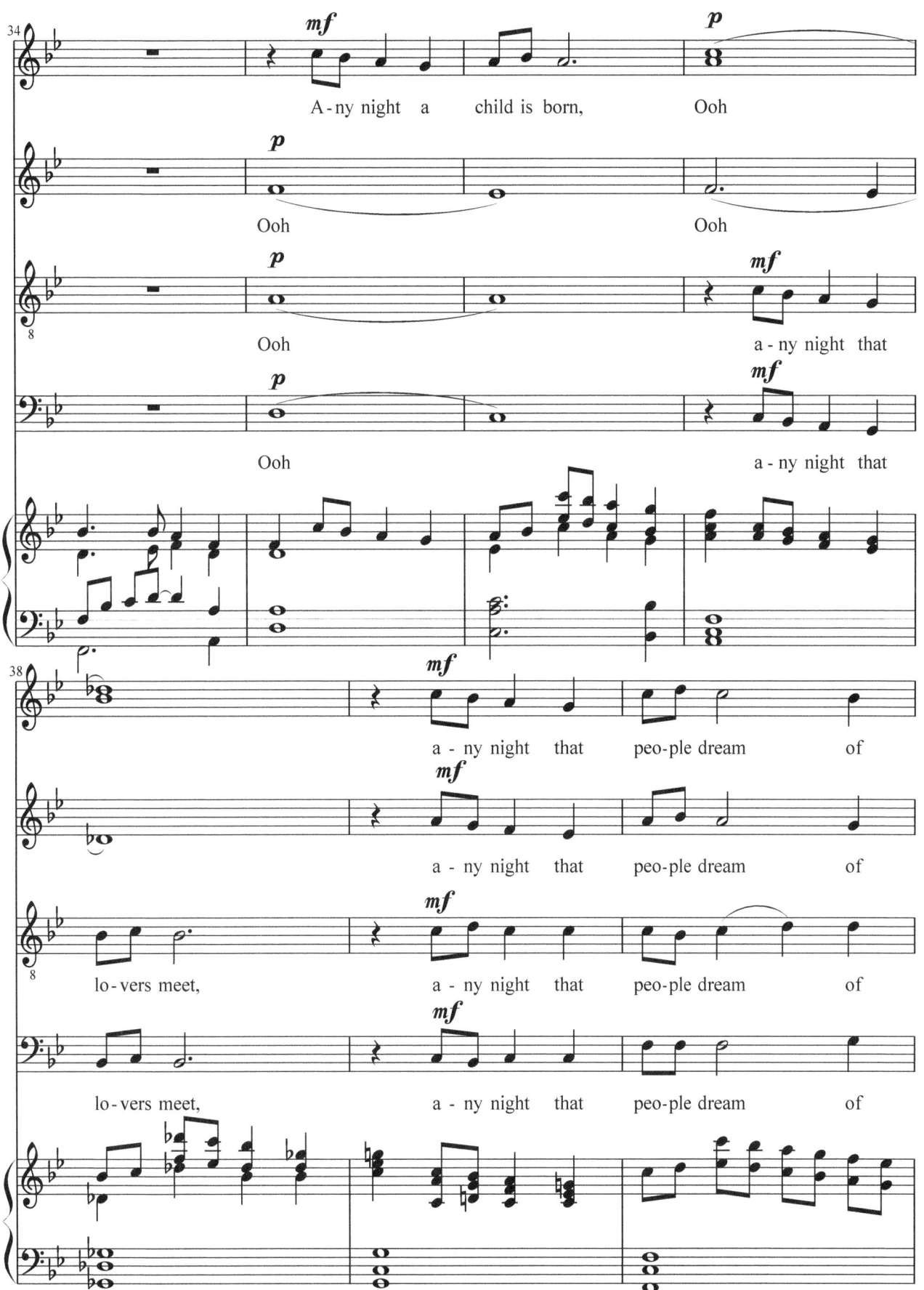

A-ny night a child is born, Ooh

Ooh Ooh

Ooh a - ny night that

a - ny night that

a - ny night that peo-ple dream of

a - ny night that peo-ple dream of

lo - vers meet, a - ny night that peo-ple dream of

lo - vers meet, a - ny night that peo-ple dream of

21

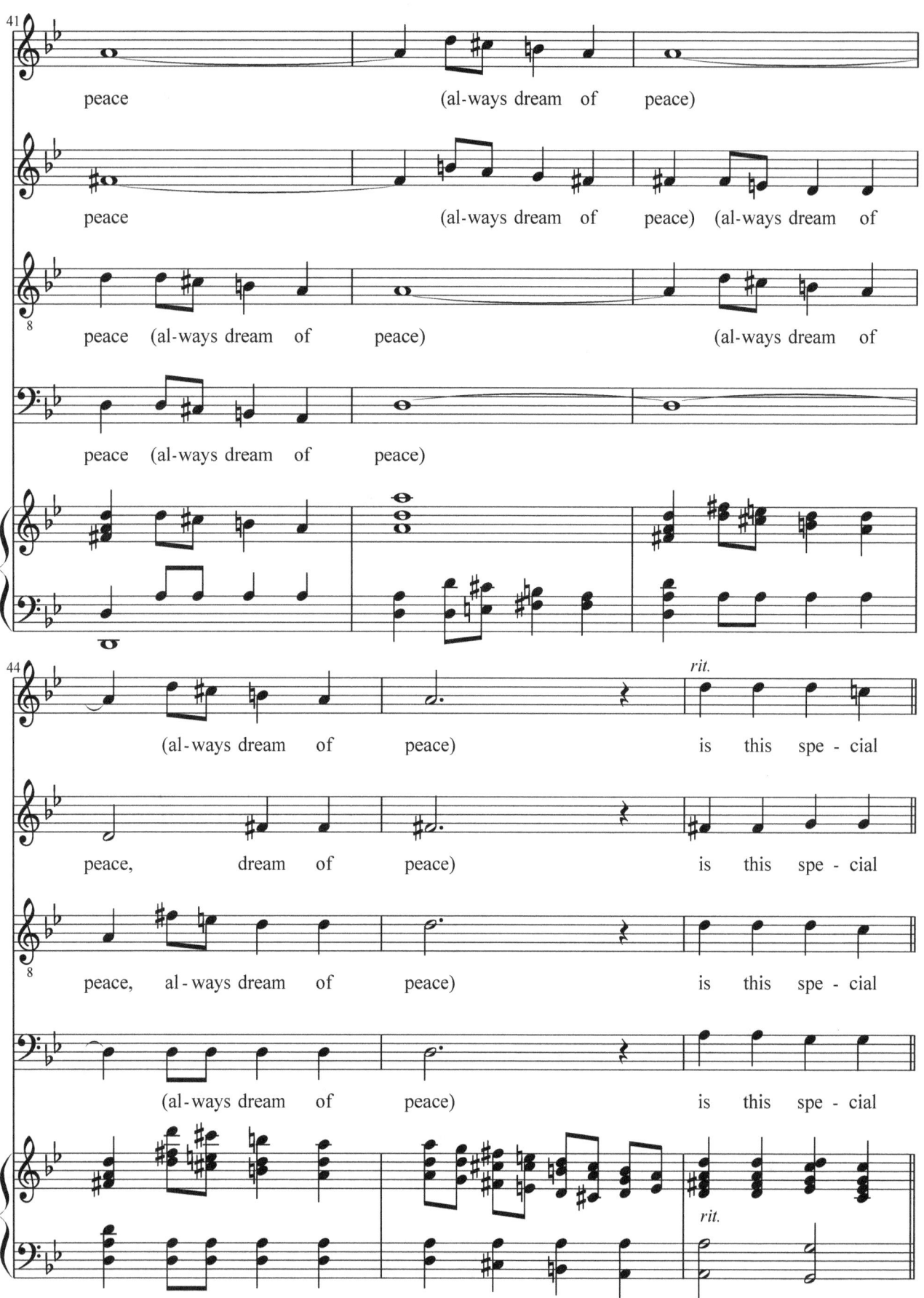

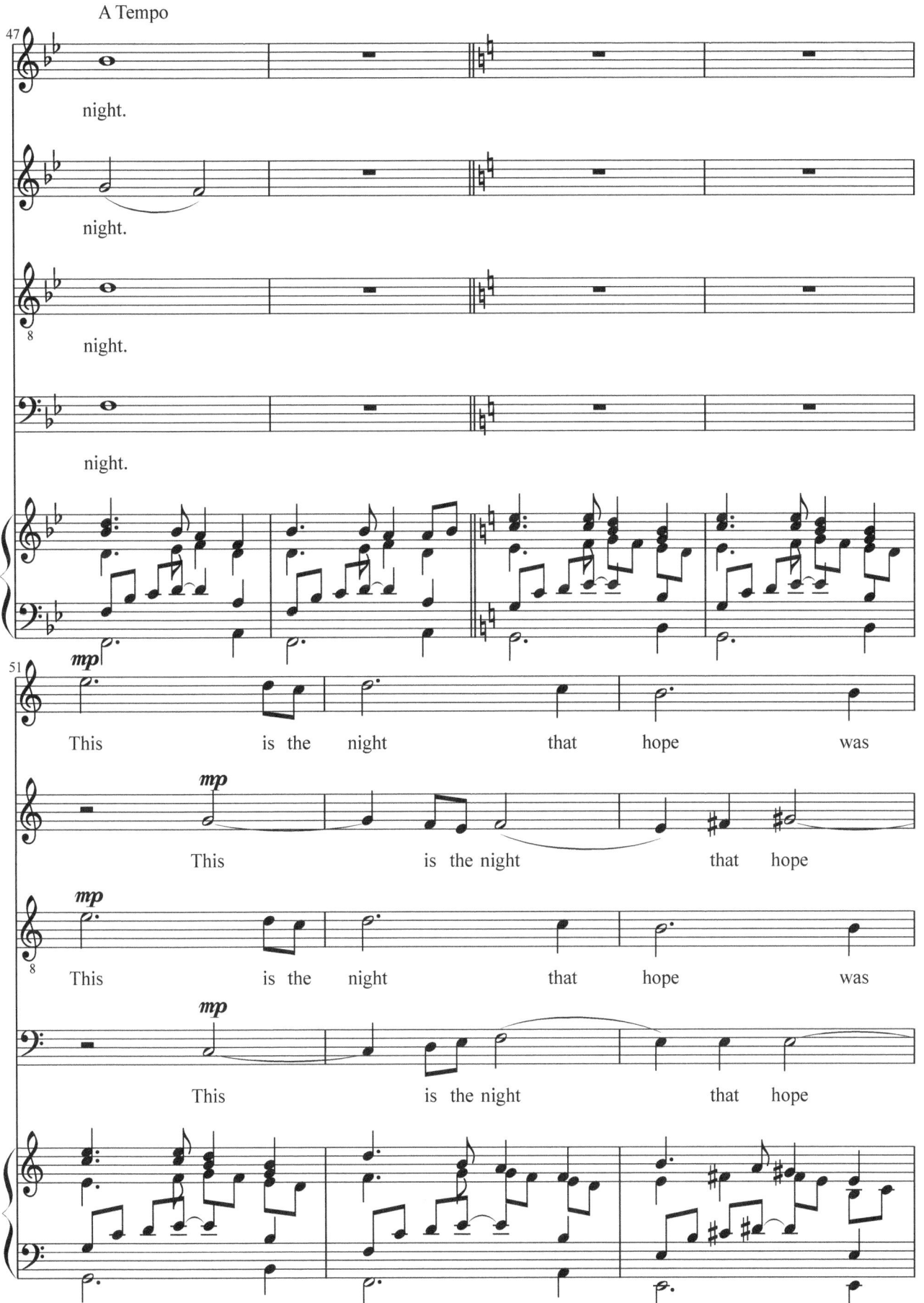

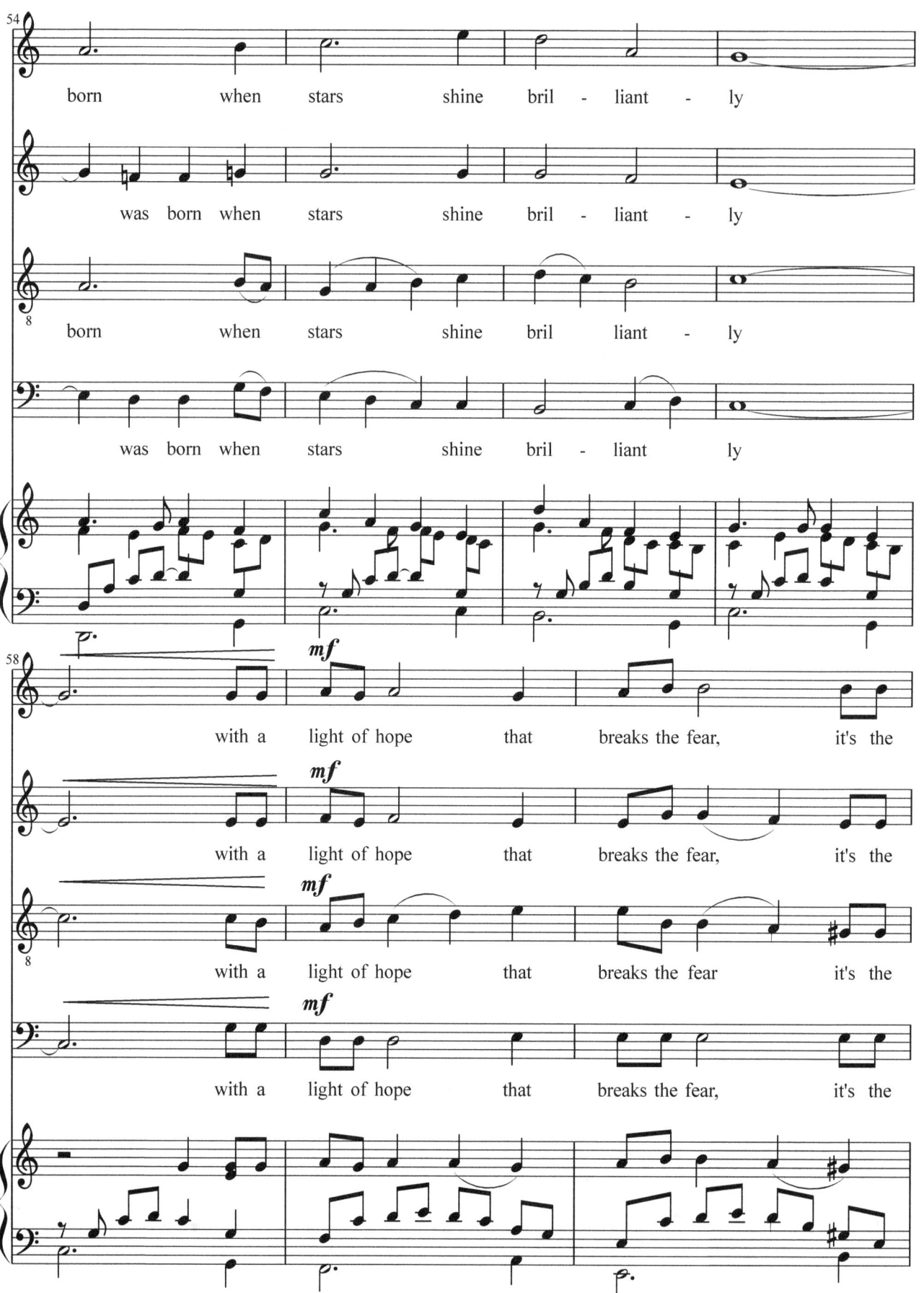

born   when   stars   shine   bril - liant - ly

was born   when   stars   shine   bril - liant - ly

born   when   stars   shine   bril   liant - ly

was born   when   stars   shine   bril - liant   ly

with a   light of hope   that   breaks the fear,   it's the

with a   light of hope   that   breaks the fear,   it's the

with a   light of hope   that   breaks the fear   it's the

with a   light of hope   that   breaks the fear,   it's the

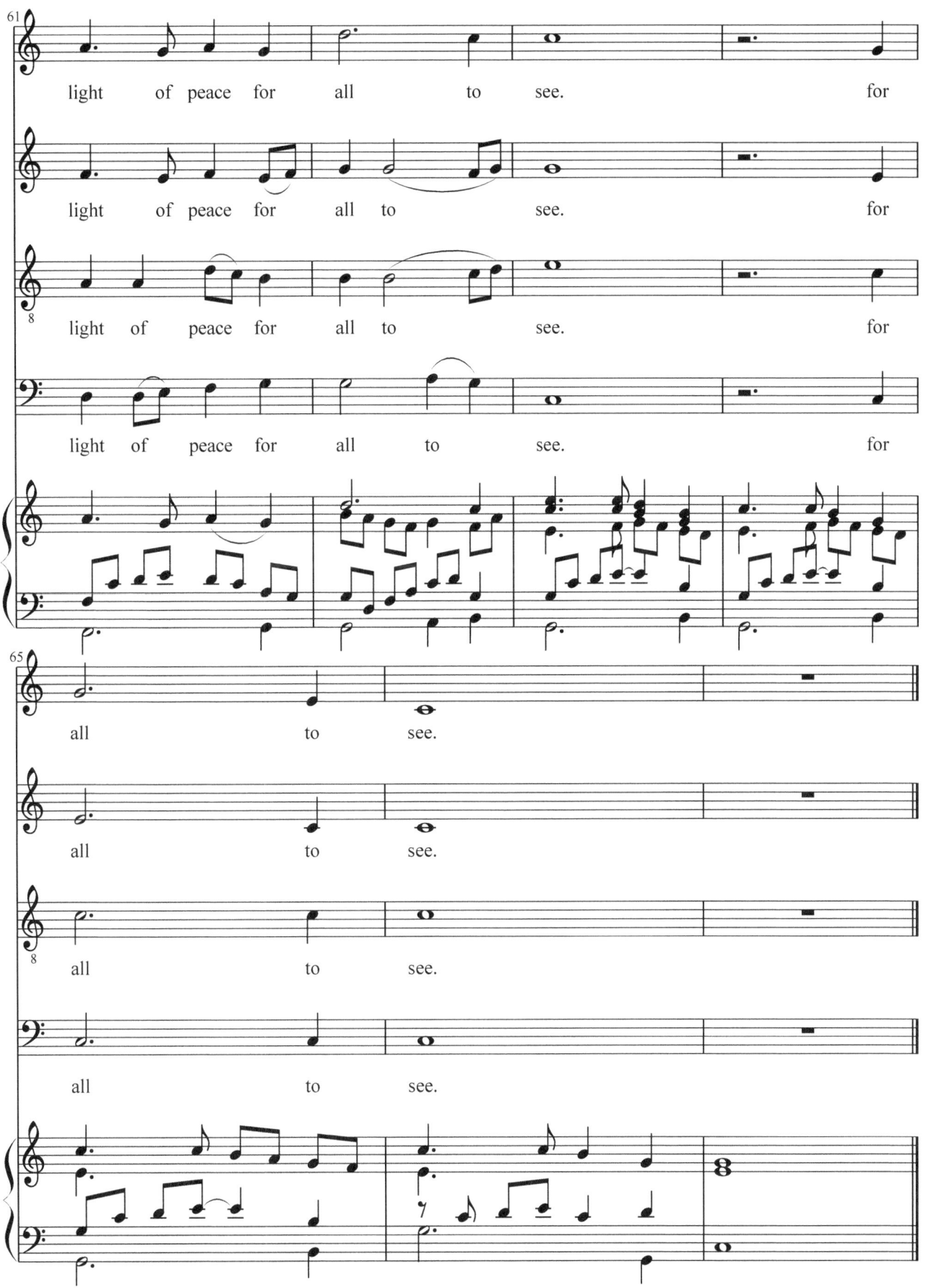

The Season of Light

Ken Langer

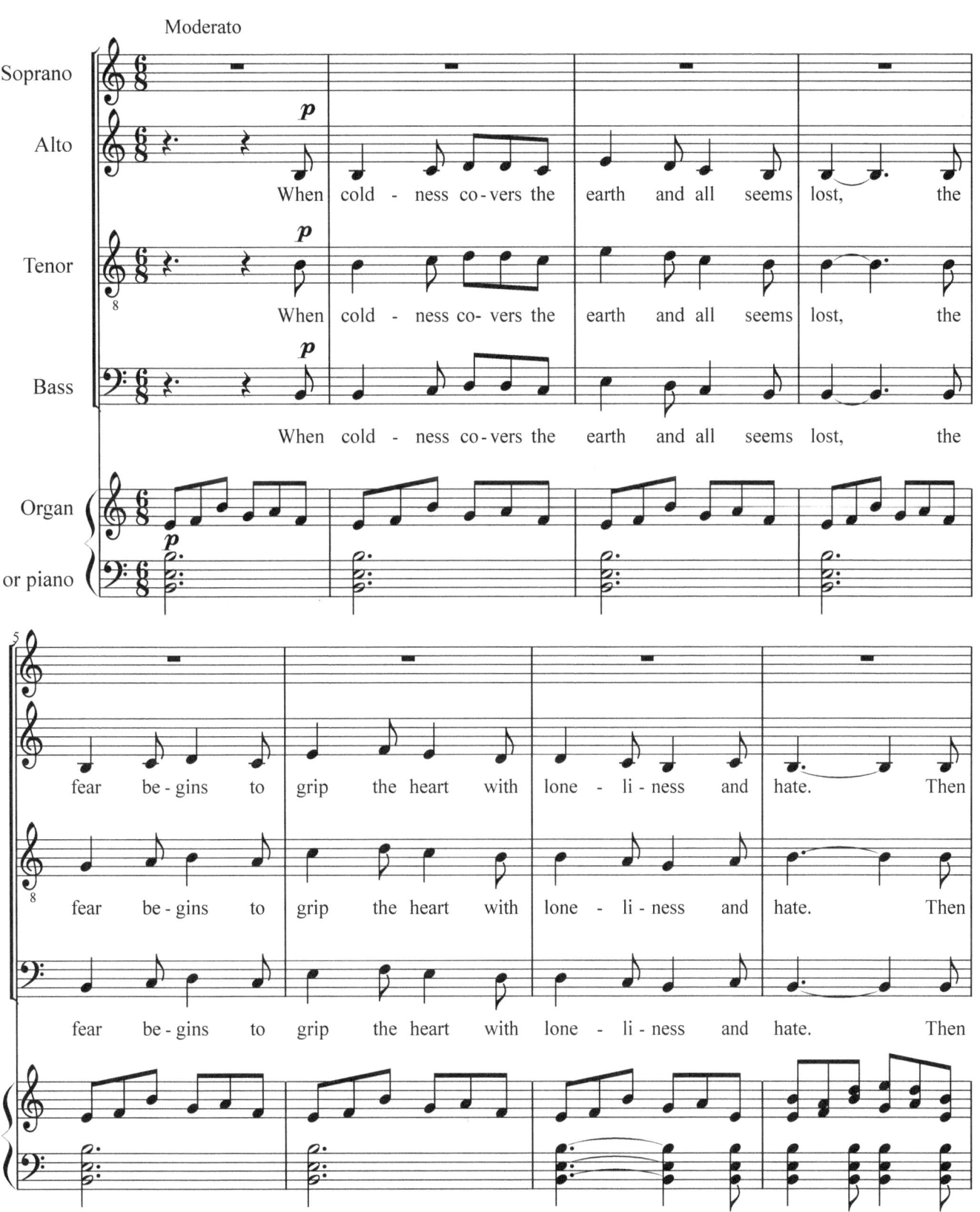

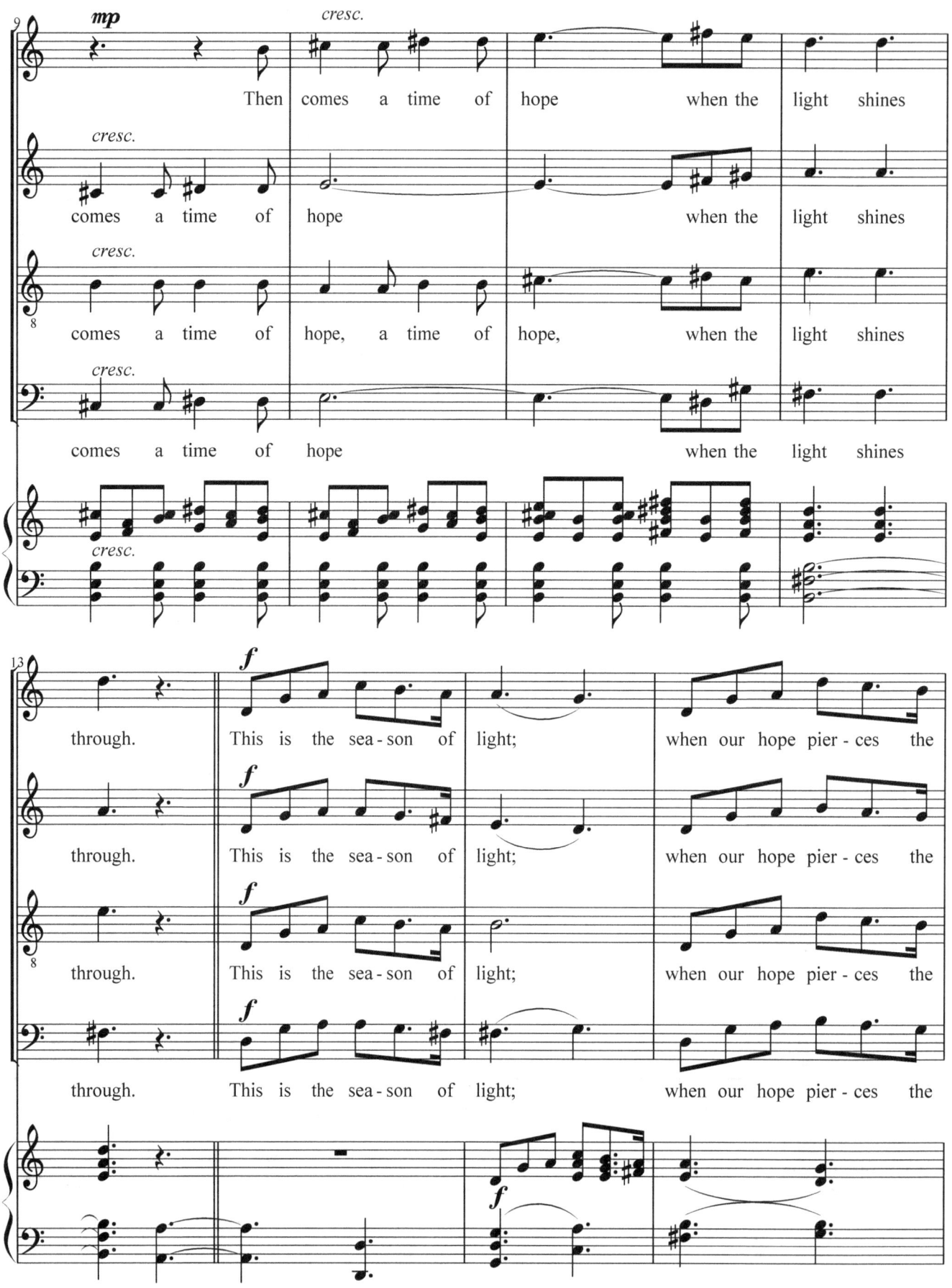

Then comes a time of hope when the light shines

comes a time of hope when the light shines

comes a time of hope, a time of hope, when the light shines

comes a time of hope when the light shines

through. This is the sea-son of light; when our hope pier-ces the

through. This is the sea-son of light; when our hope pier-ces the

through. This is the sea-son of light; when our hope pier-ces the

through. This is the sea-son of light; when our hope pier-ces the

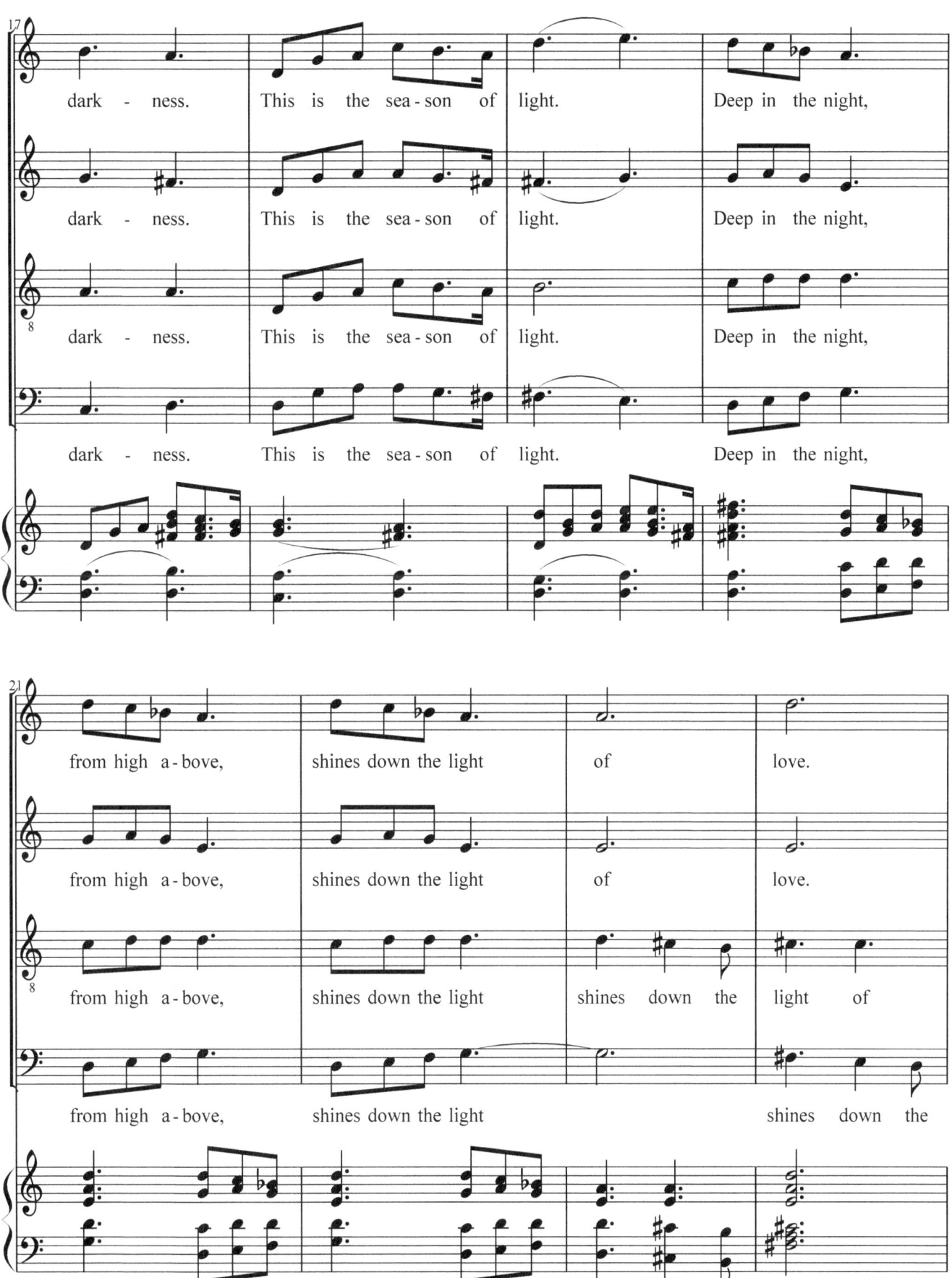

darkness. This is the sea-son of light. Deep in the night,

from high a-bove, shines down the light of love.

from high a-bove, shines down the light of love.

from high a-bove, shines down the light shines down the light of

from high a-bove, shines down the light shines down the

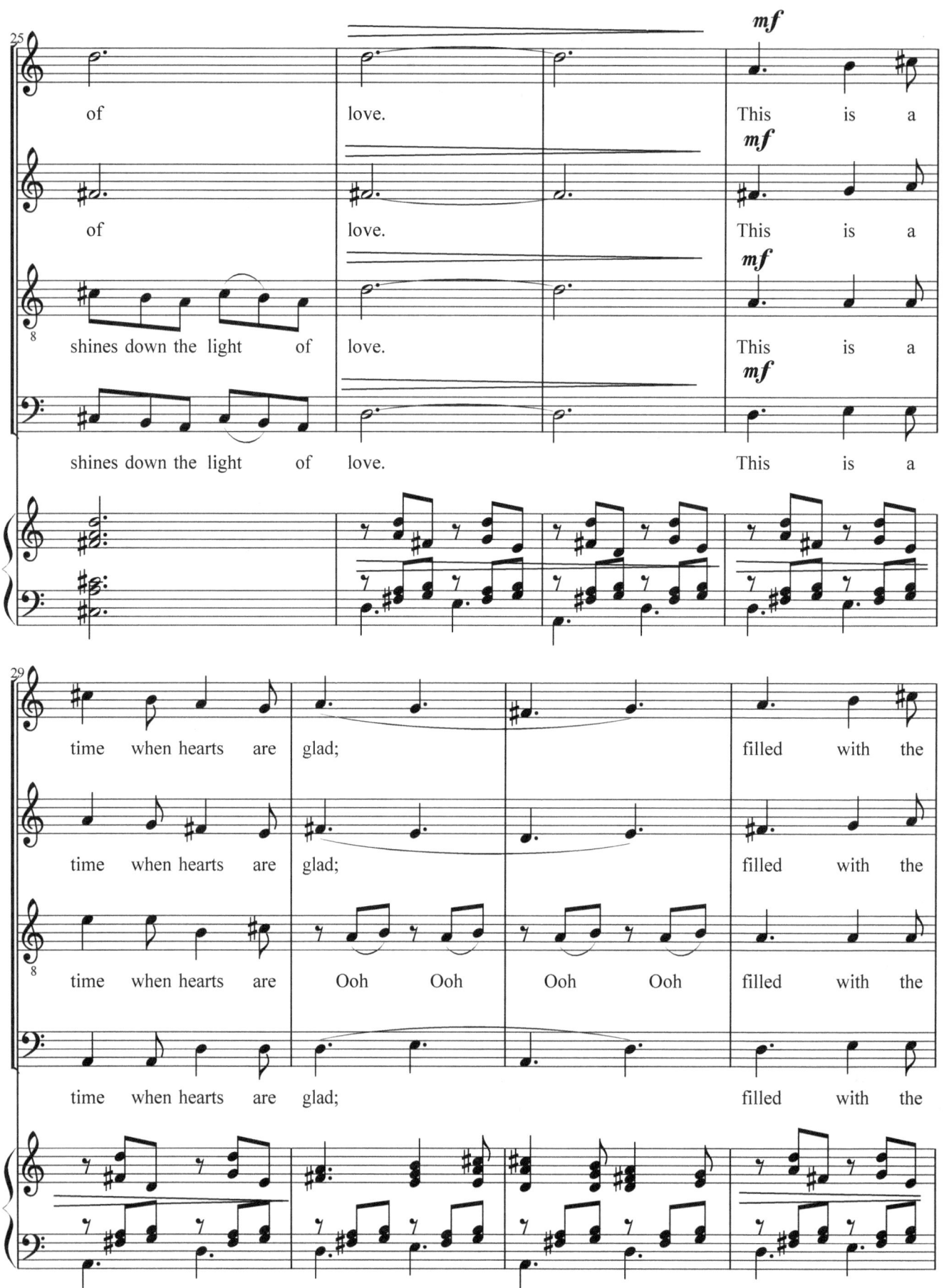

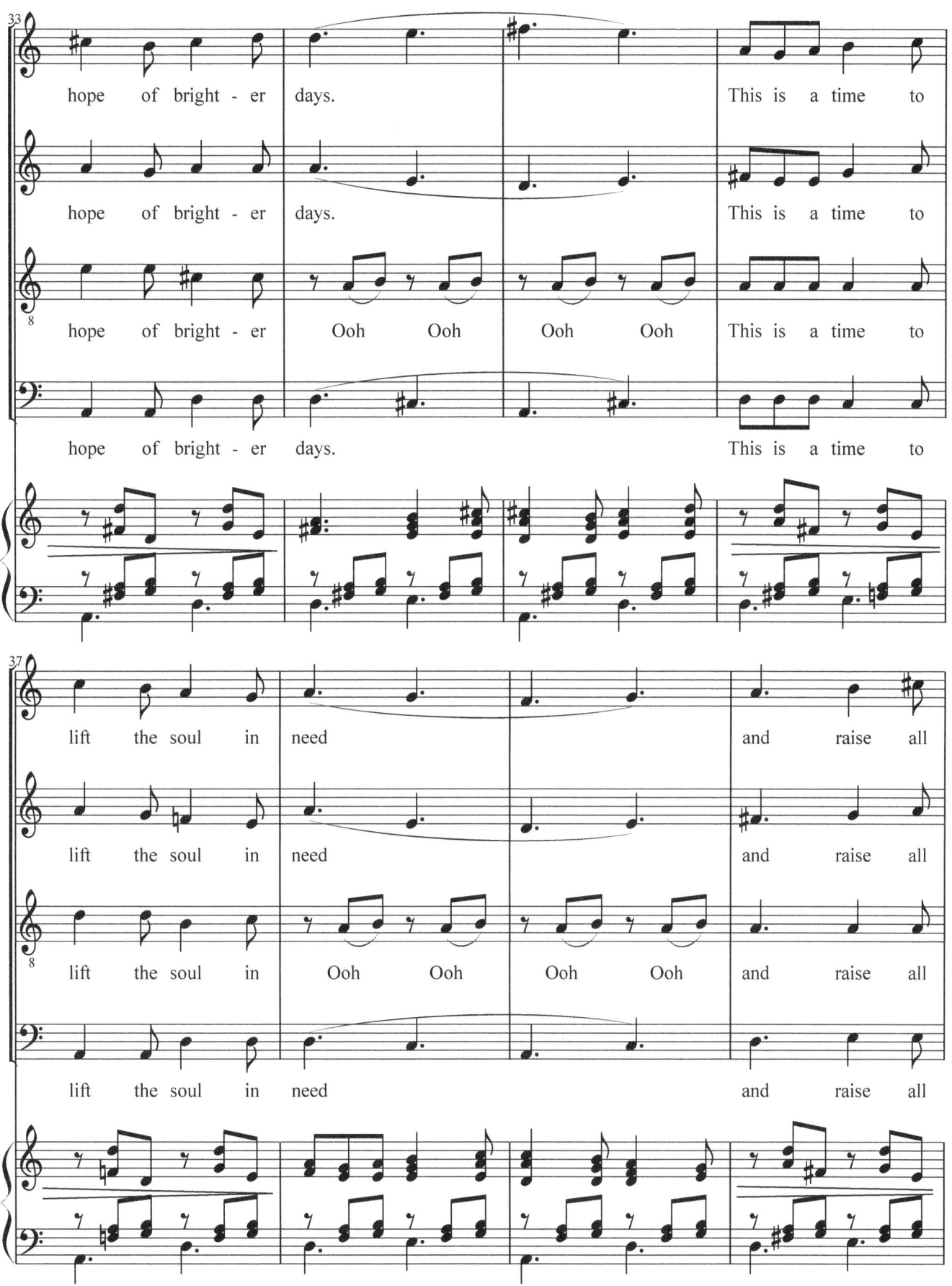

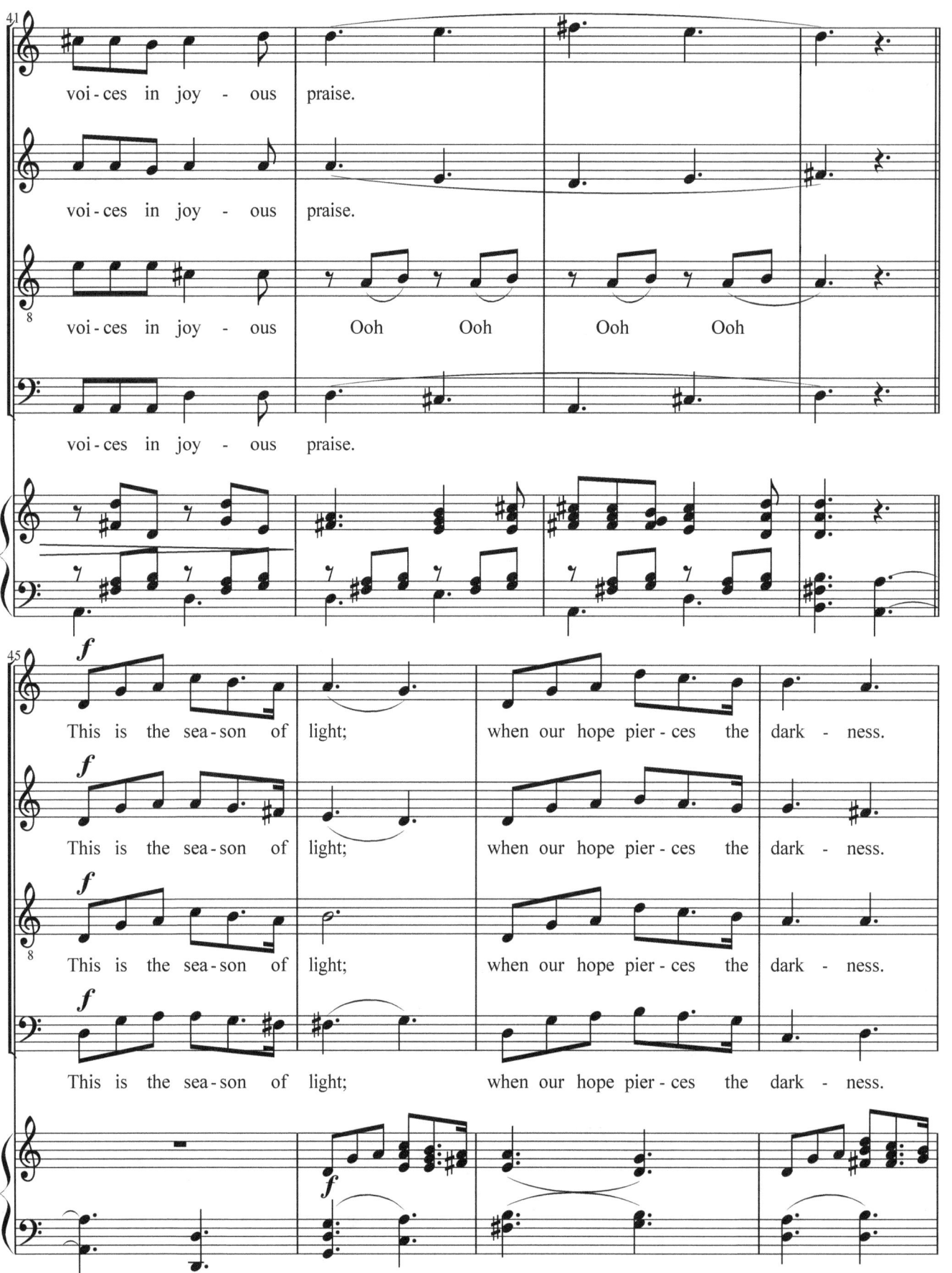

voi - ces in joy - ous praise.

voi - ces in joy - ous praise.

voi - ces in joy - ous Ooh Ooh Ooh Ooh

voi - ces in joy - ous praise.

This is the sea - son of light; when our hope pier - ces the dark - ness.

This is the sea - son of light; when our hope pier - ces the dark - ness.

This is the sea - son of light; when our hope pier - ces the dark - ness.

This is the sea - son of light; when our hope pier - ces the dark - ness.

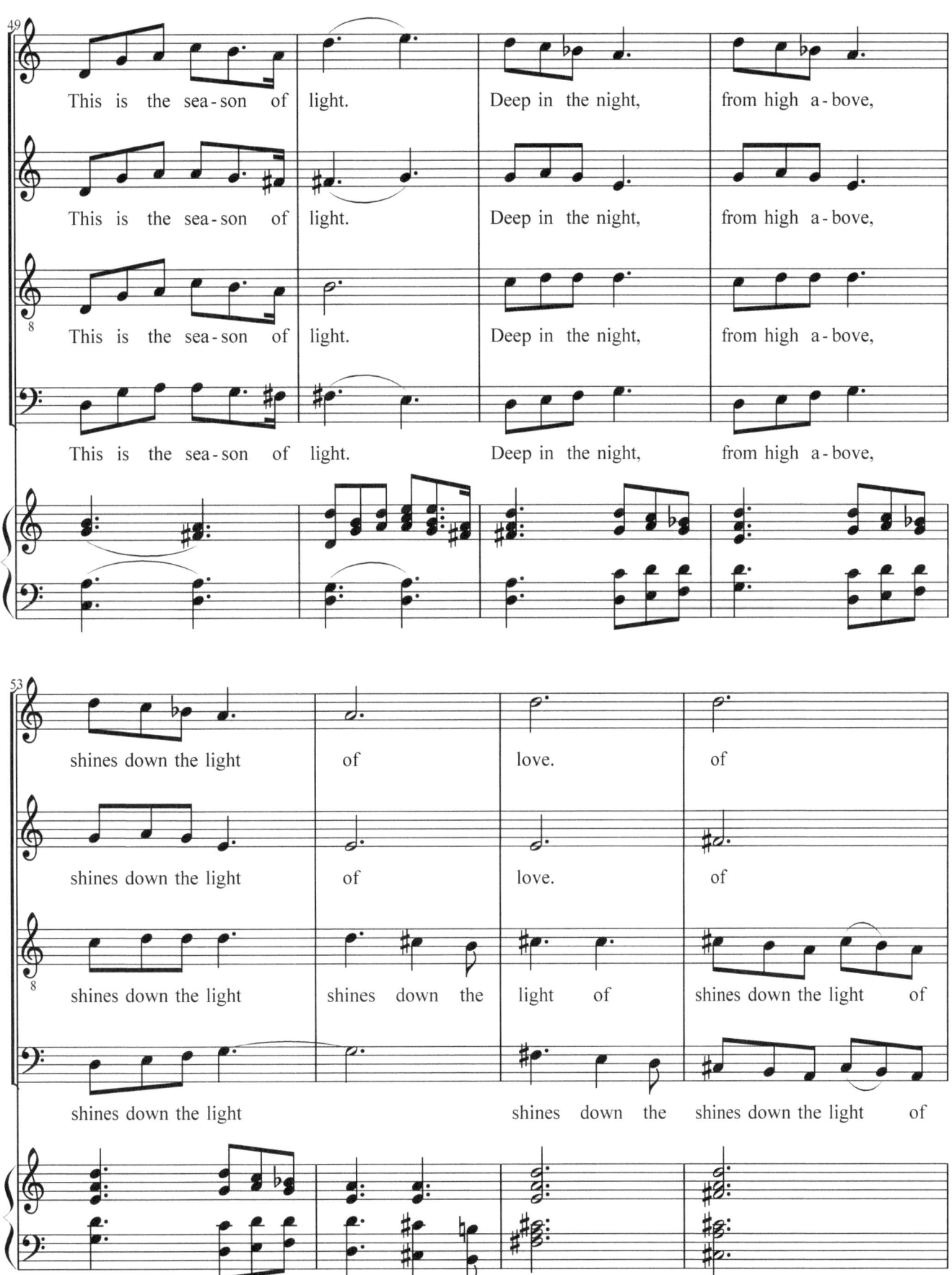

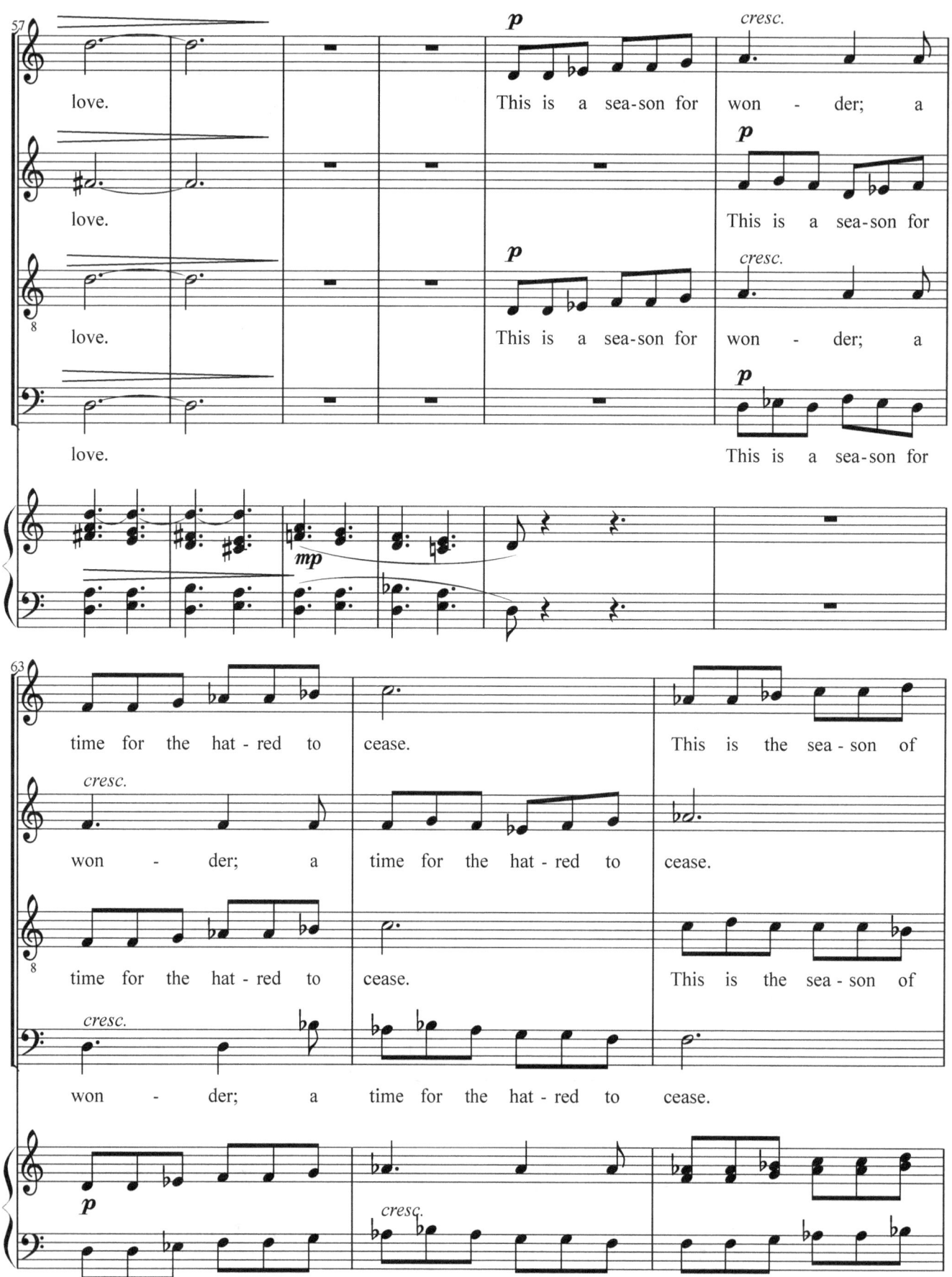

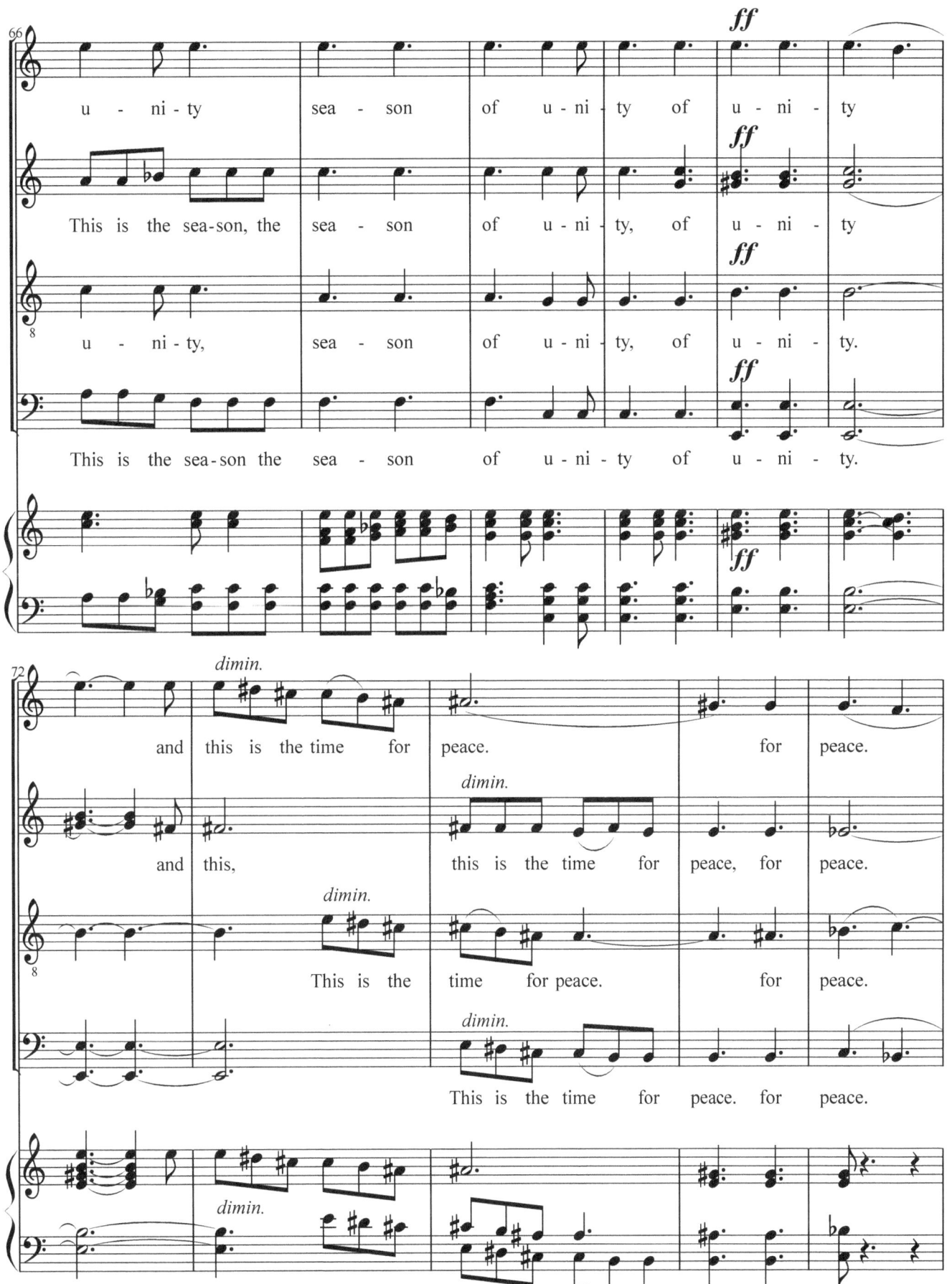

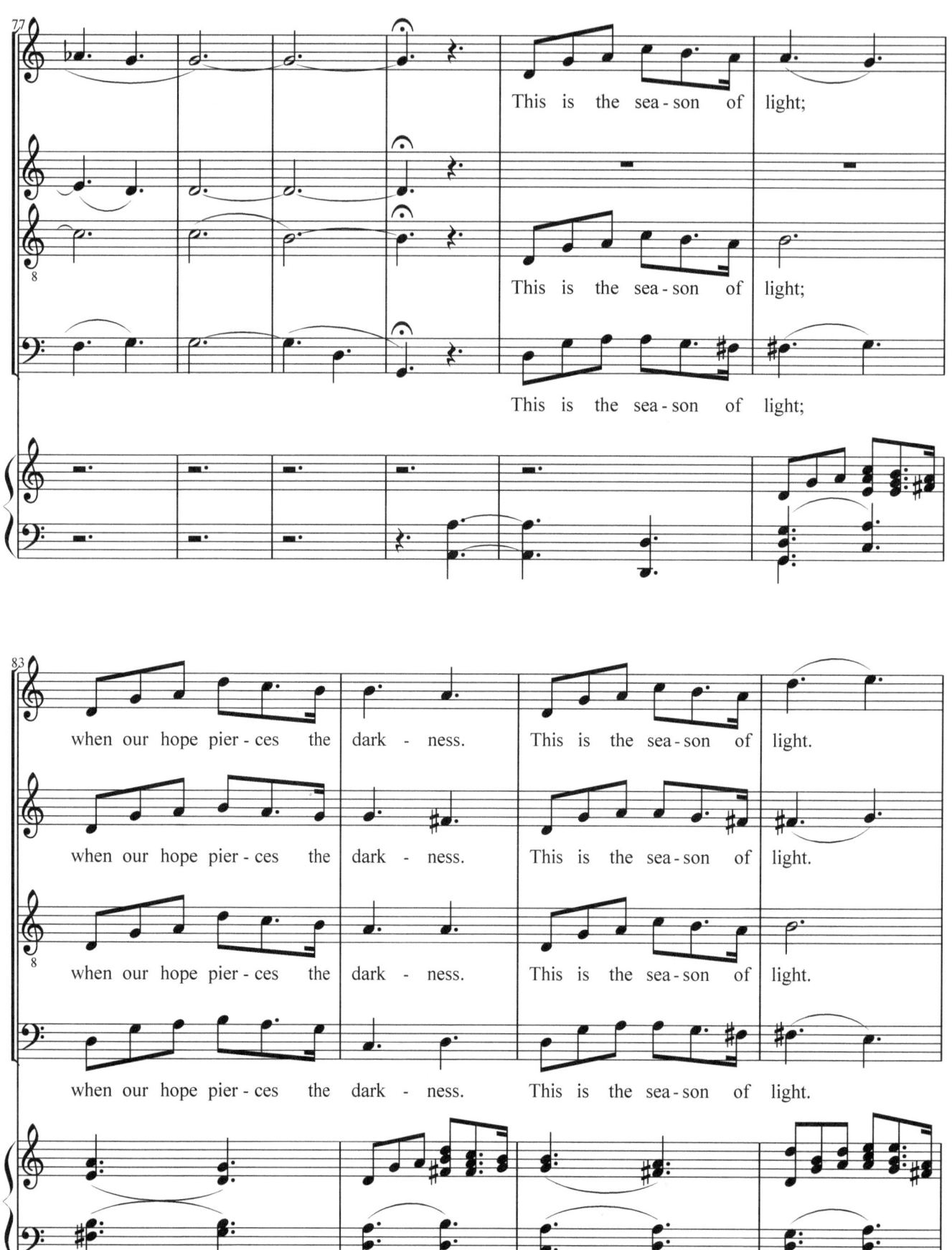

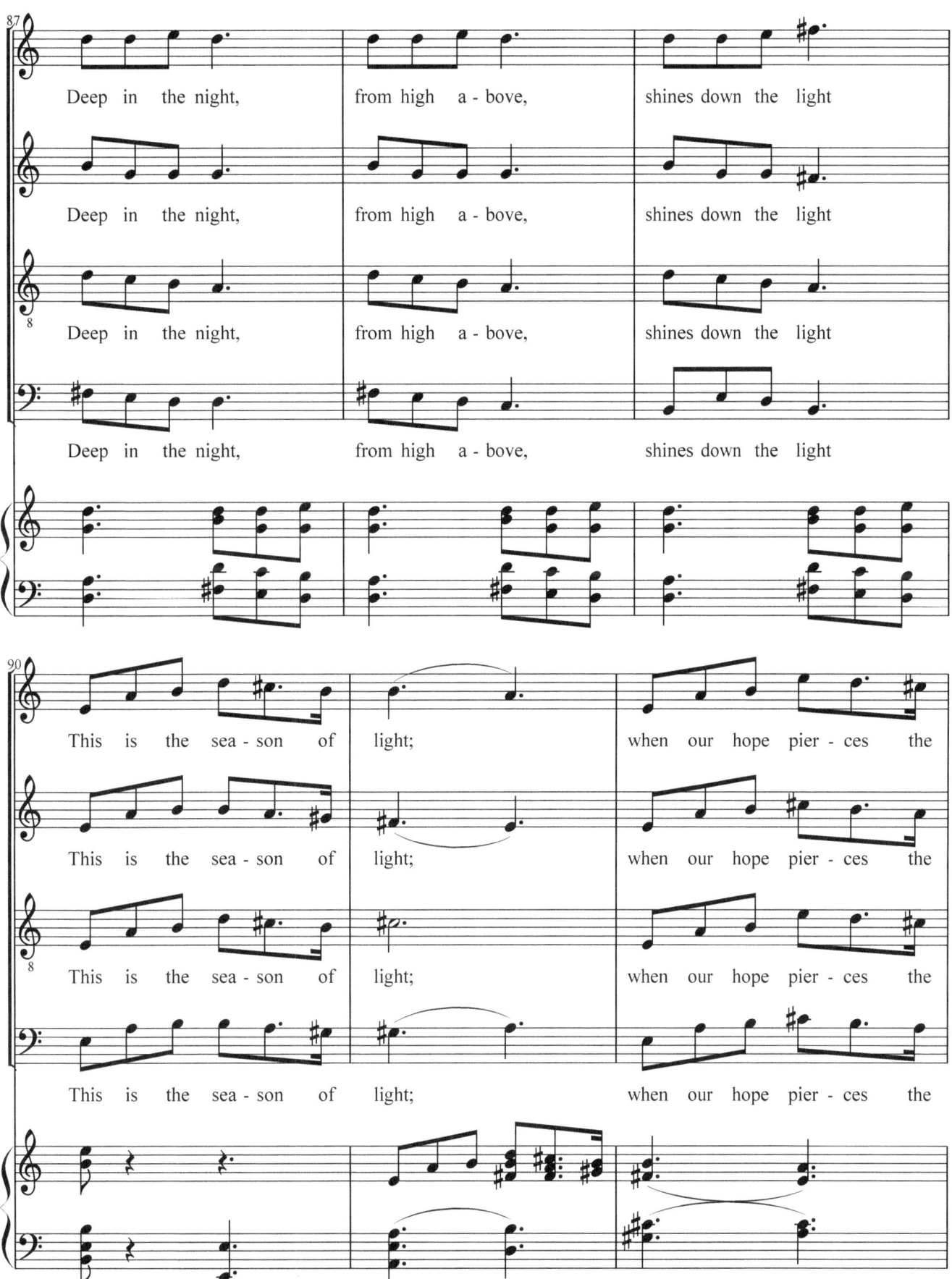

Deep in the night, from high a - bove, shines down the light

Deep in the night, from high a - bove, shines down the light

Deep in the night, from high a - bove, shines down the light

Deep in the night, from high a - bove, shines down the light

This is the sea - son of light; when our hope pier - ces the

This is the sea - son of light; when our hope pier - ces the

This is the sea - son of light; when our hope pier - ces the

This is the sea - son of light; when our hope pier - ces the

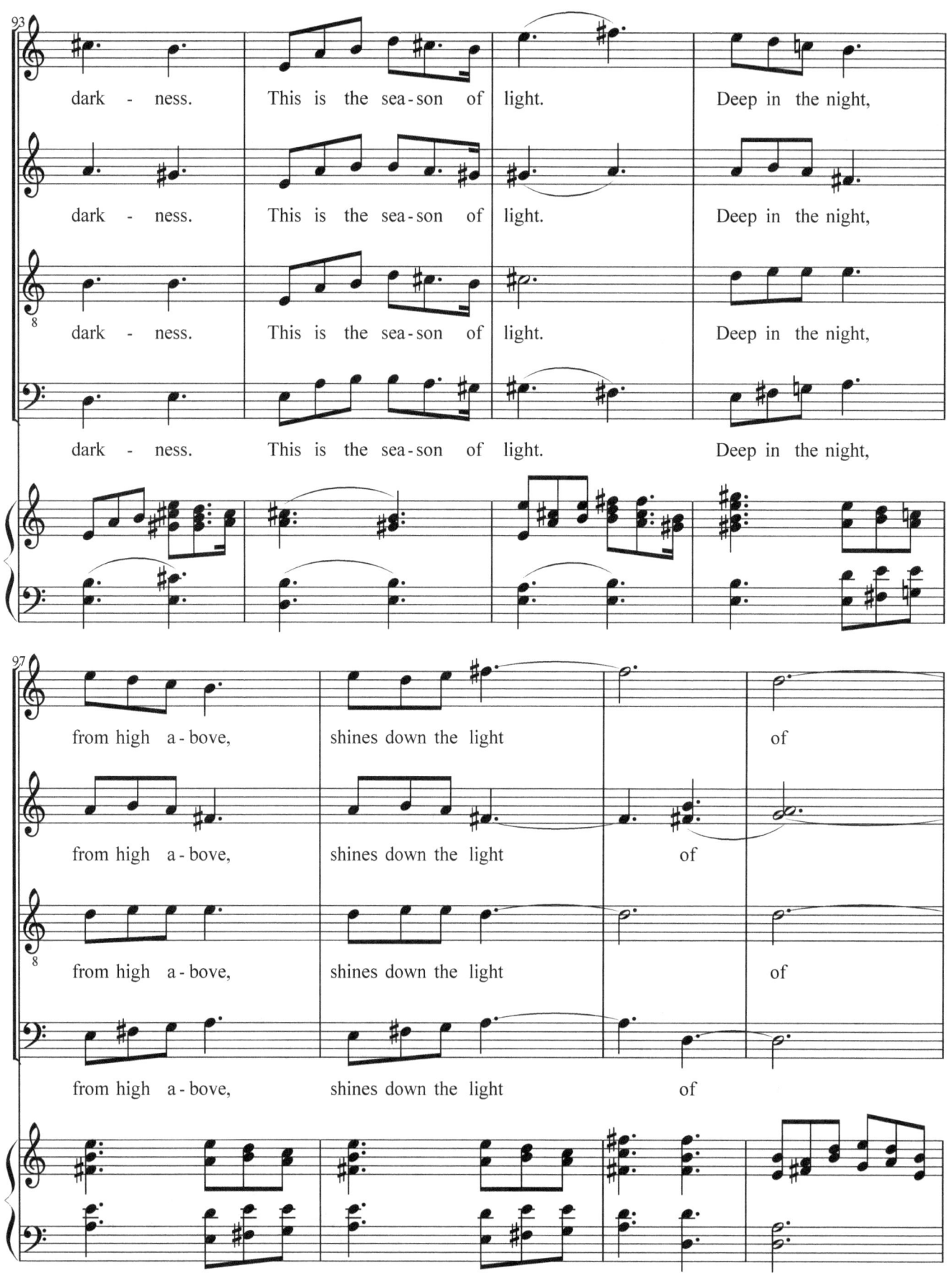

darkness. This is the sea-son of light. Deep in the night,

darkness. This is the sea-son of light. Deep in the night,

darkness. This is the sea-son of light. Deep in the night,

darkness. This is the sea-son of light. Deep in the night,

from high a-bove, shines down the light of

from high a-bove, shines down the light of

from high a-bove, shines down the light of

from high a-bove, shines down the light of

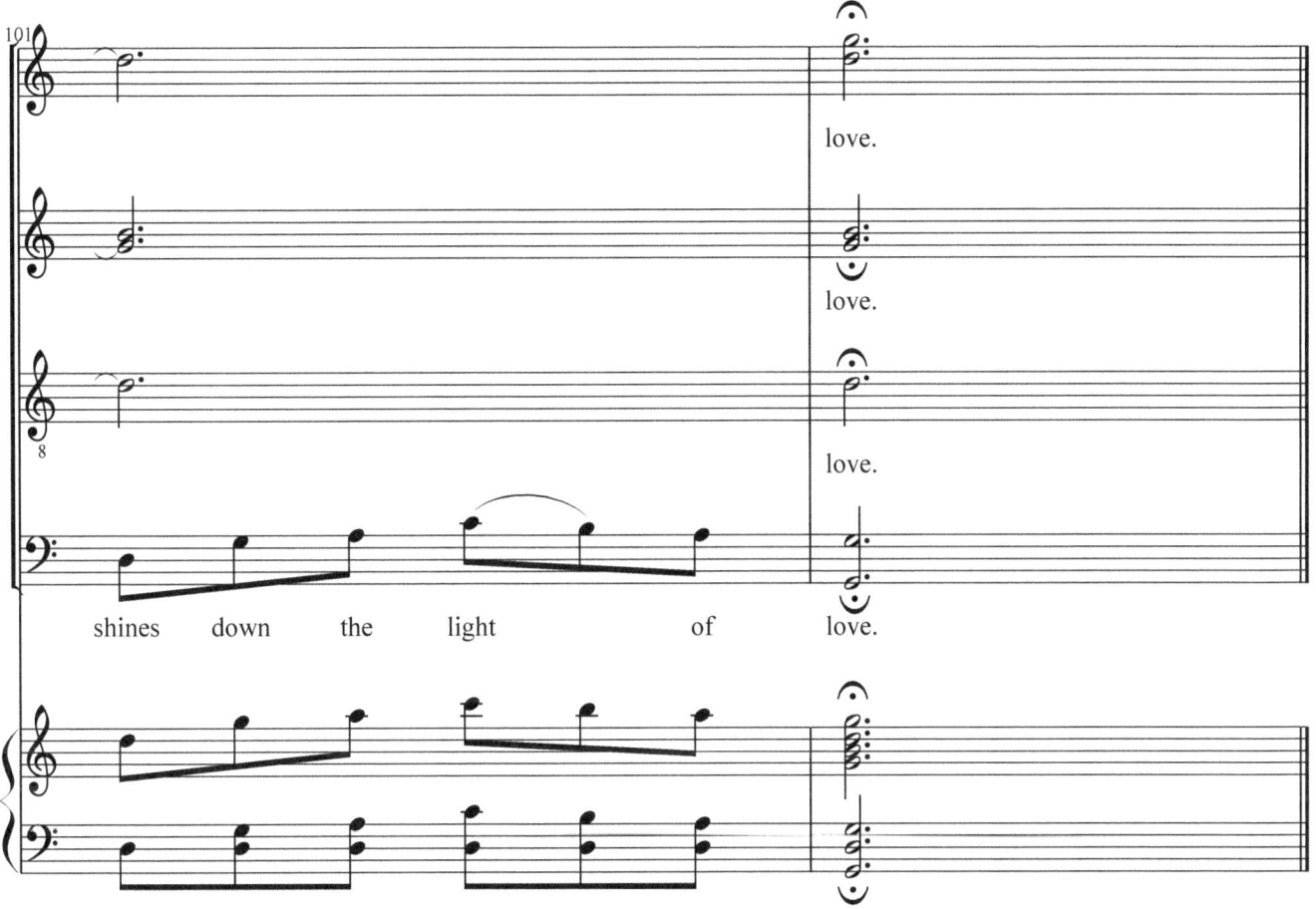

love.

love.

love.

shines   down   the   light   of   love.

Ring Out Those New Year's Bells

Ken Langer

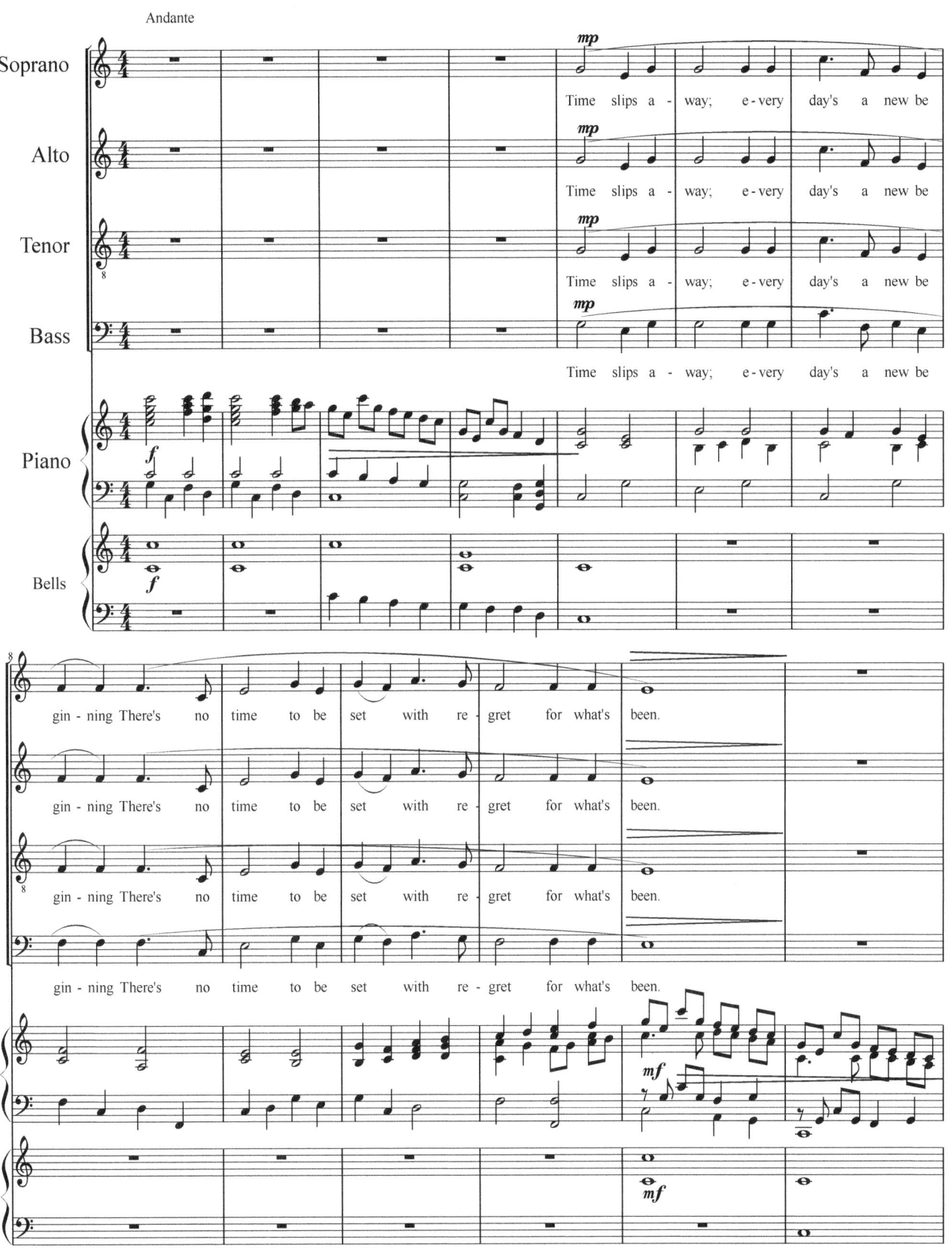

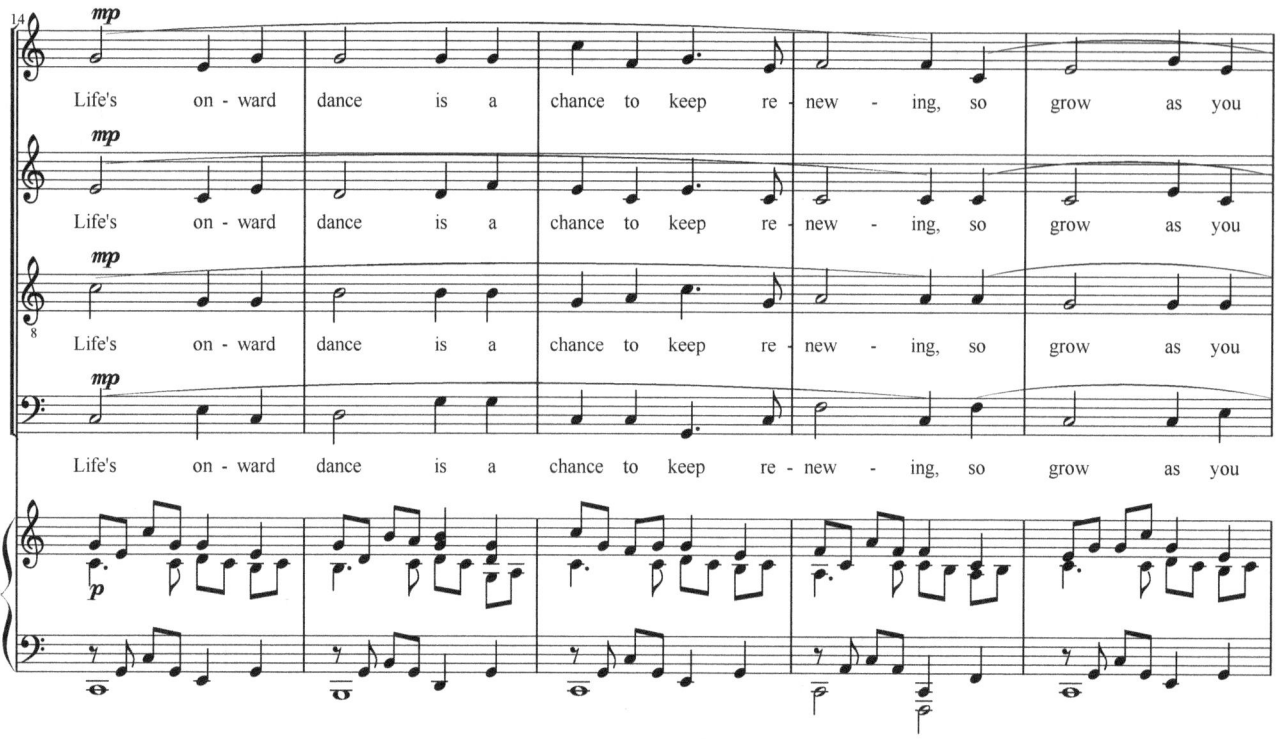

Life's on-ward dance is a chance to keep re-new - ing, so grow as you
Life's on-ward dance is a chance to keep re-new - ing, so grow as you
Life's on-ward dance is a chance to keep re-new - ing, so grow as you
Life's on-ward dance is a chance to keep re-new - ing, so grow as you

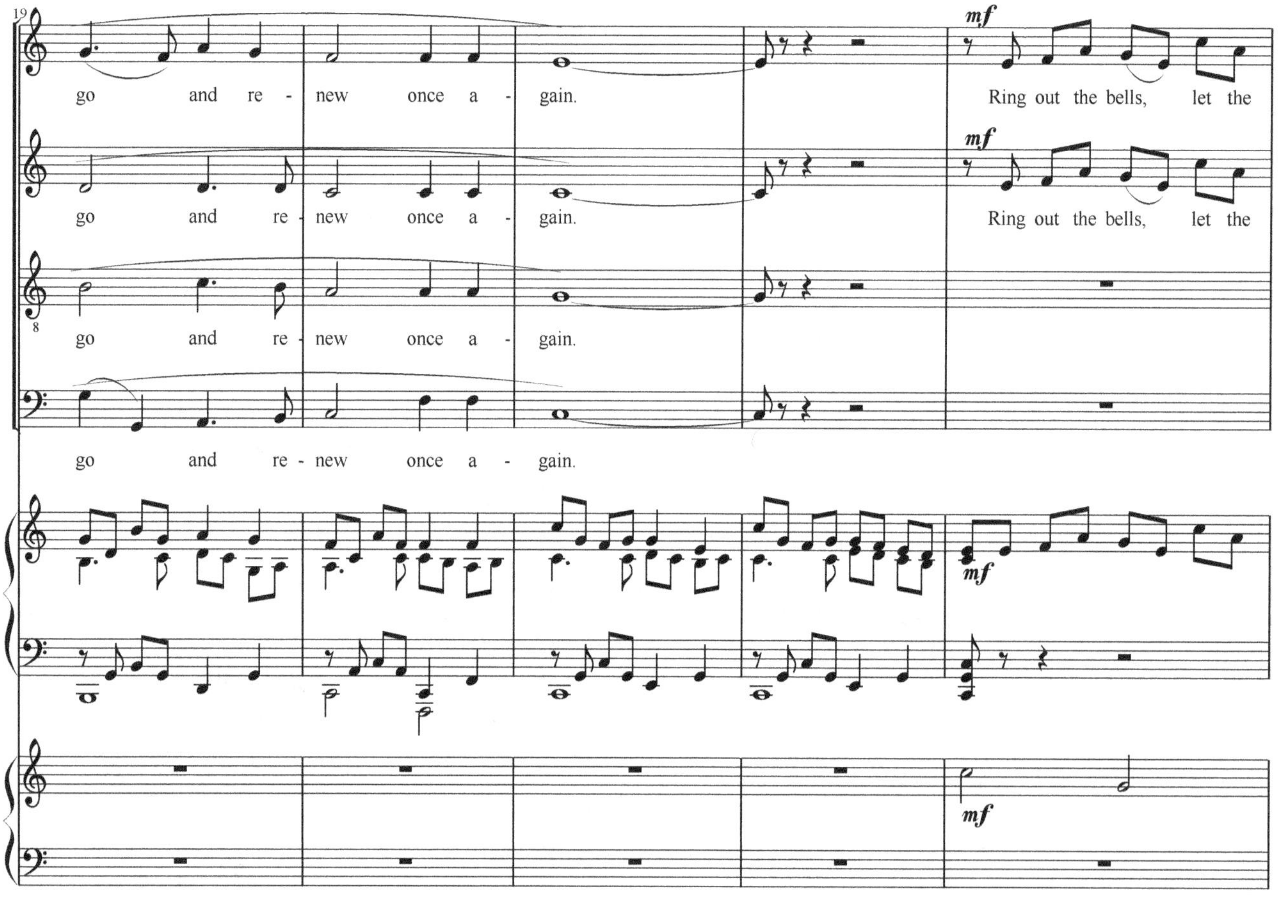

go and re - new once a - gain. Ring out the bells, let the
go and re - new once a - gain. Ring out the bells, let the
go and re - new once a - gain.
go and re - new once a - gain.

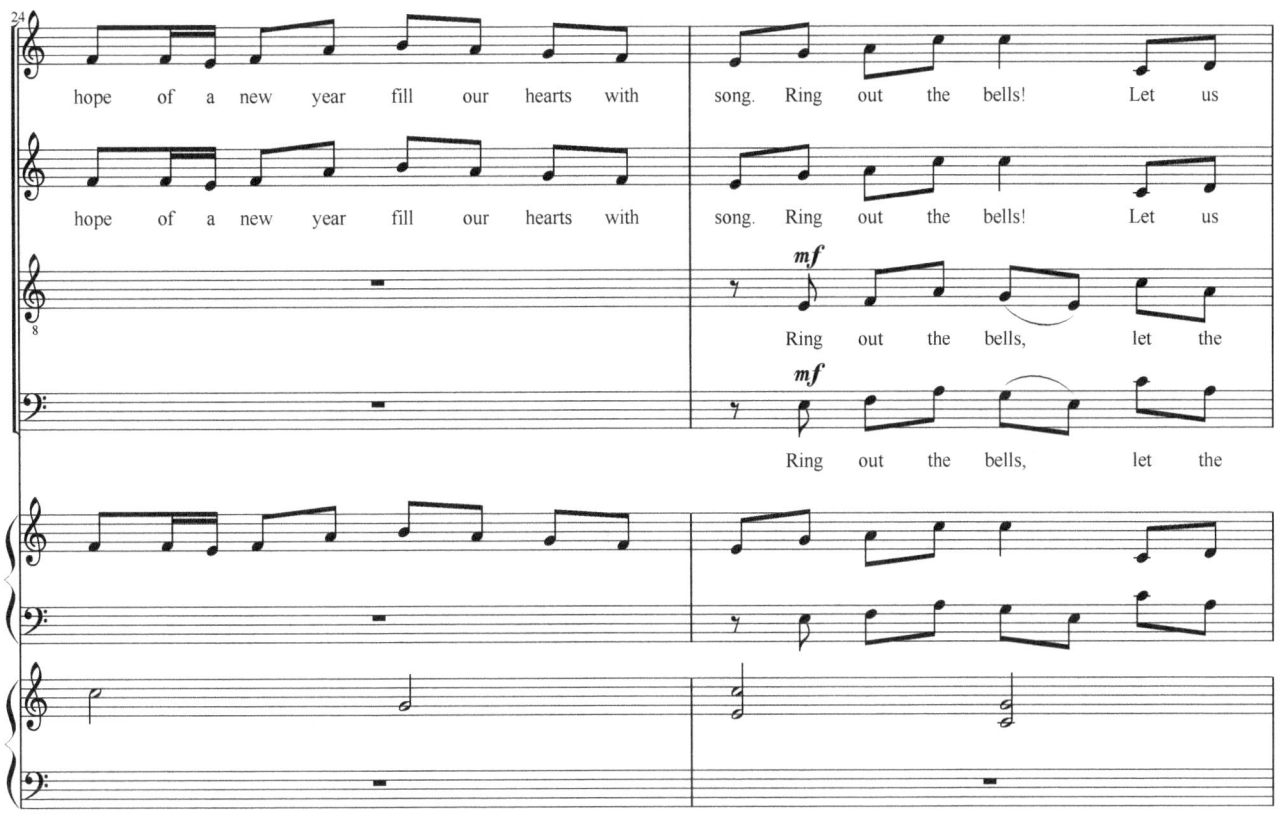

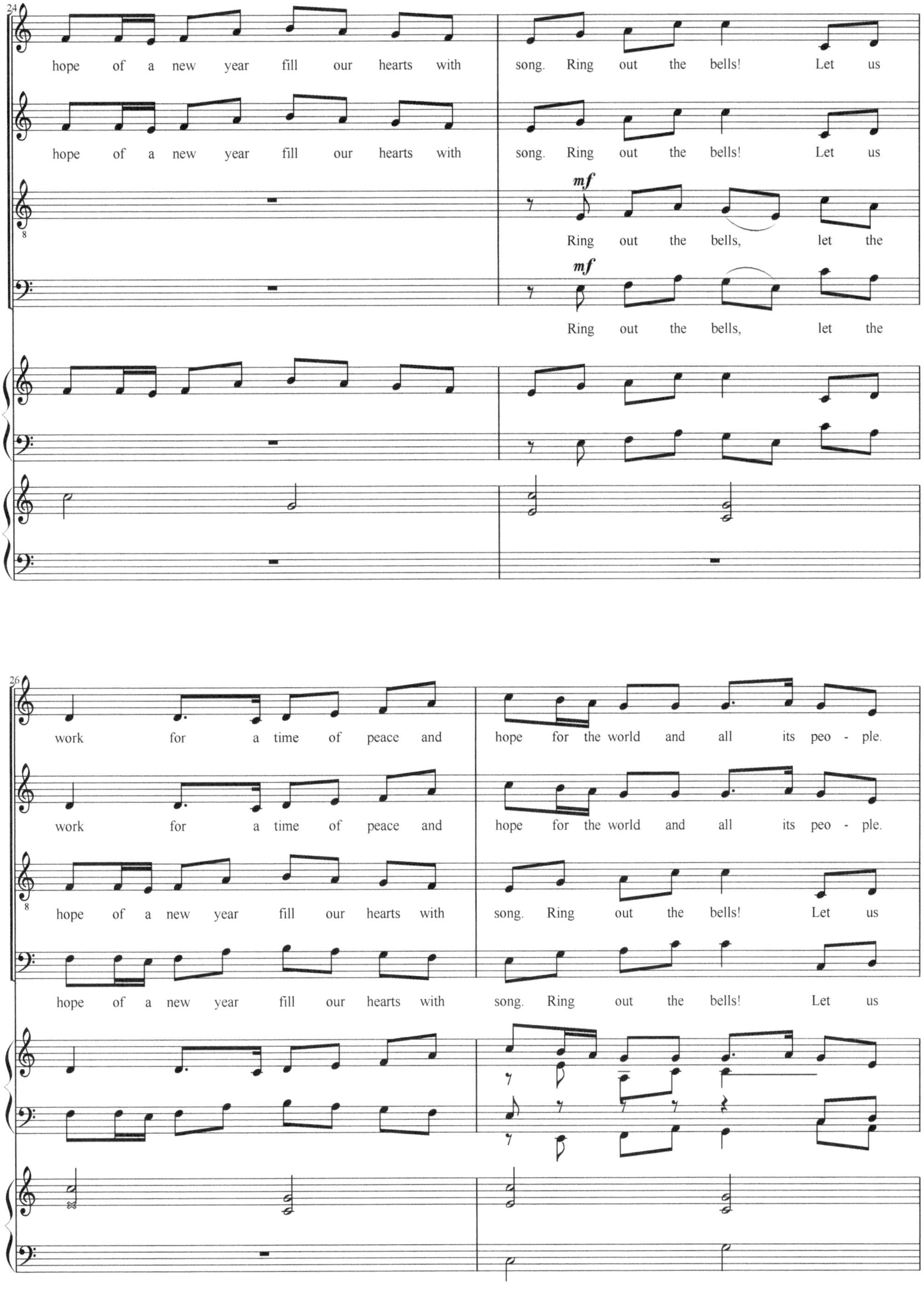

hope of a new year fill our hearts with song. Ring out the bells! Let us

hope of a new year fill our hearts with song. Ring out the bells! Let us

mf Ring out the bells, let the

mf Ring out the bells, let the

work for a time of peace and hope for the world and all its peo - ple.

work for a time of peace and hope for the world and all its peo - ple.

hope of a new year fill our hearts with song. Ring out the bells! Let us

hope of a new year fill our hearts with song. Ring out the bells! Let us

43

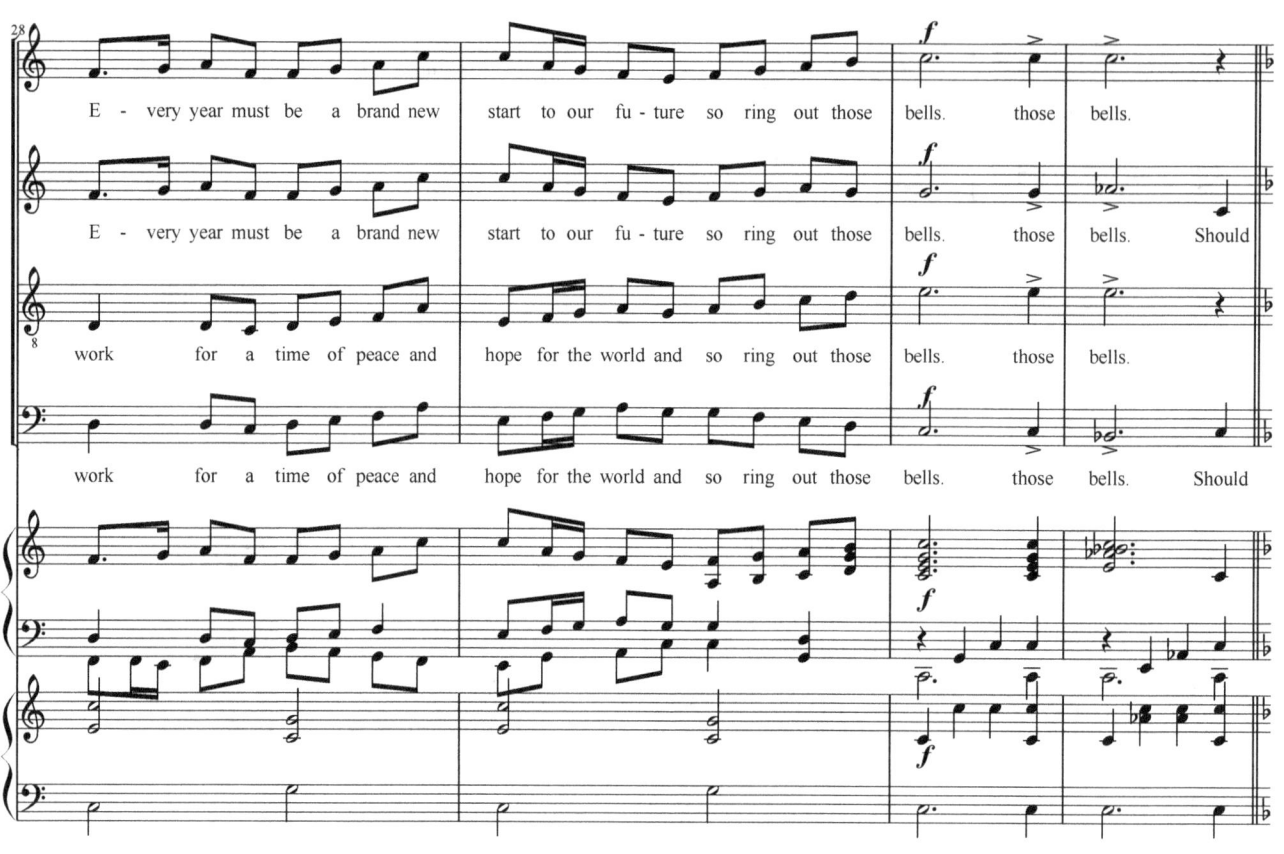

E - very year must be a brand new start to our fu - ture so ring out those bells. those bells.

E - very year must be a brand new start to our fu - ture so ring out those bells. those bells. Should

work for a time of peace and hope for the world and so ring out those bells. those bells.

work for a time of peace and hope for the world and so ring out those bells. those bells. Should

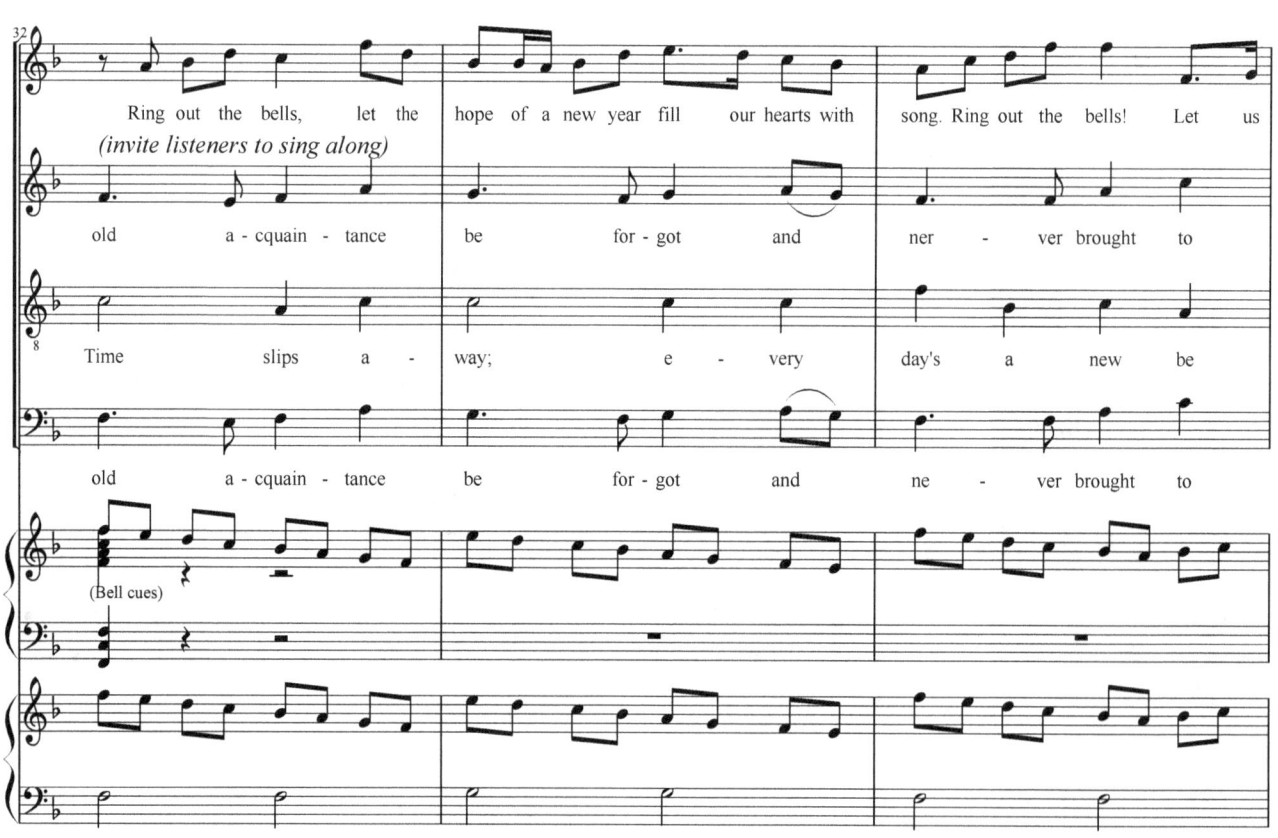

(invite listeners to sing along)

Ring out the bells, let the hope of a new year fill our hearts with song. Ring out the bells! Let us

old a - cquain - tance be for - got and ne - ver brought to

Time slips a - way; e - very day's a new be

old a - cquain - tance be for - got and ne - ver brought to

(Bell cues)

44

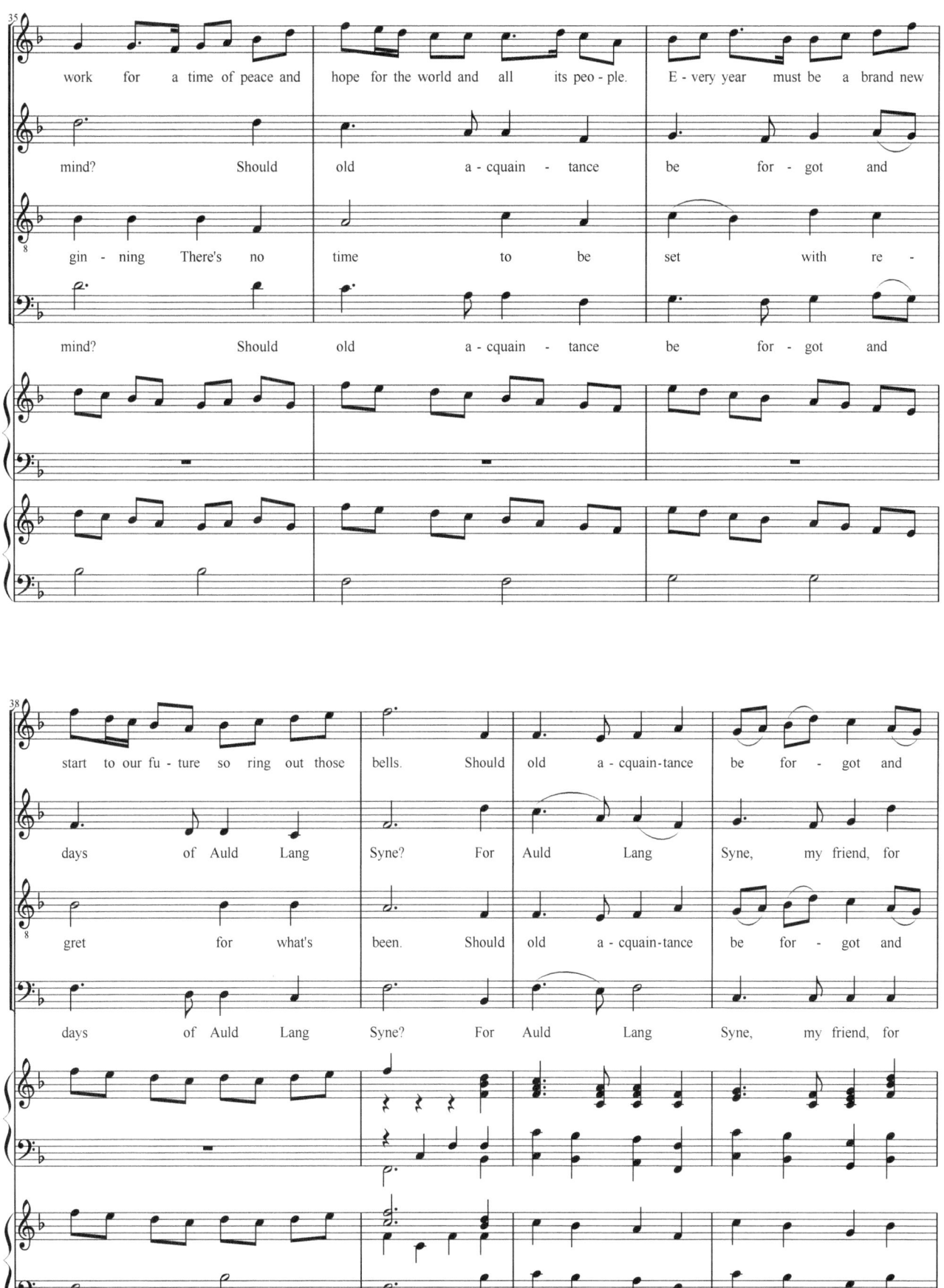

45

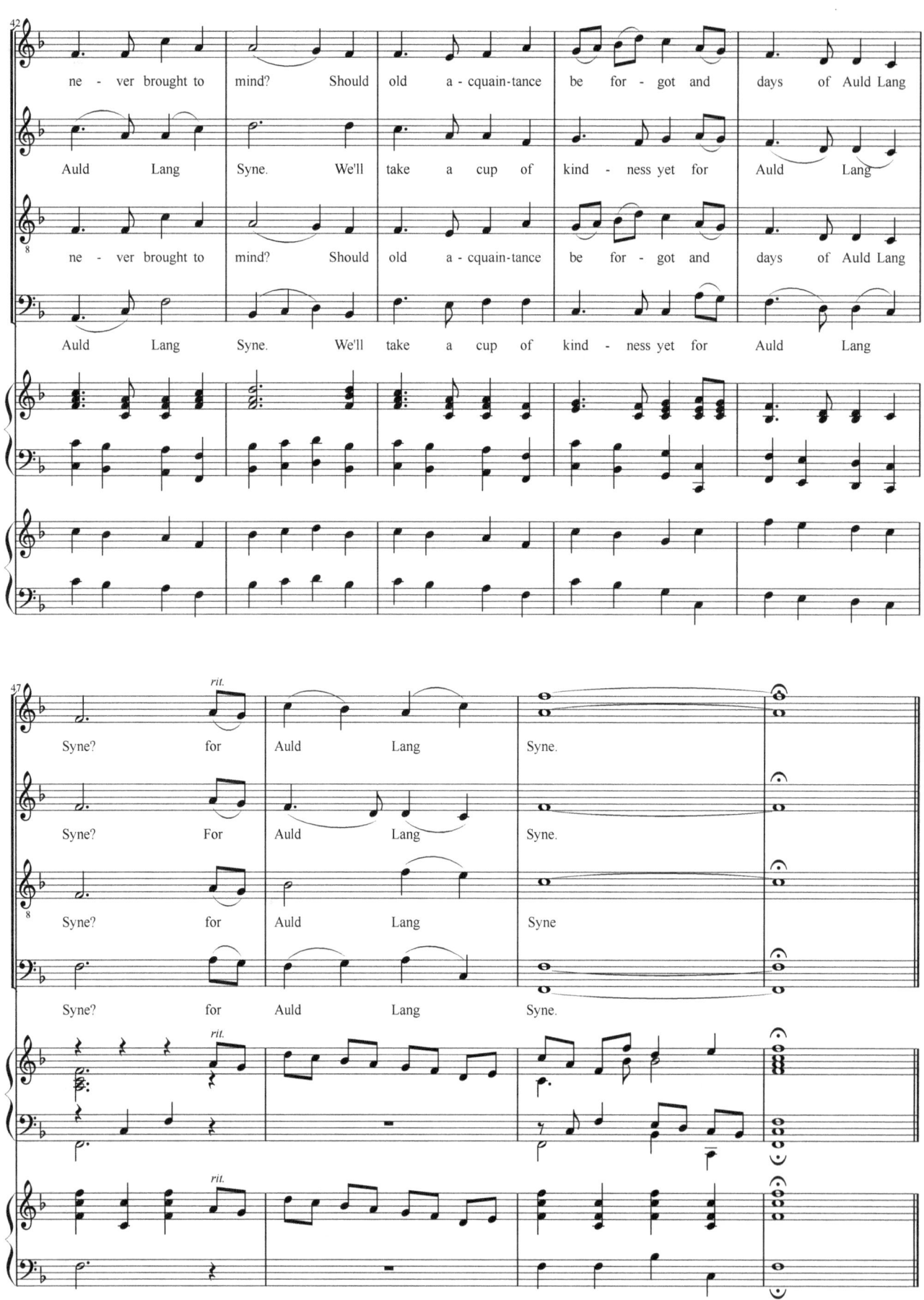

A Time of Jubilation

Ken Langer

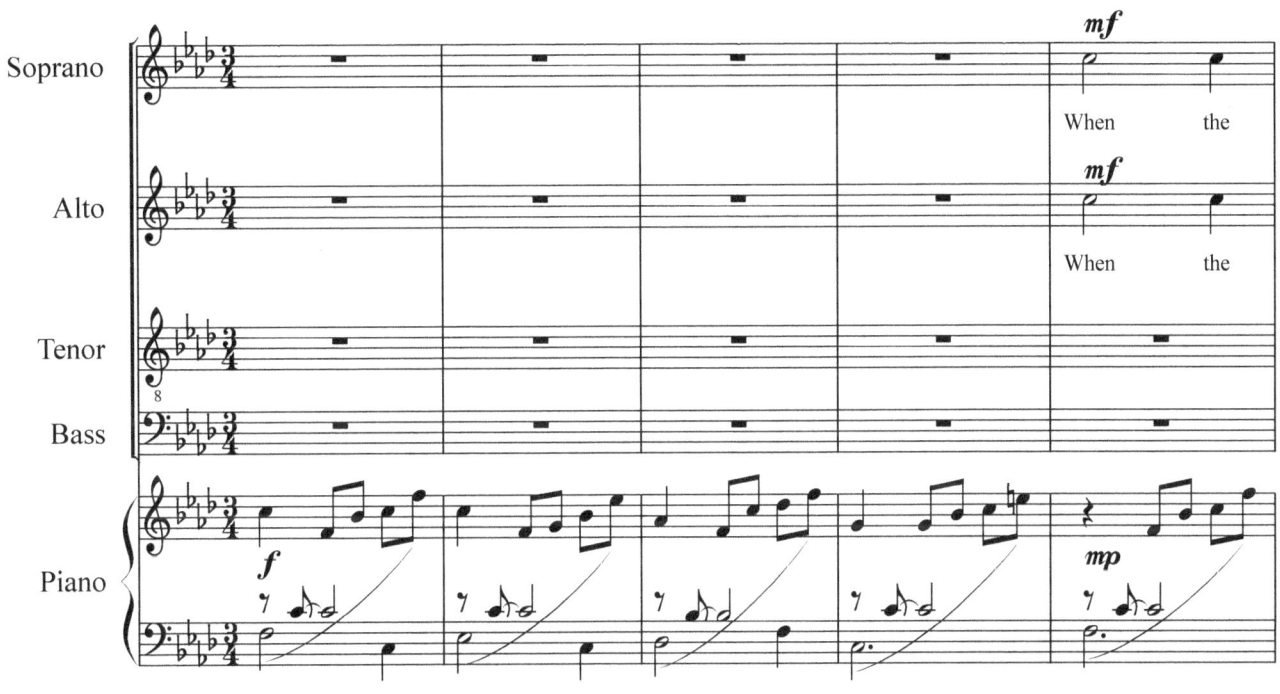

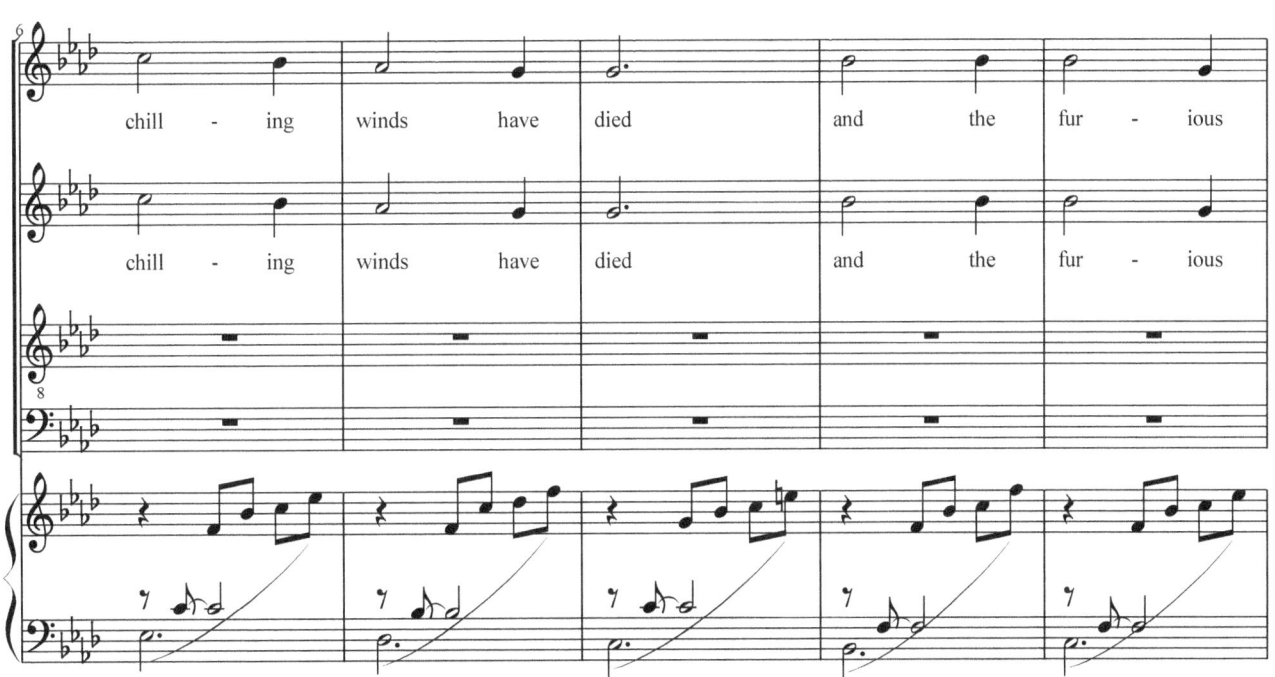

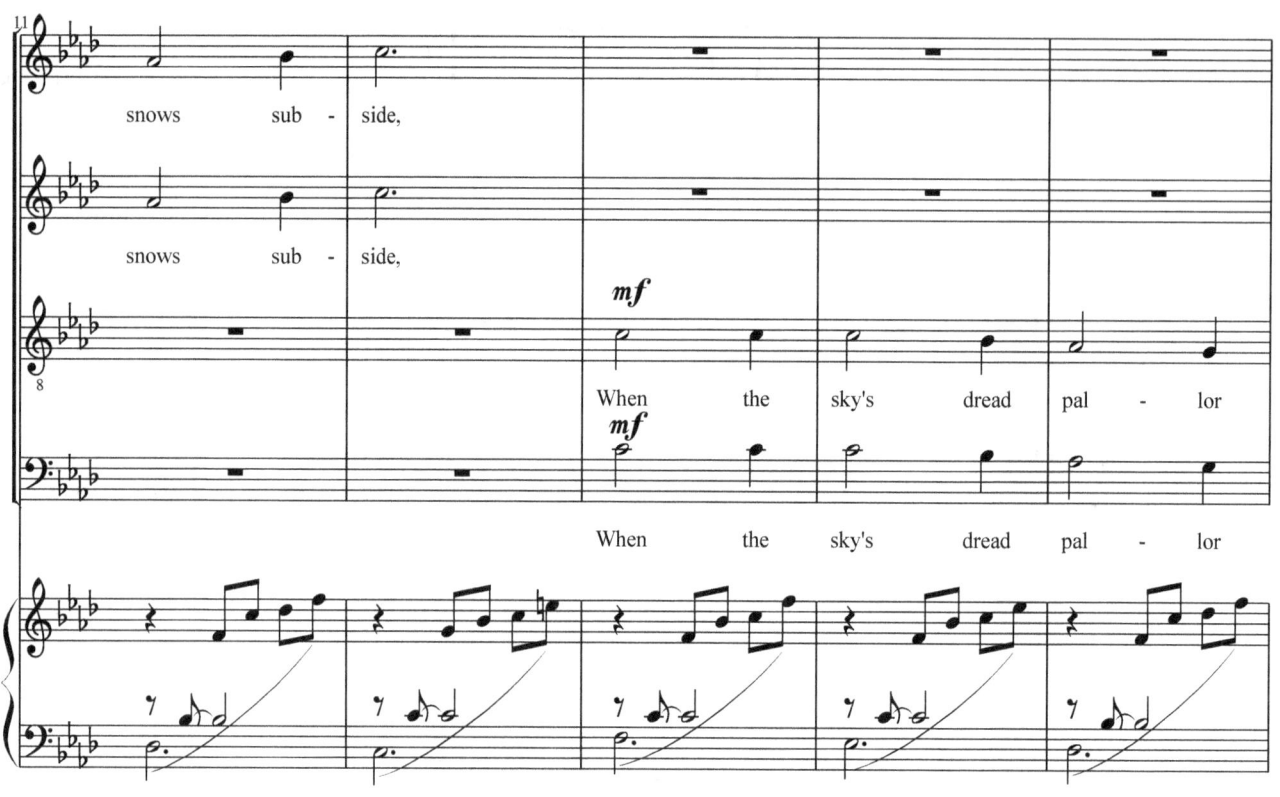

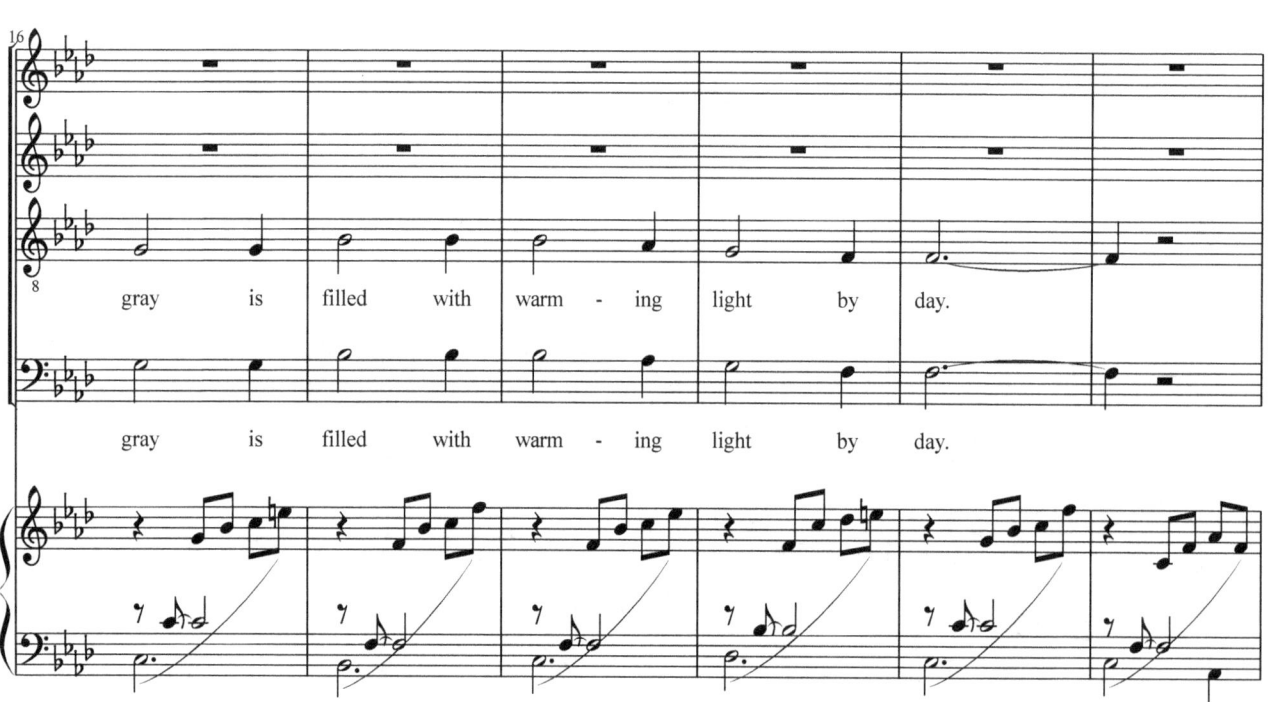

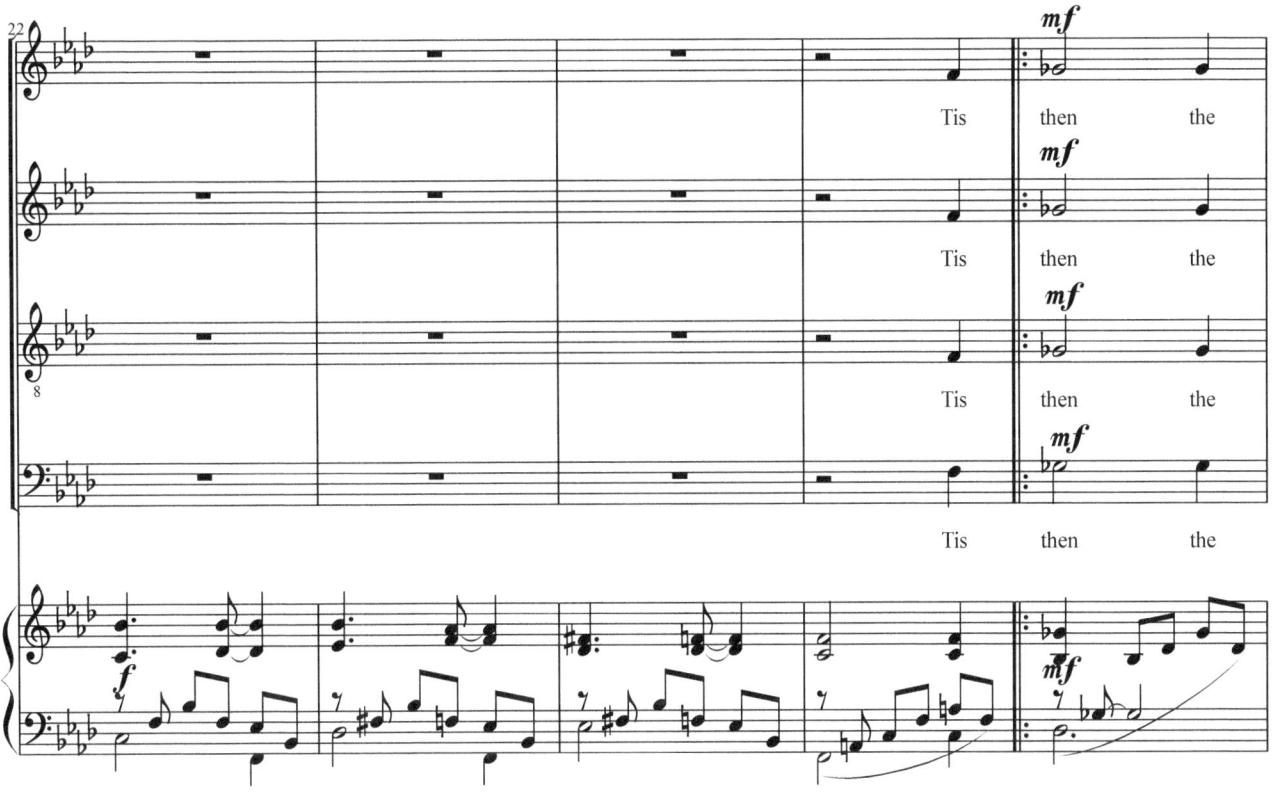

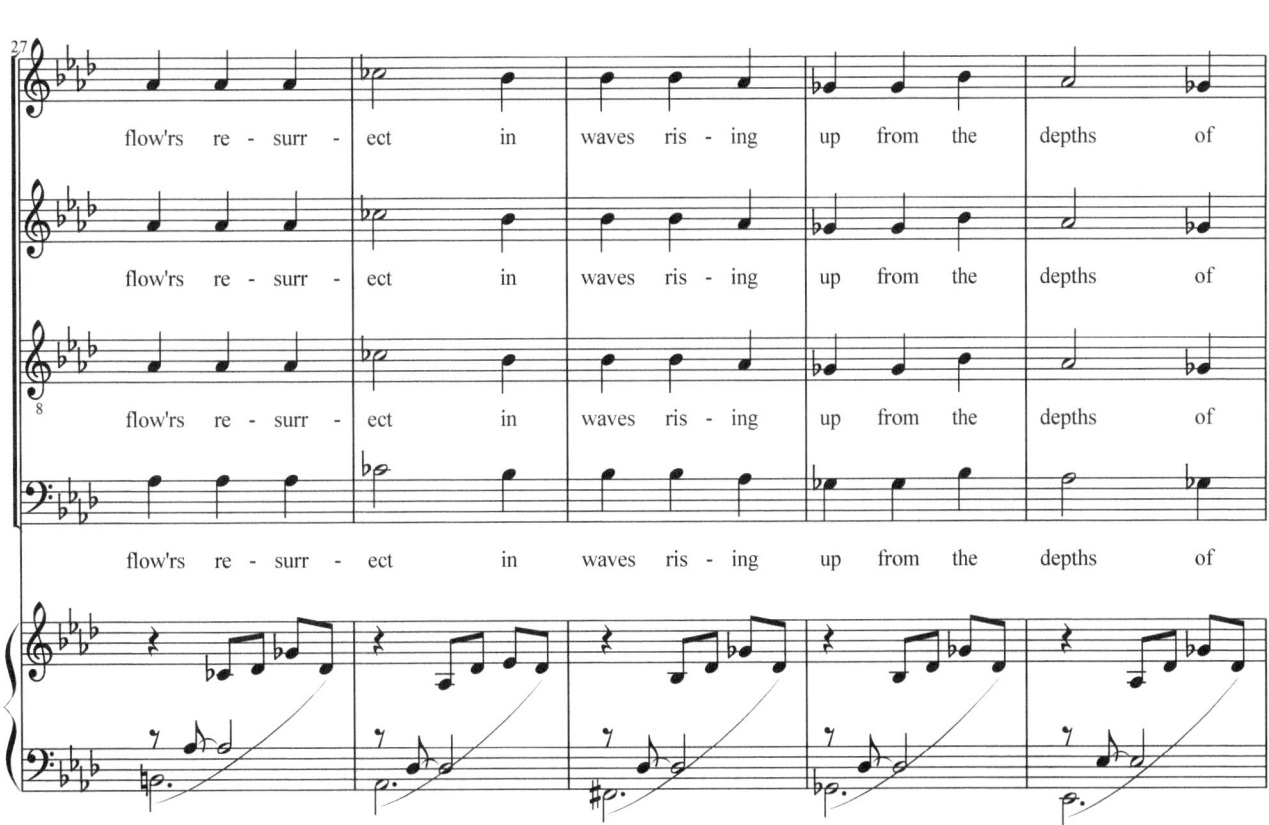

49

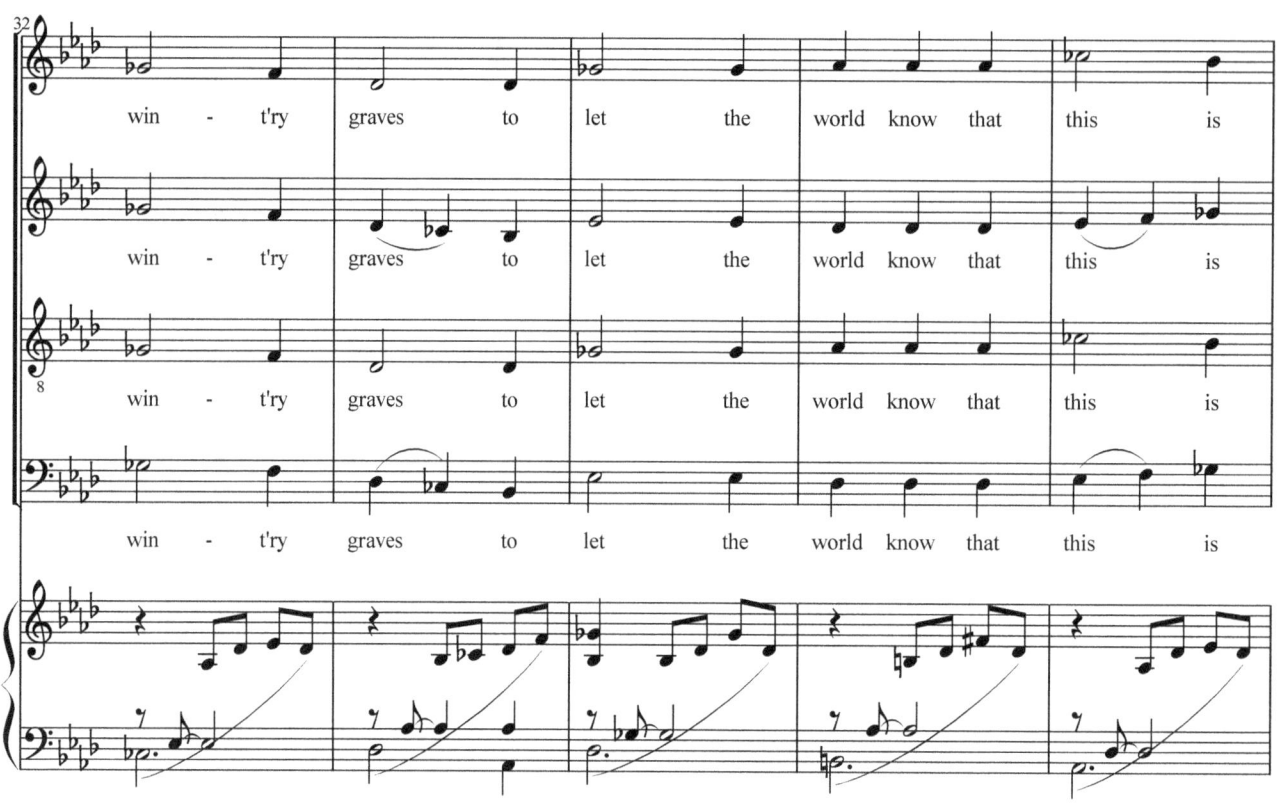

win - t'ry graves to let the world know that this is

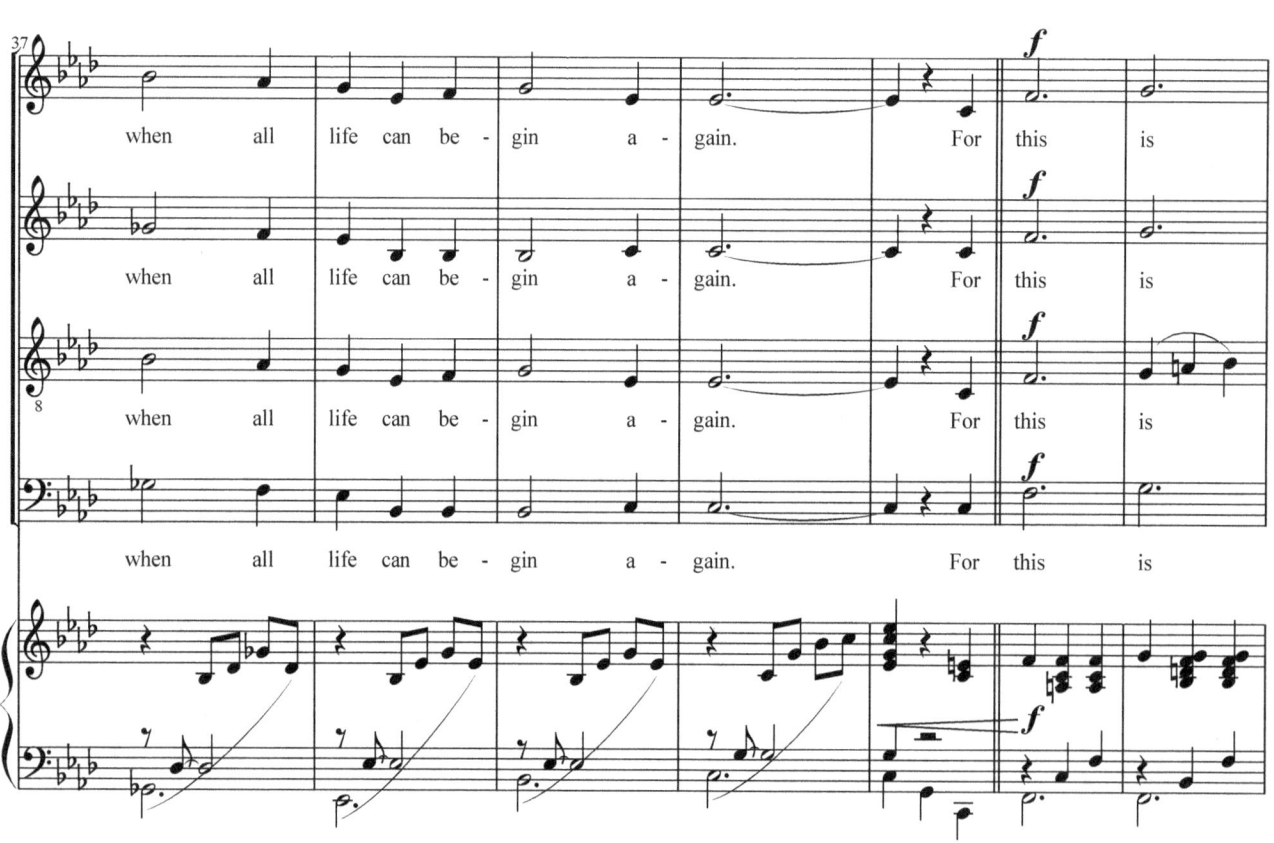

when all life can be - gin a - gain. For this is

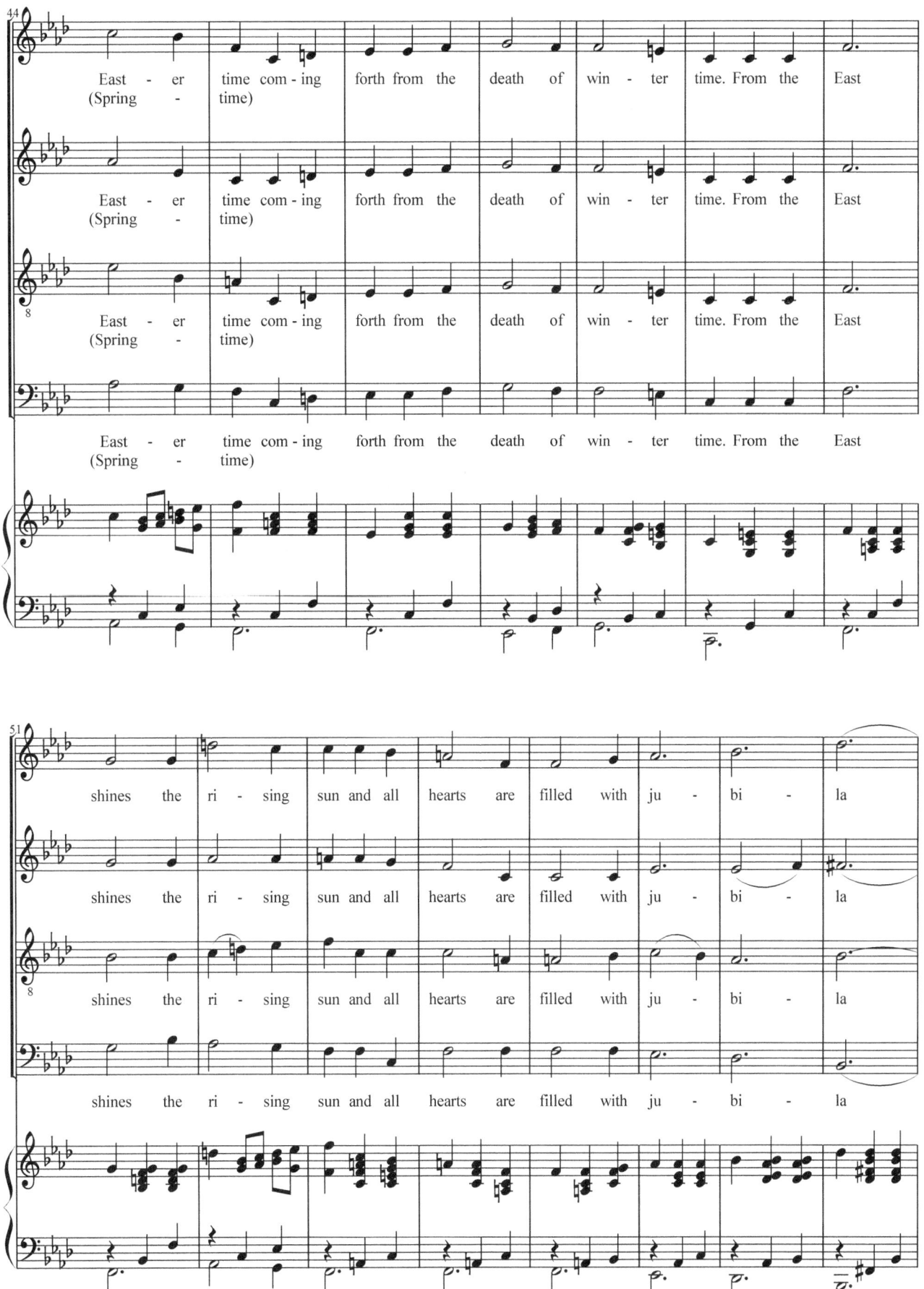

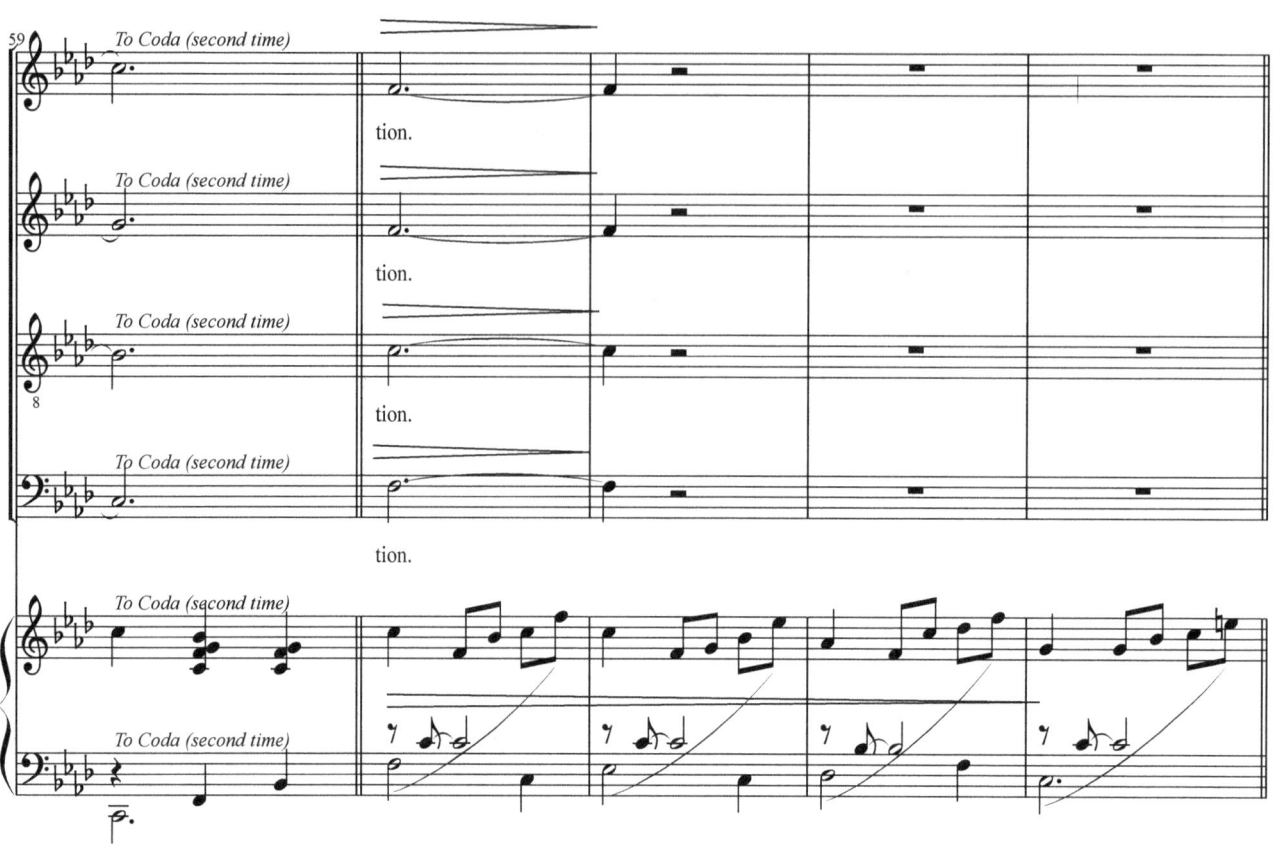

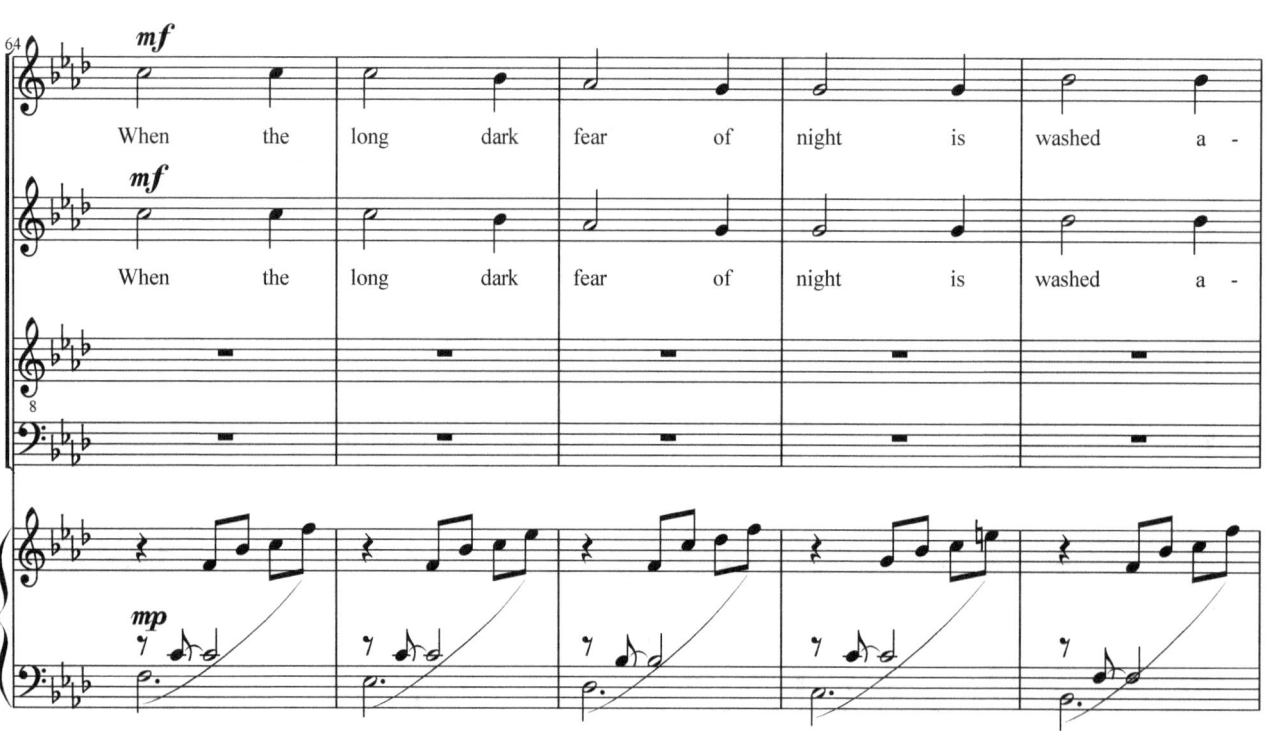

52

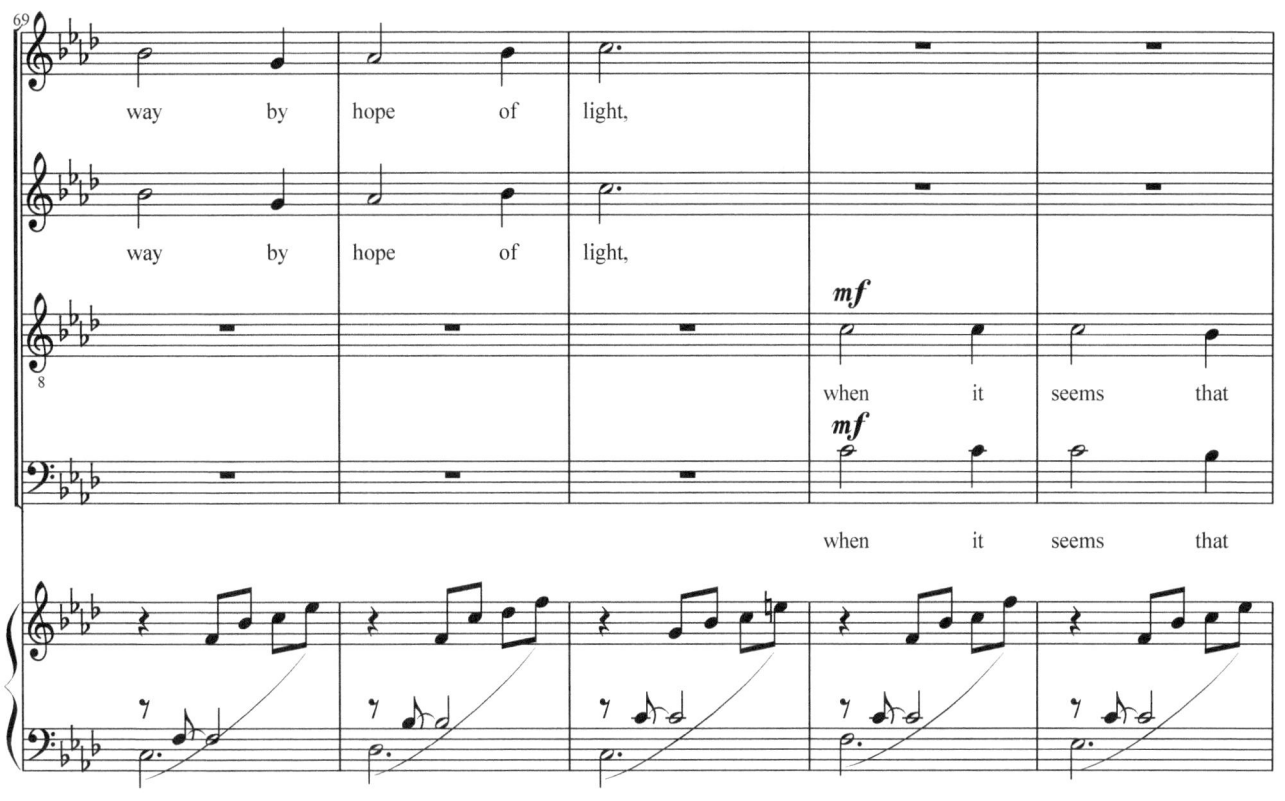

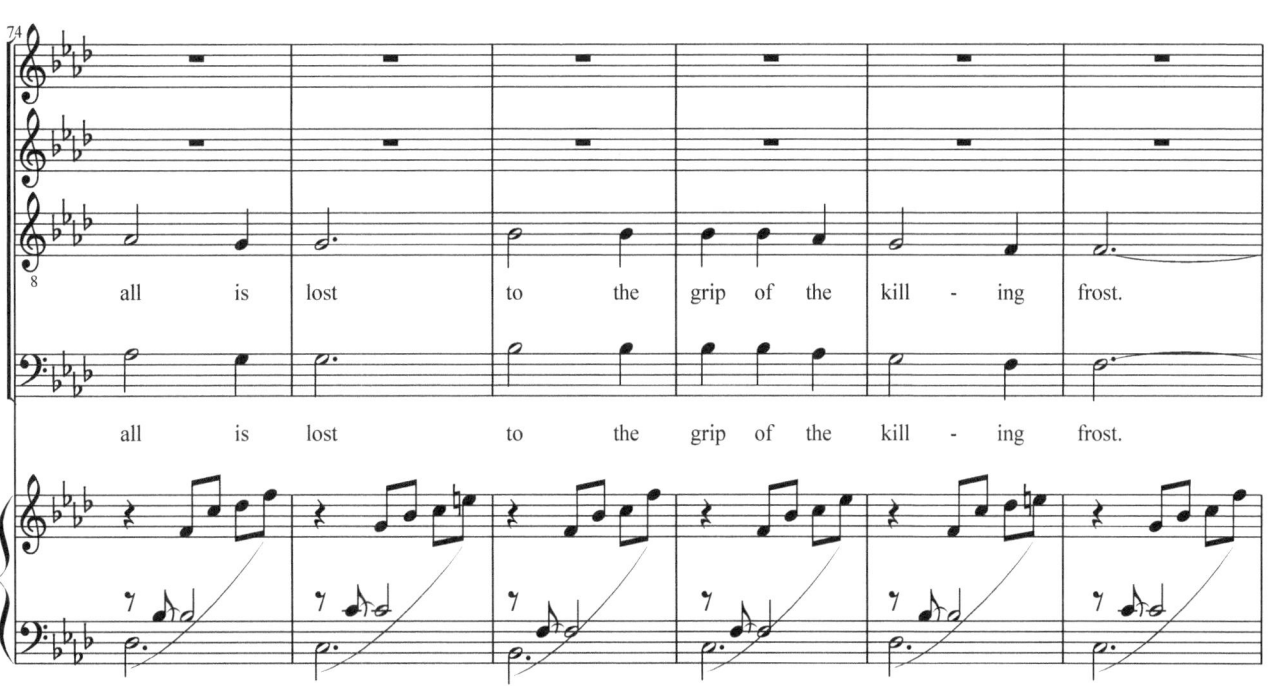

53

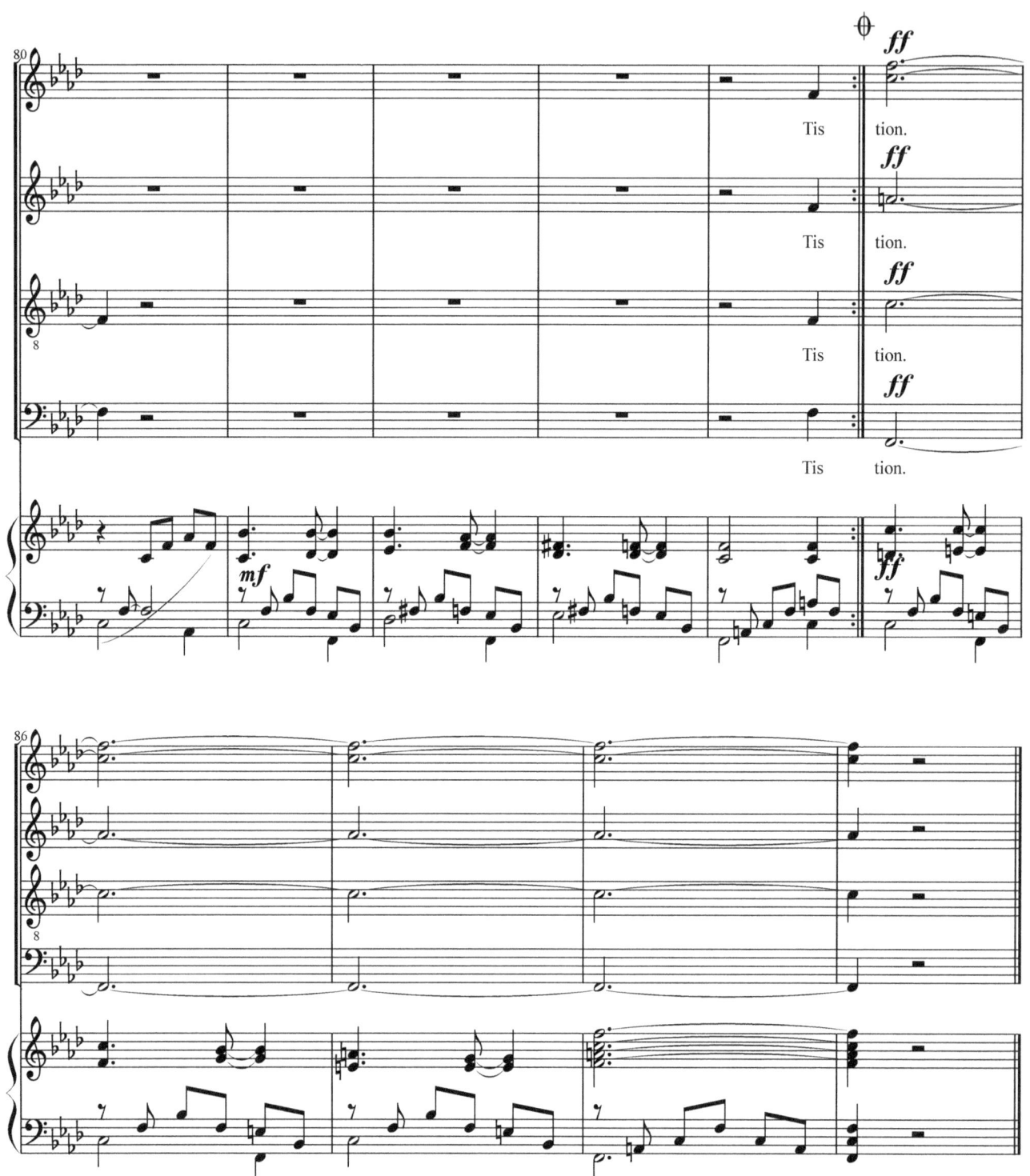

Tis   tion.

Tis   tion.

Tis   tion.

Tis   tion.

Spiritual Songs

Table of Contents

Desires Like Weeds

from the Dhammapada - 24

from "Spiritual Songs"

Ken Langer

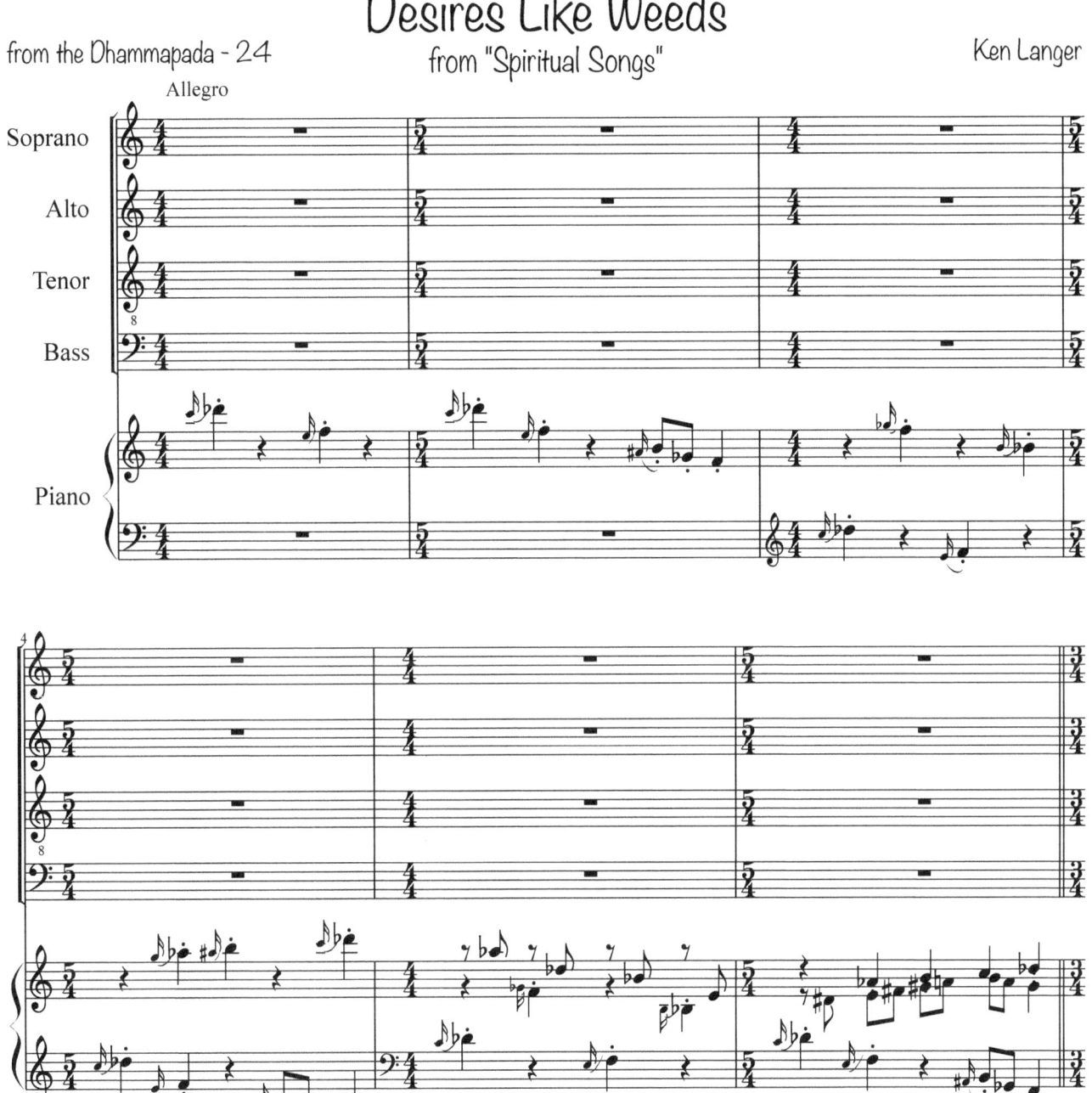

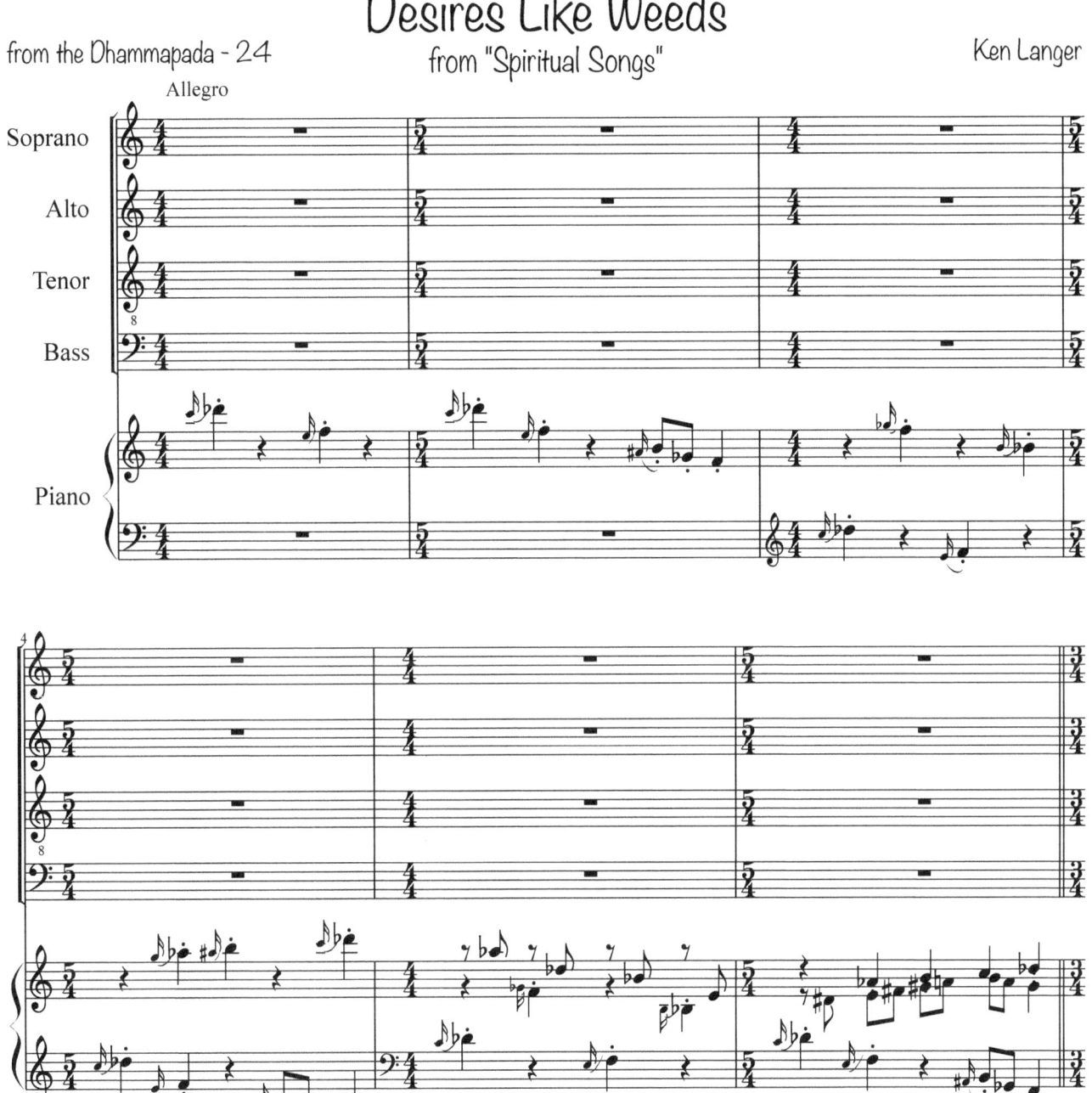

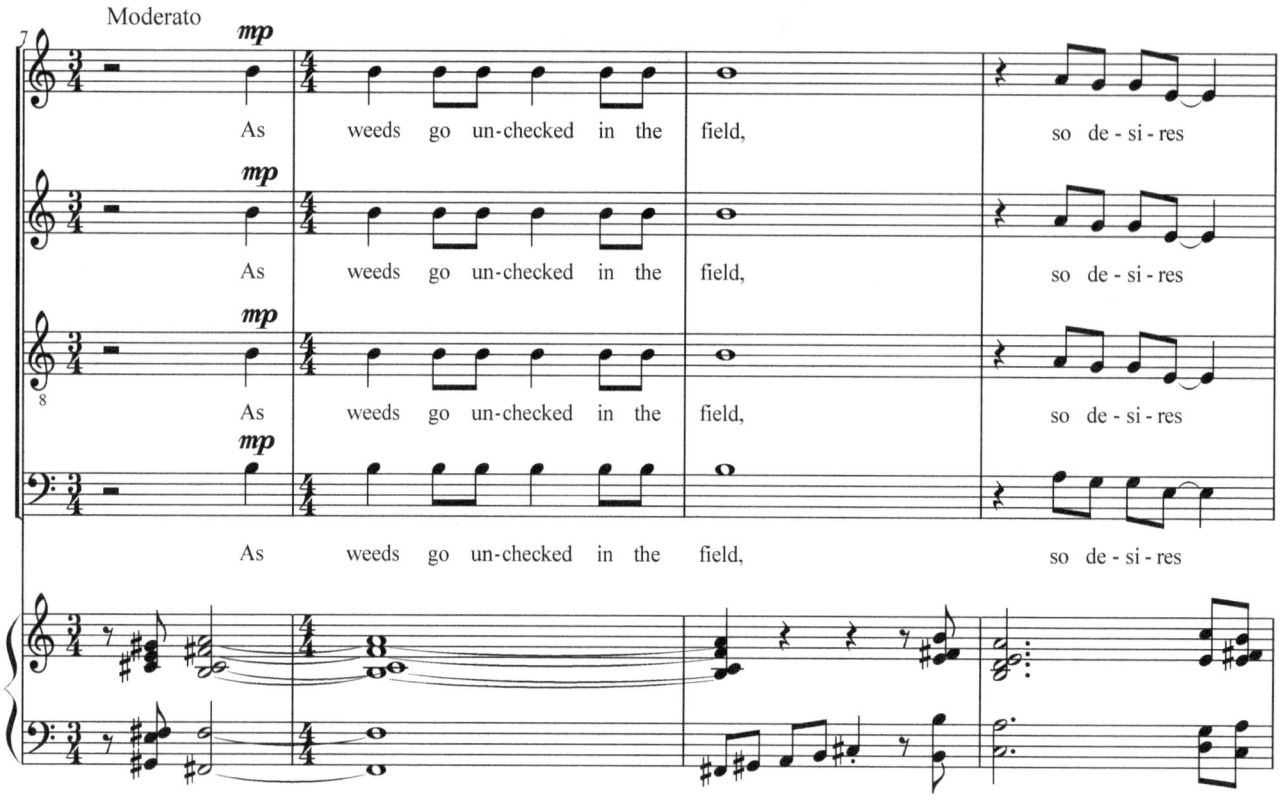

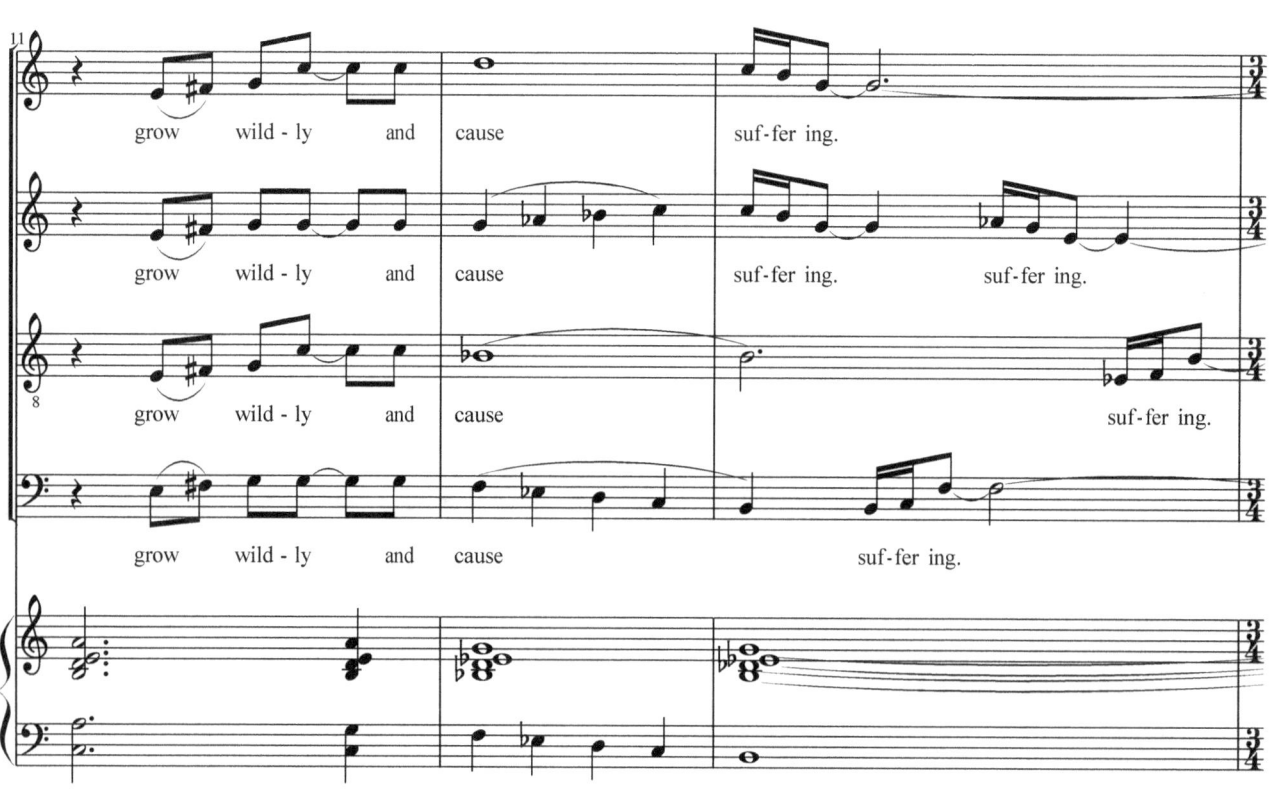

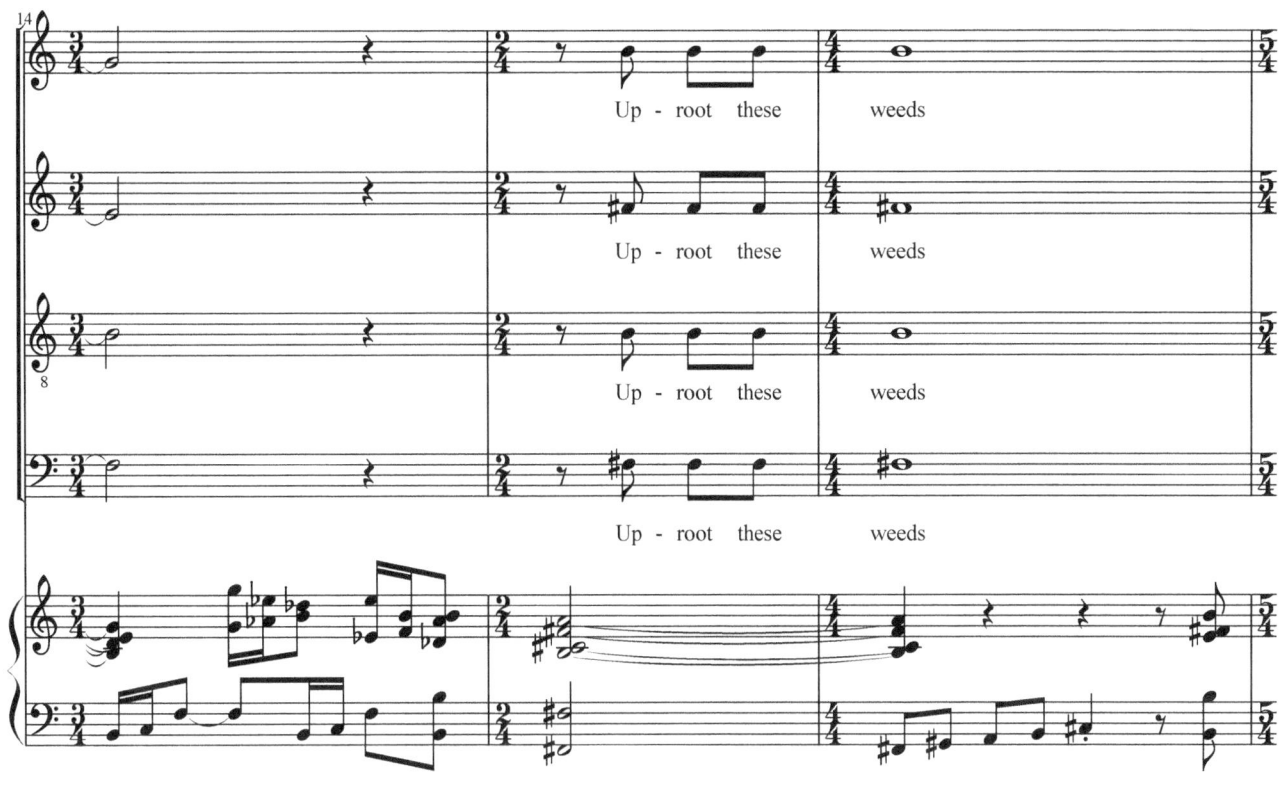

Up - root these weeds

Up - root these weeds

Up - root these weeds

Up - root these weeds

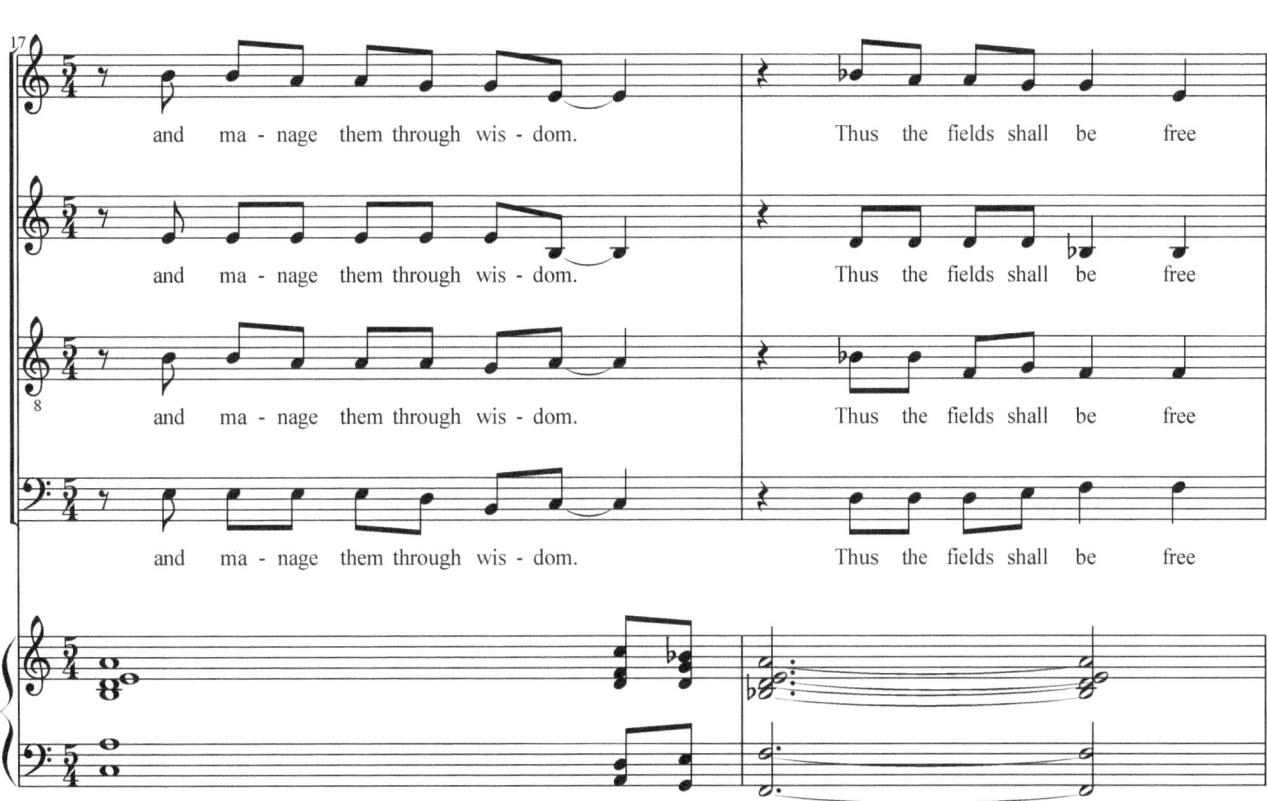

and ma - nage them through wis - dom.   Thus the fields shall be free

and ma - nage them through wis - dom.   Thus the fields shall be free

and ma - nage them through wis - dom.   Thus the fields shall be free

and ma - nage them through wis - dom.   Thus the fields shall be free

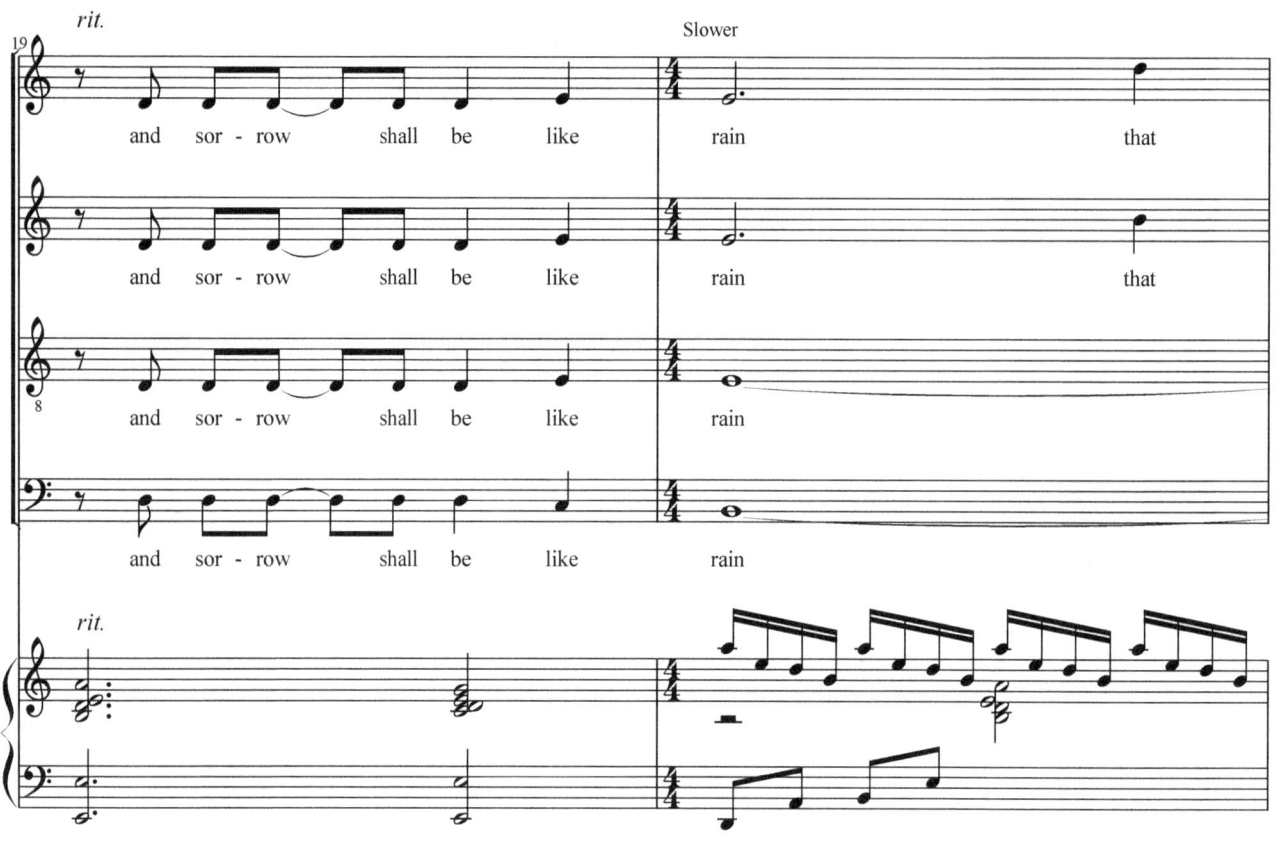

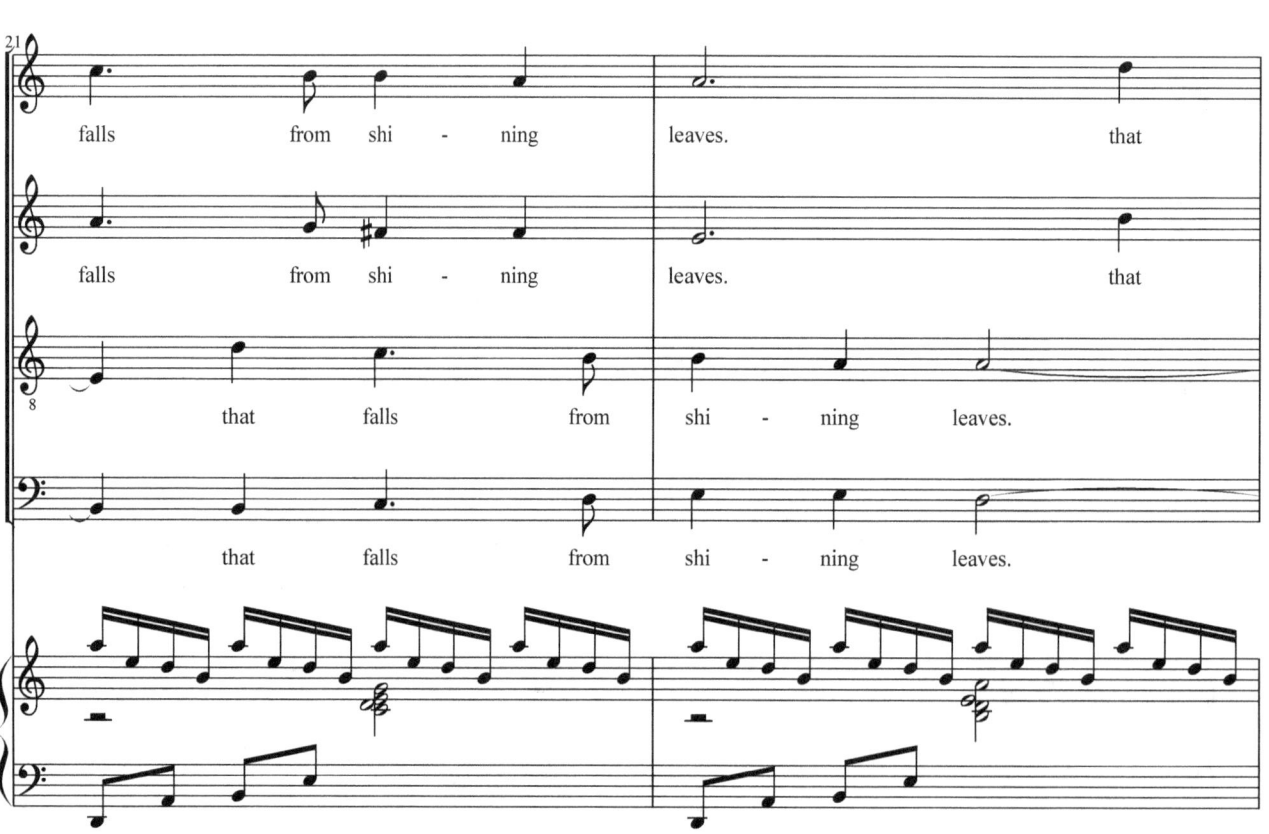

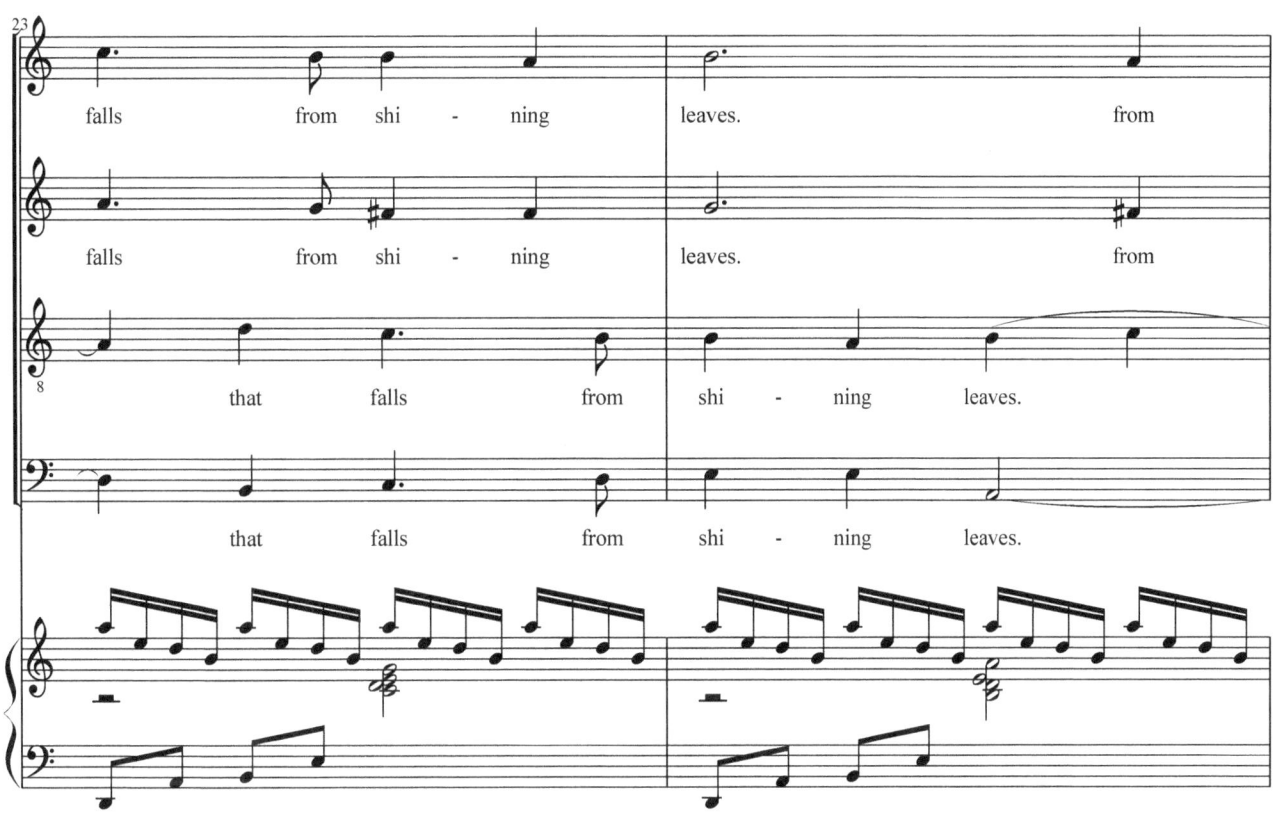

falls   from shi - ning   leaves.   from
falls   from shi - ning   leaves.   from
that falls   from shi - ning   leaves.
that falls   from shi - ning   leaves.

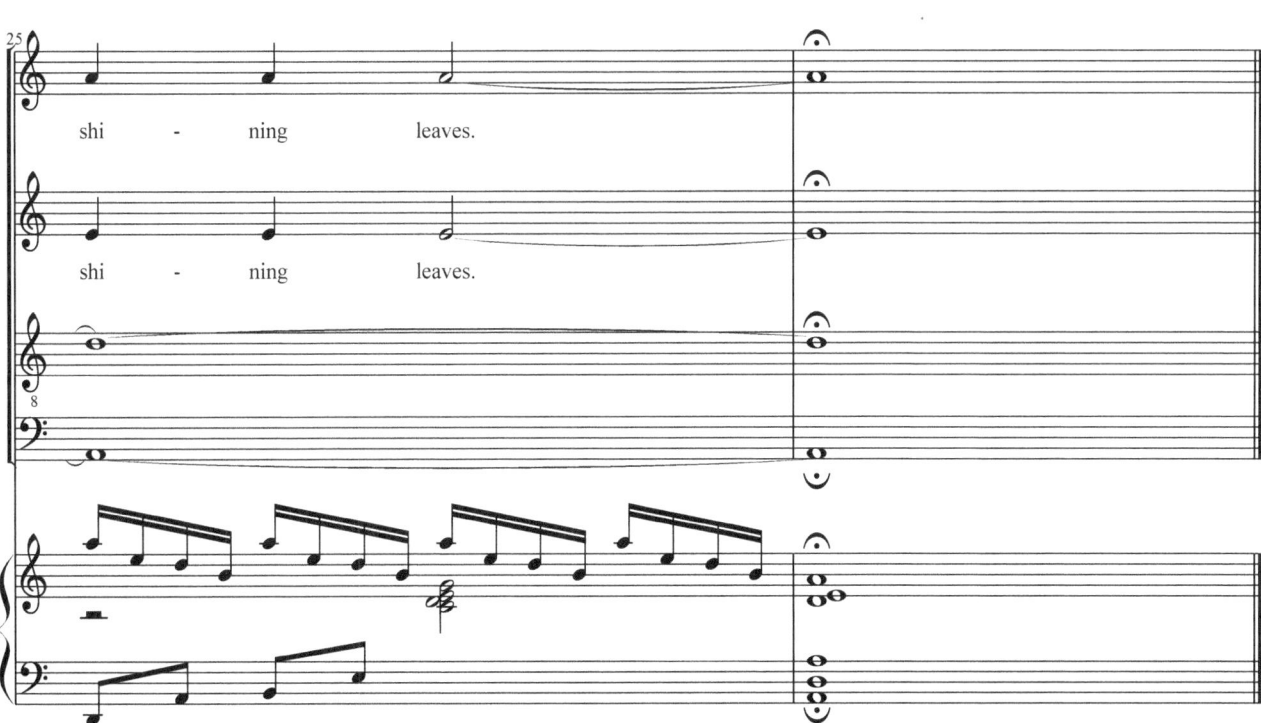

shi - ning   leaves.
shi - ning   leaves.

The Earth Am I

Navajo chant and Pagan blessing

from "Spiritual Songs"

music by Ken Langer

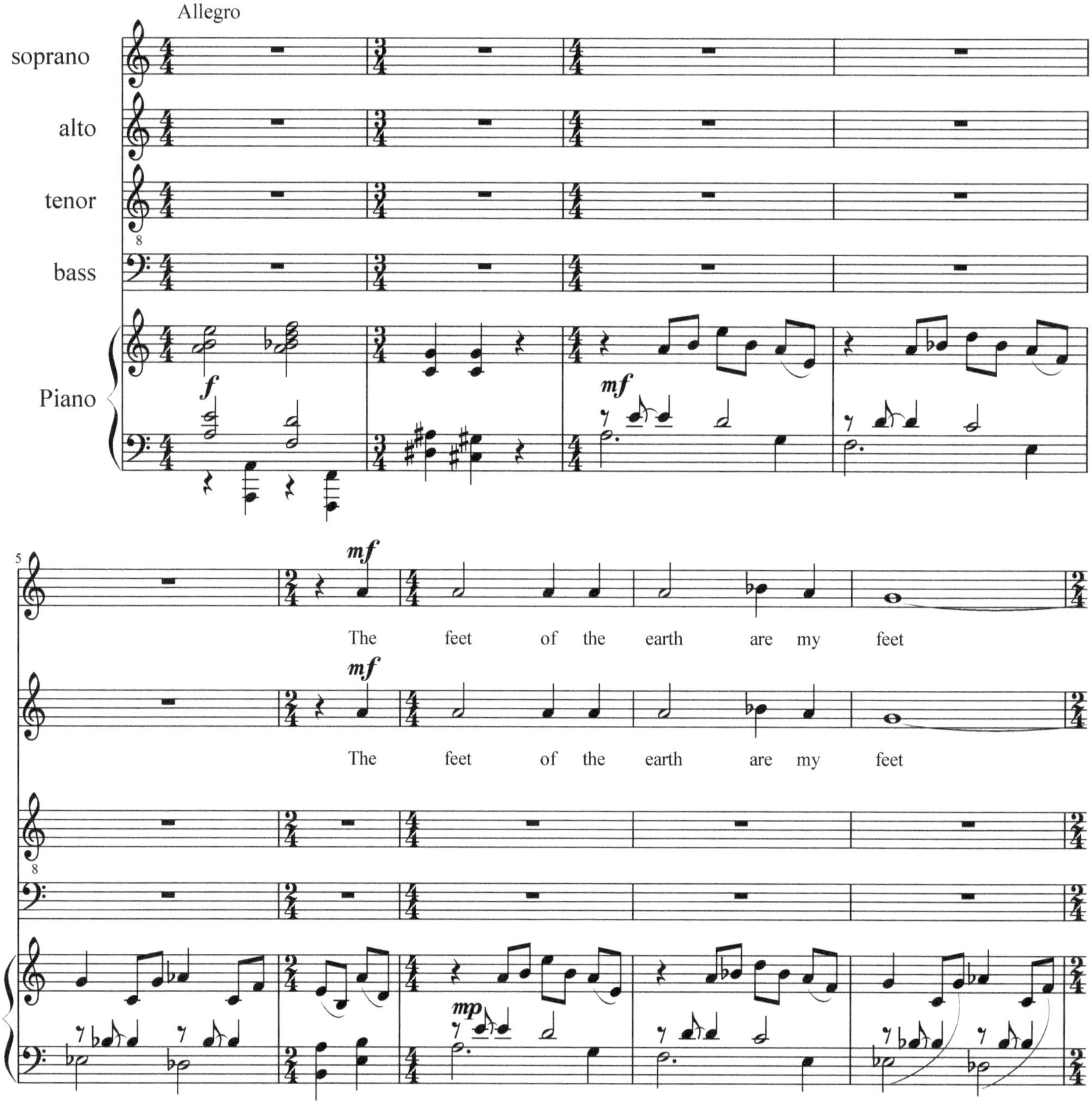
Allegro
soprano
alto
tenor
bass
Piano
f
mf
mp
The feet of the earth are my feet
The feet of the earth are my feet

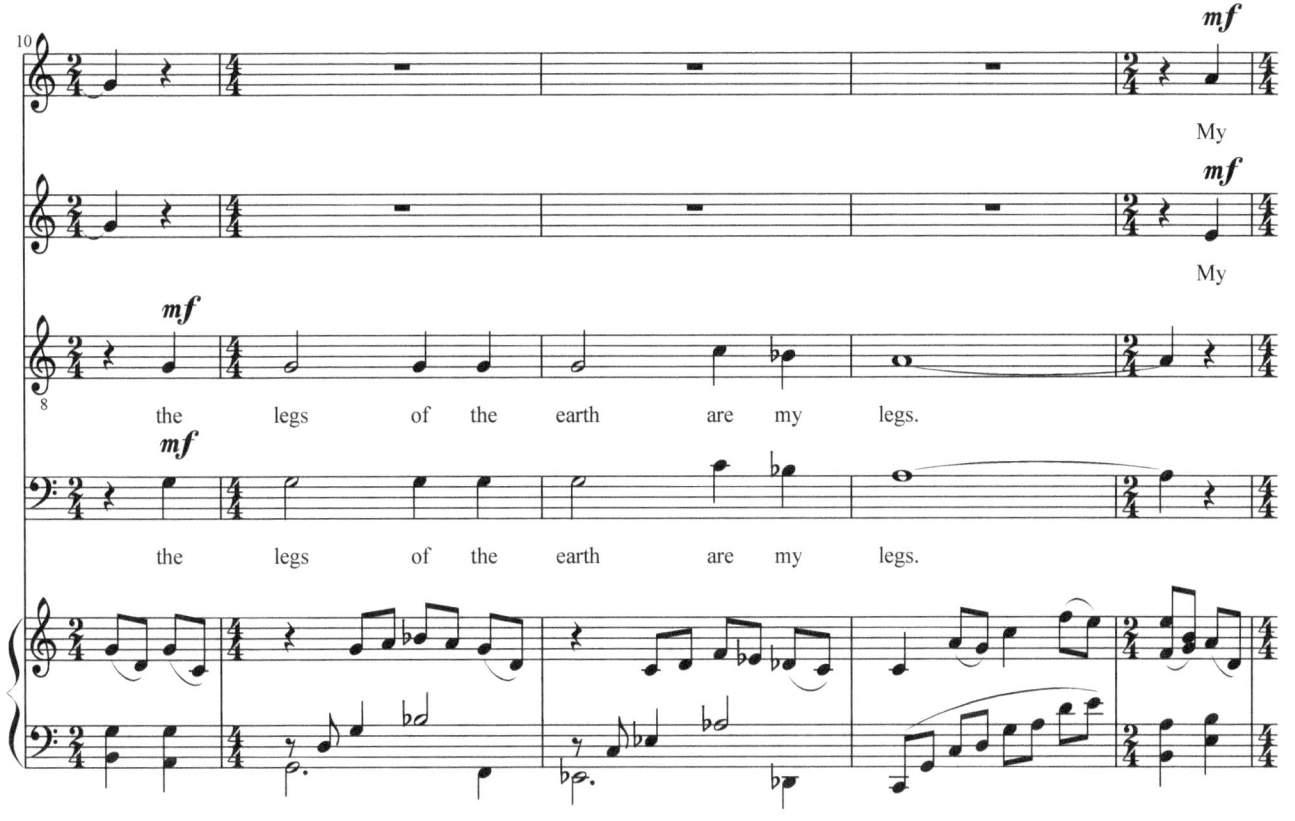

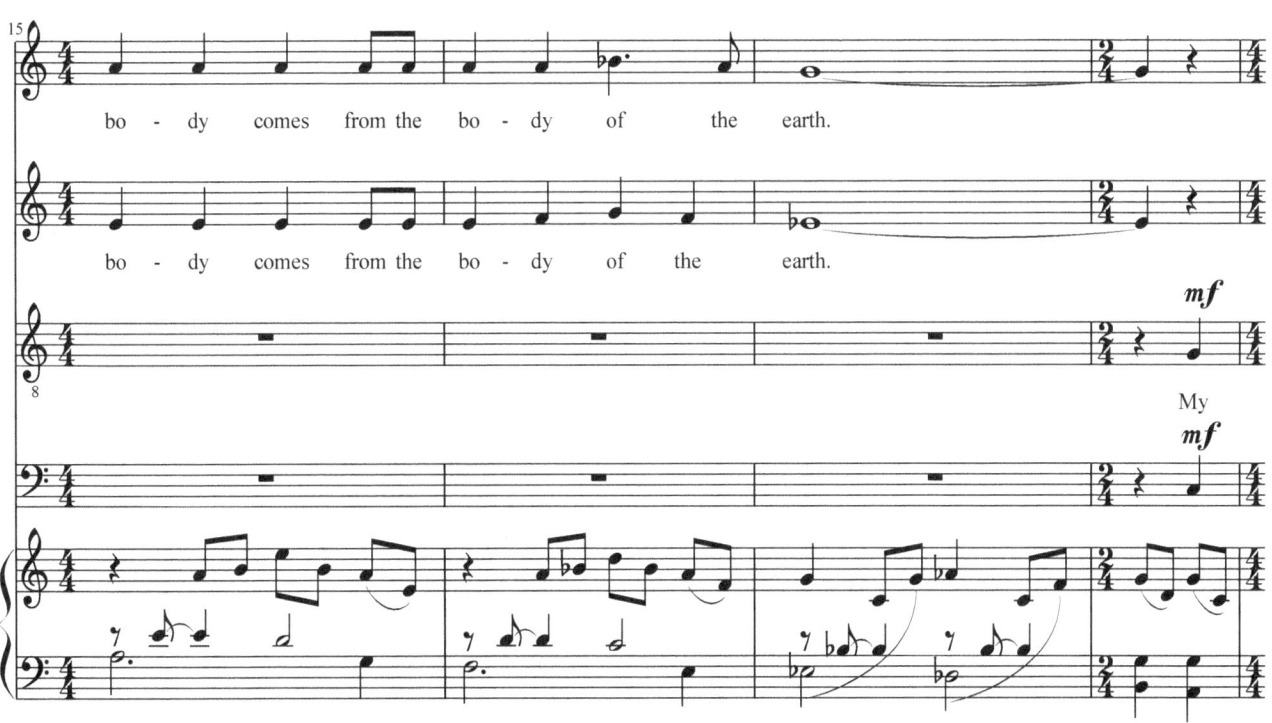

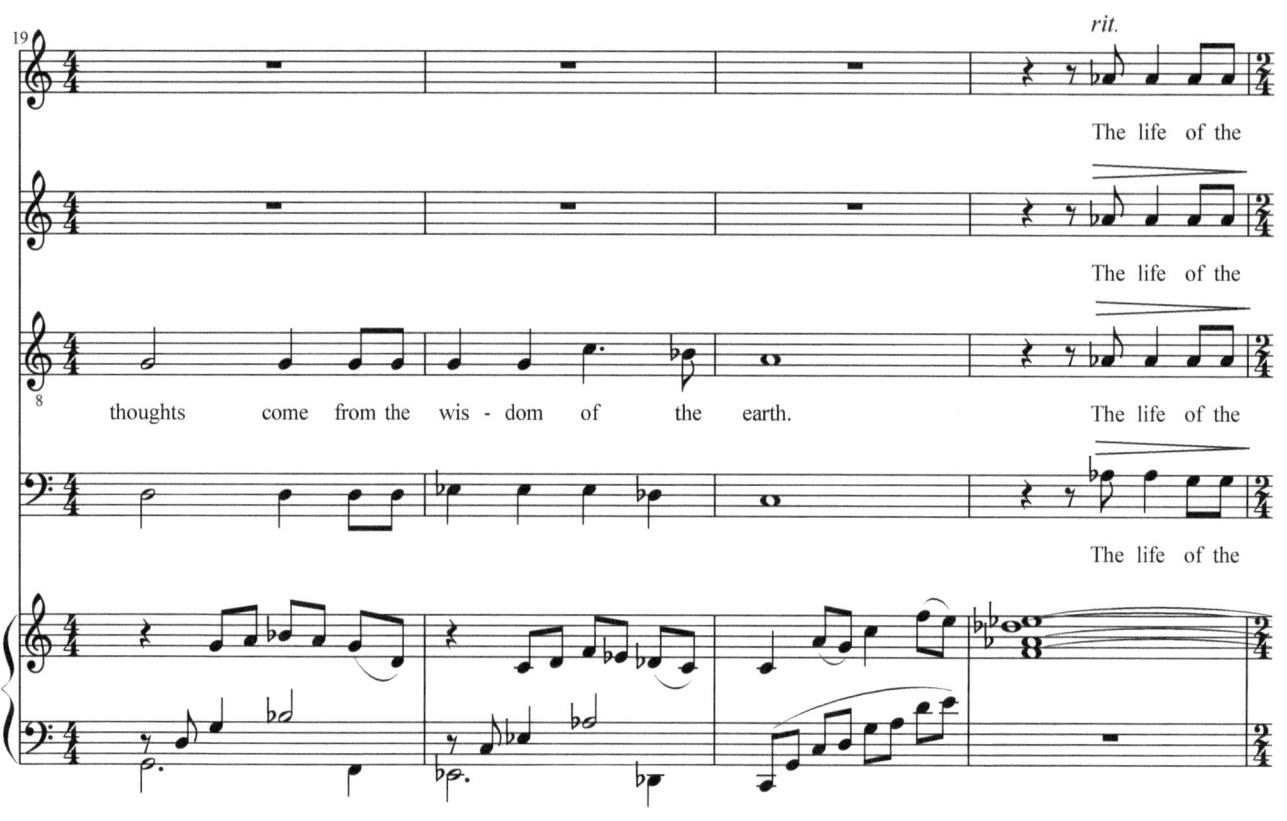

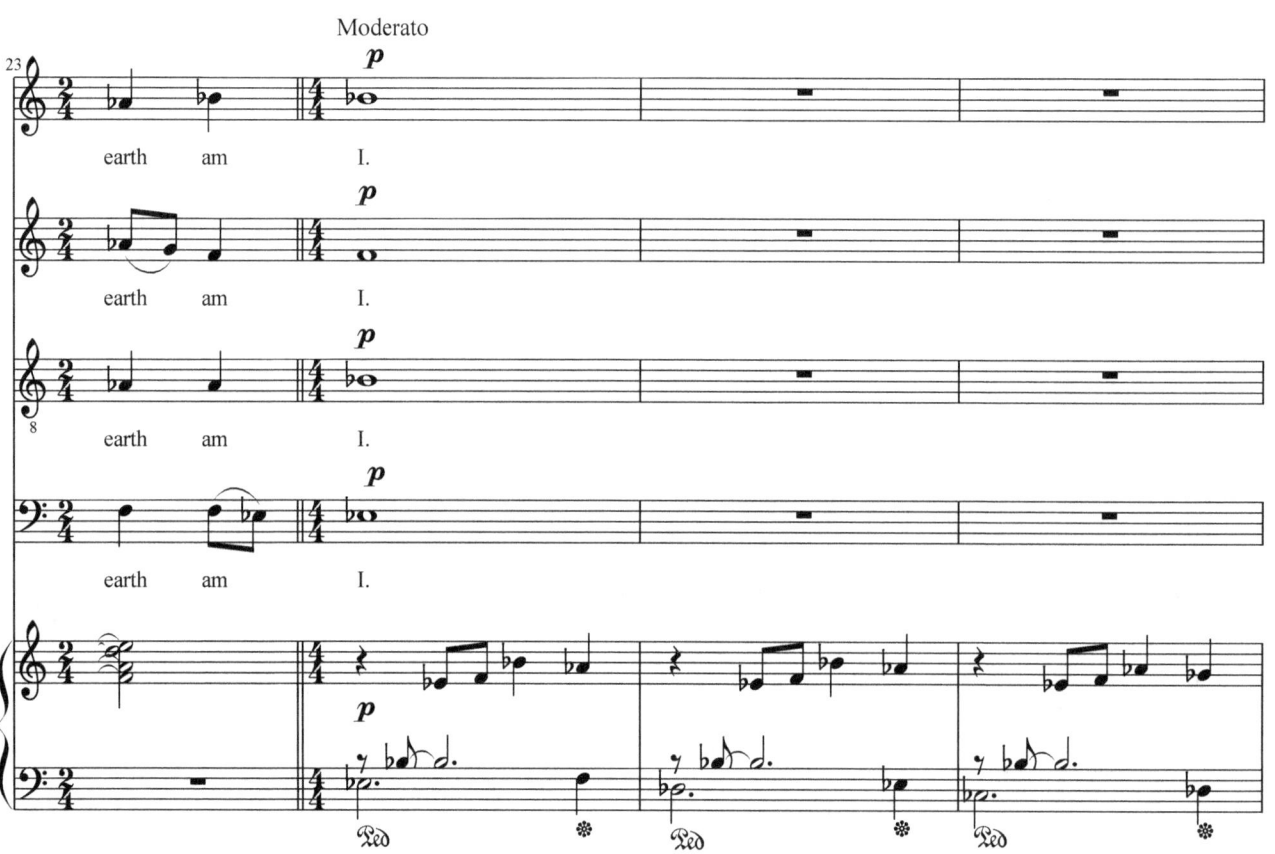

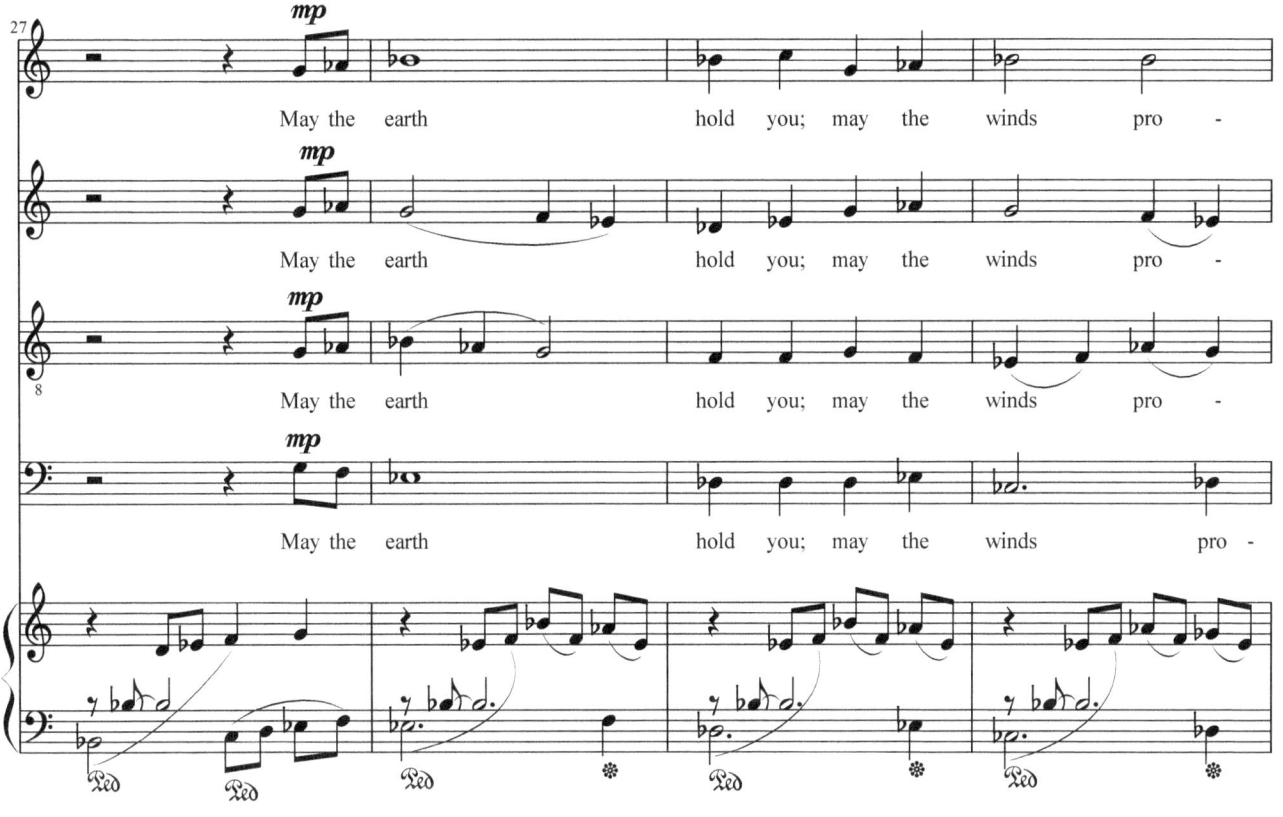

May the earth hold you; may the winds pro -

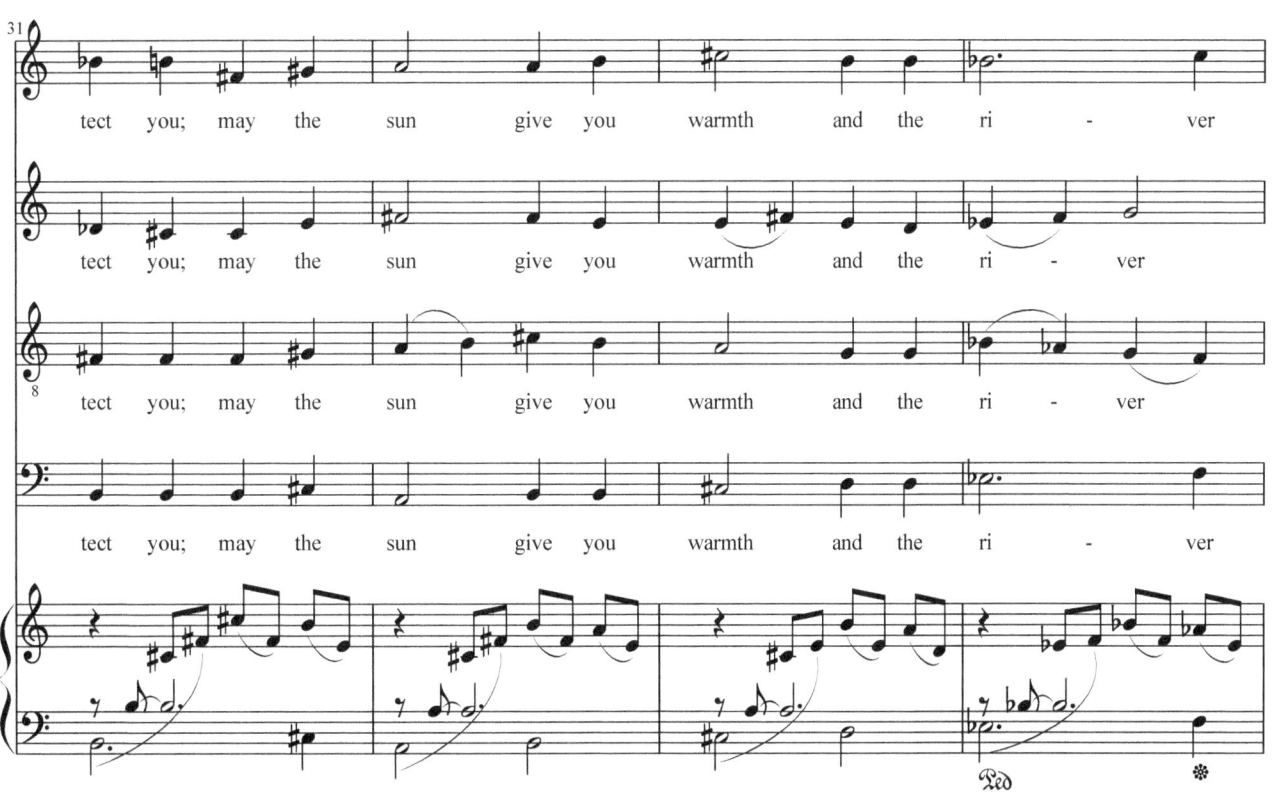

tect you; may the sun give you warmth and the ri - ver

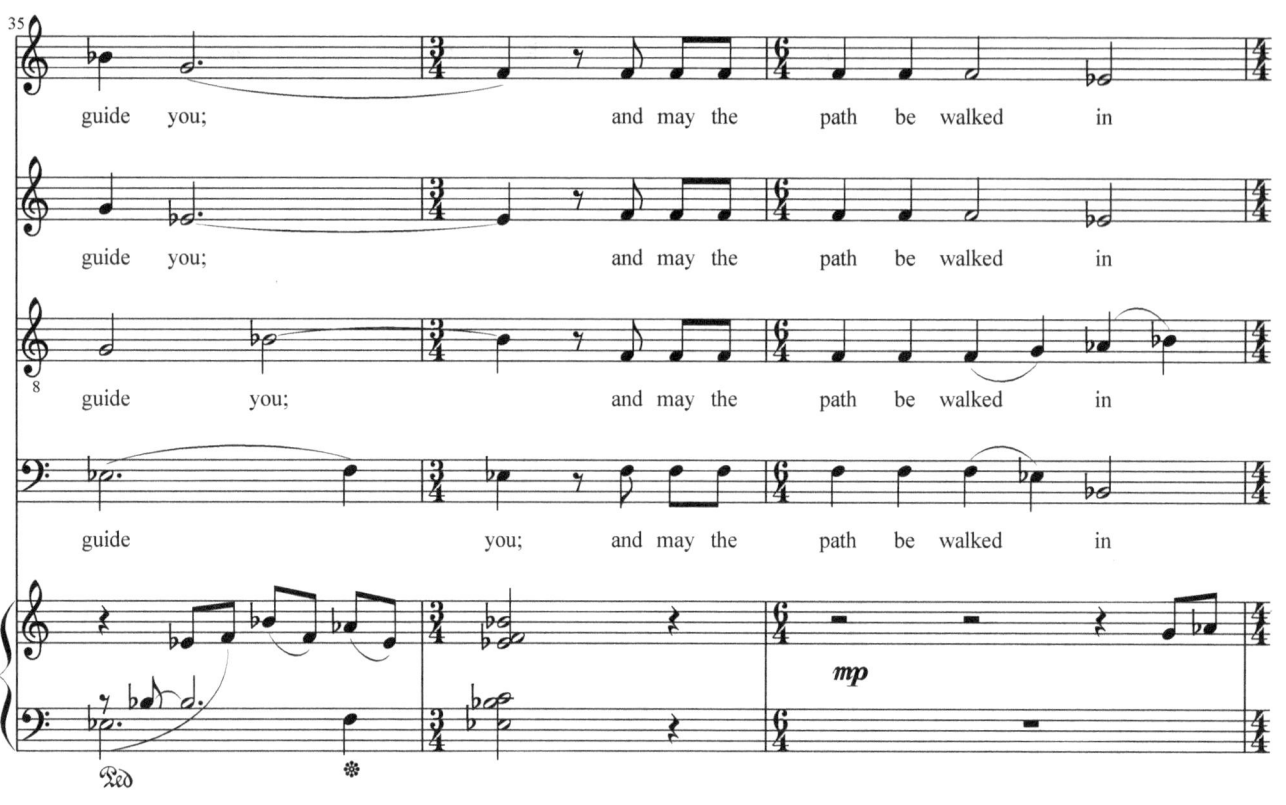

guide you; and may the path be walked in

guide you; and may the path be walked in

guide you; and may the path be walked in

guide you; and may the path be walked in

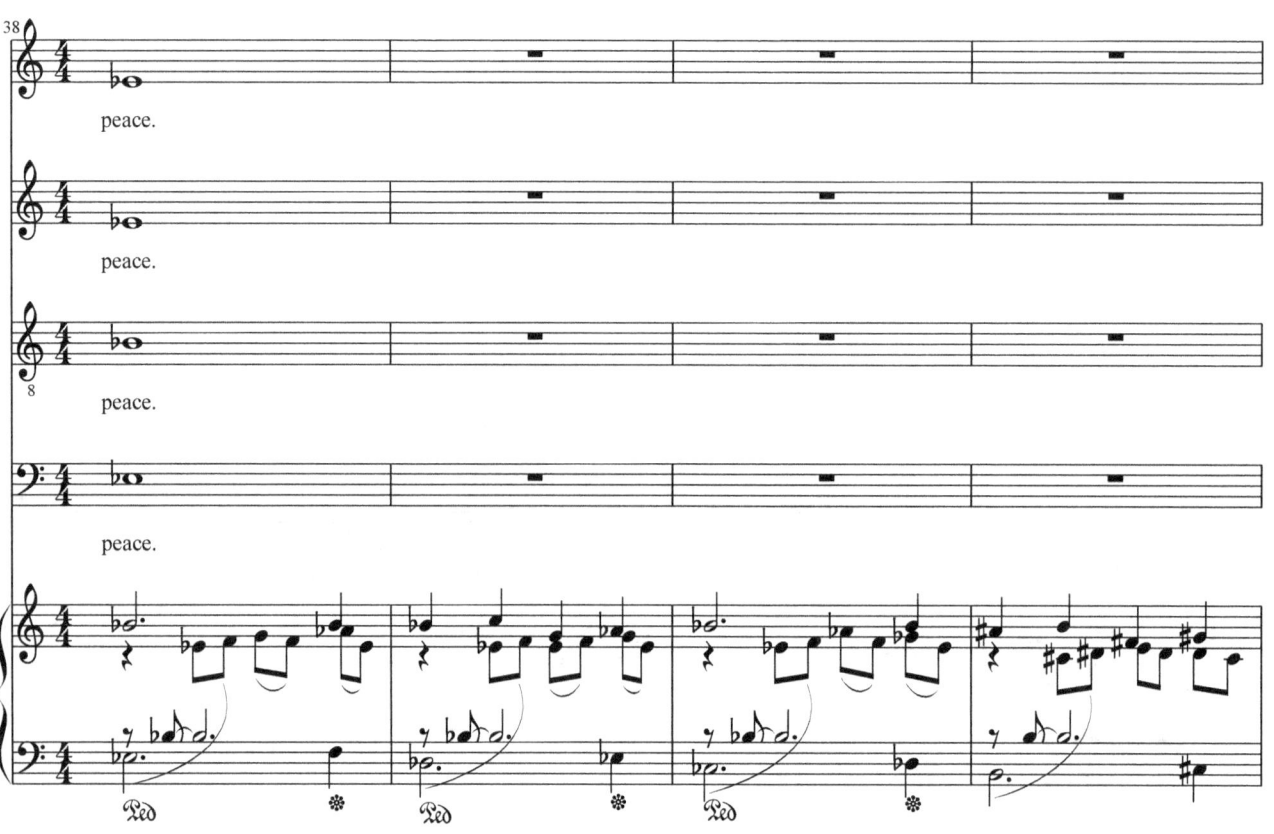

peace.

peace.

peace.

peace.

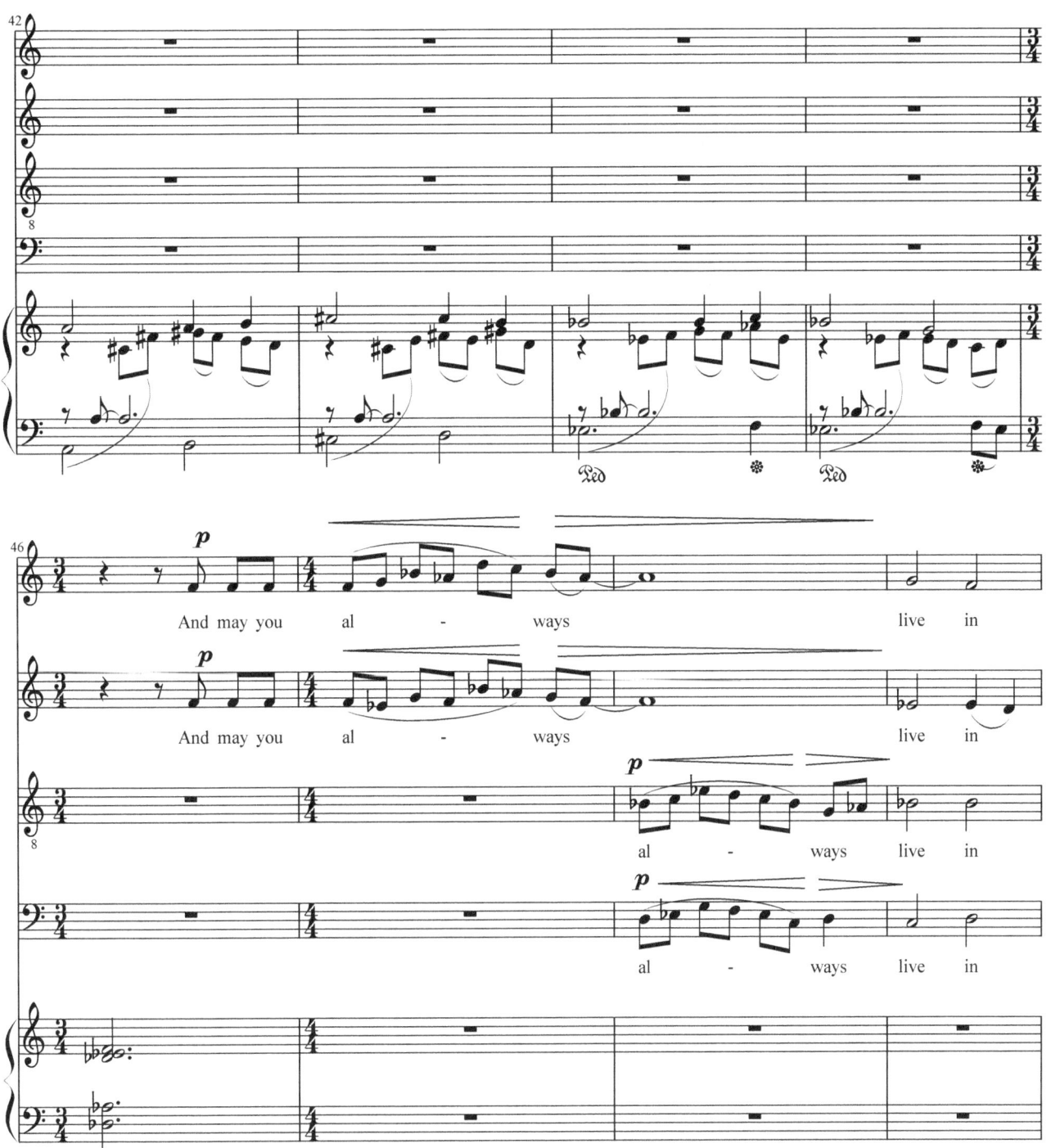

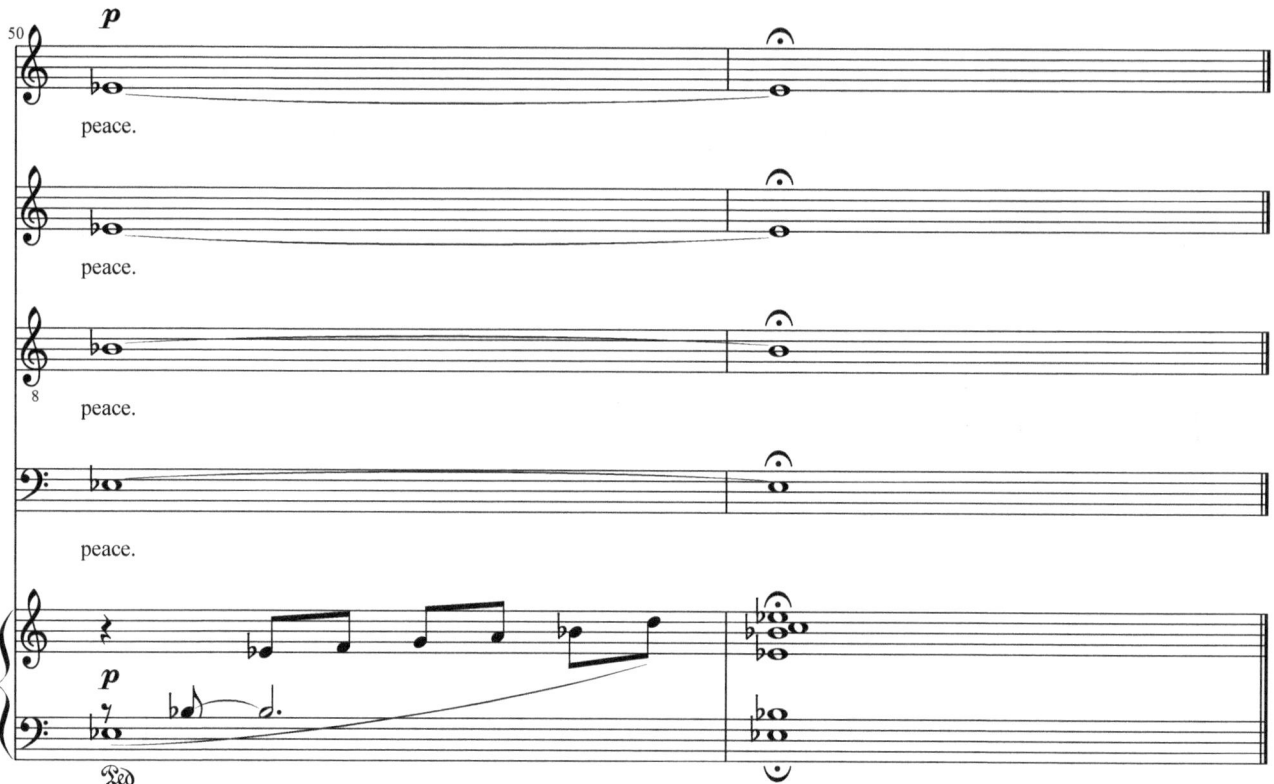

peace.

peace.

peace.

peace.

From Love We Come

from the Bible John 4:16

from "Spiritual Songs"

Ken Langer

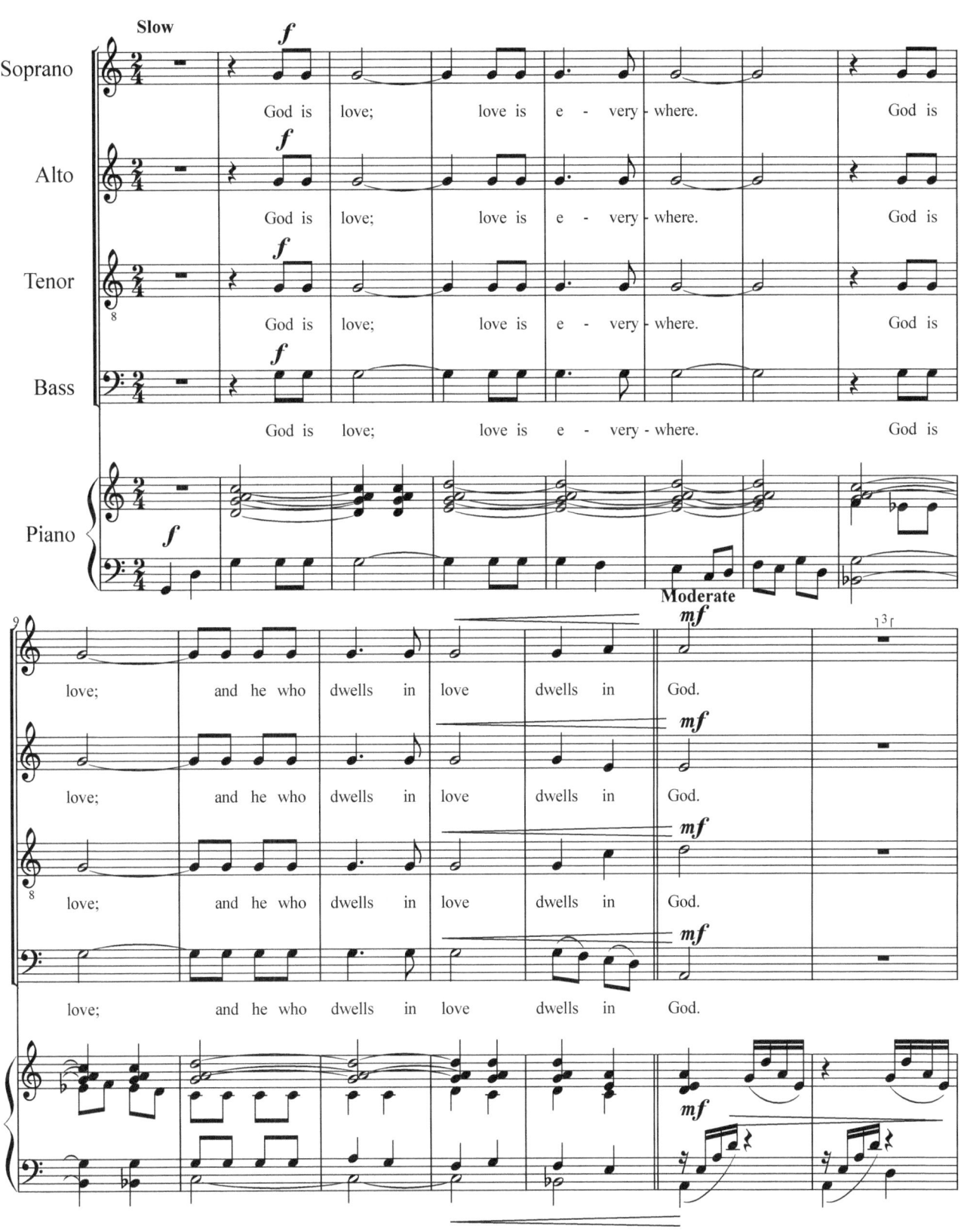

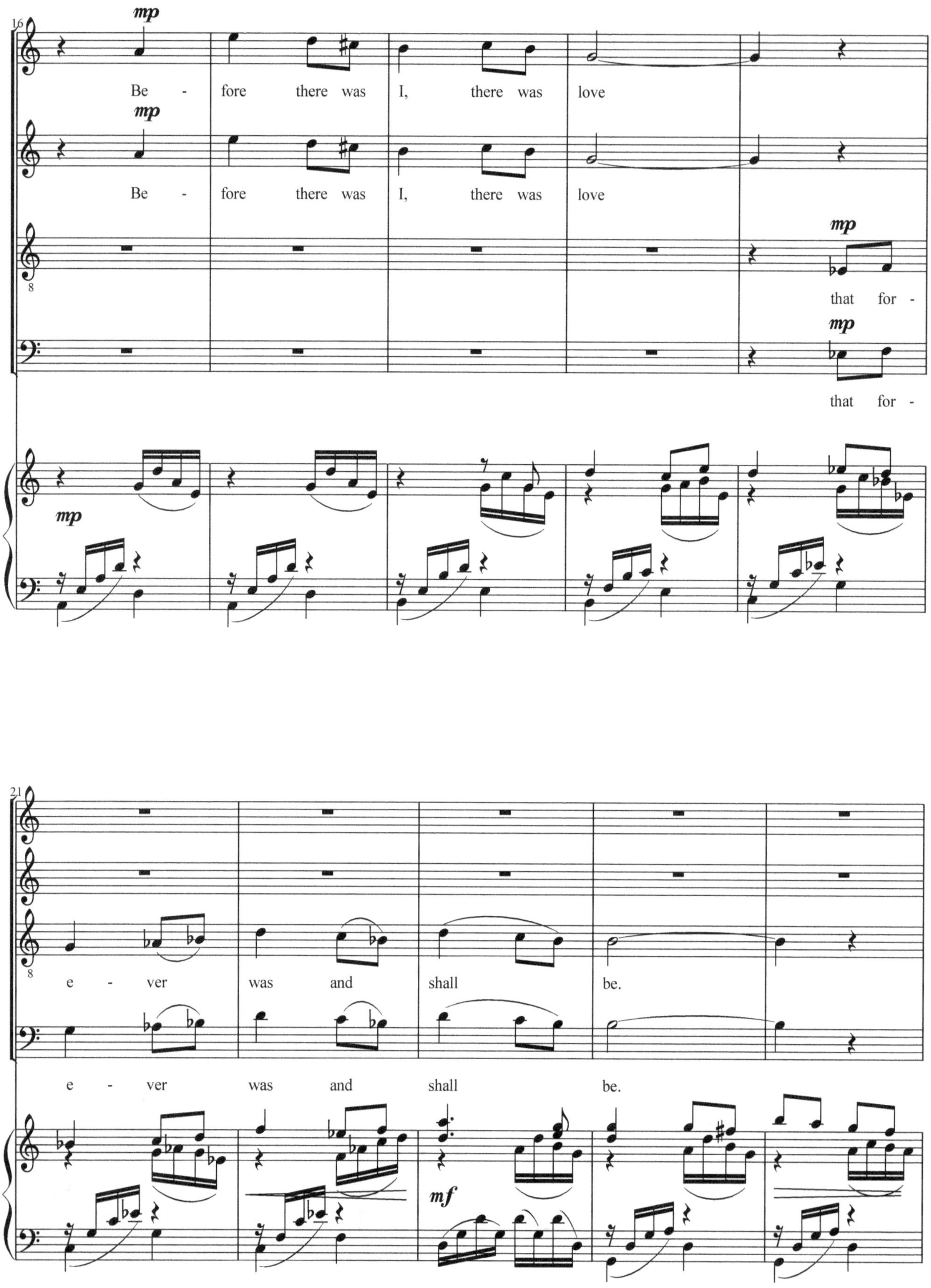

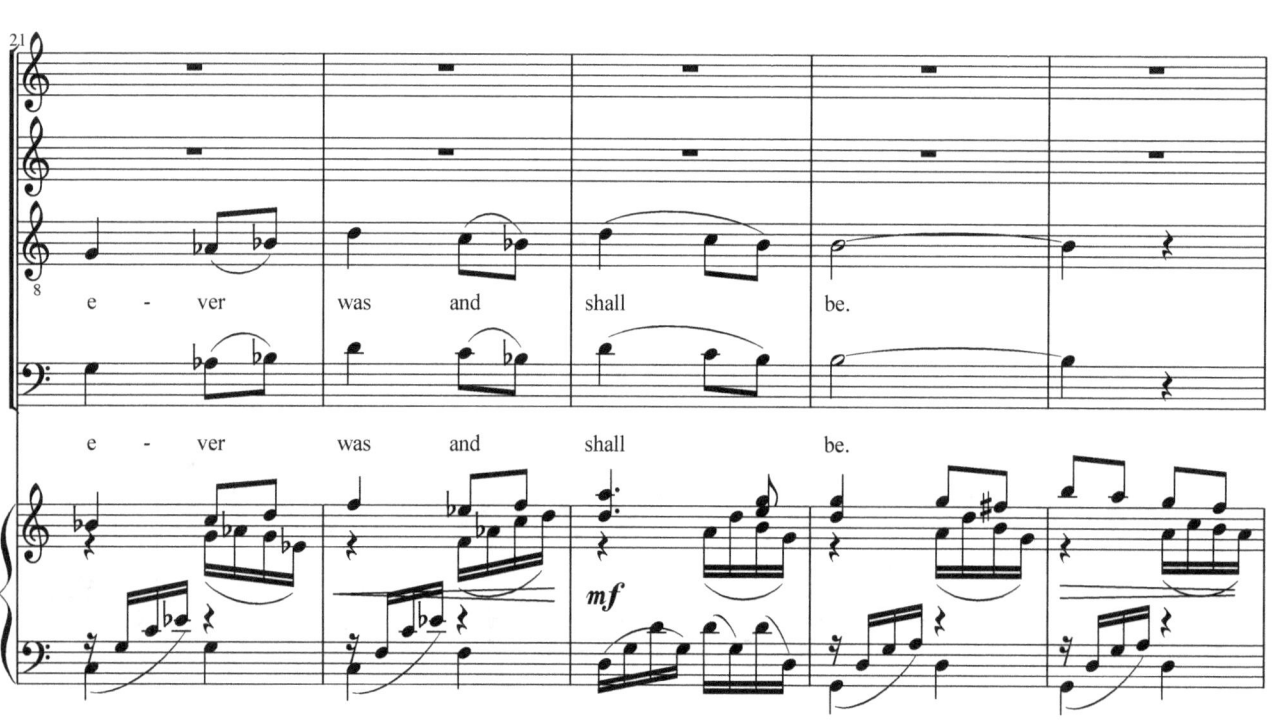

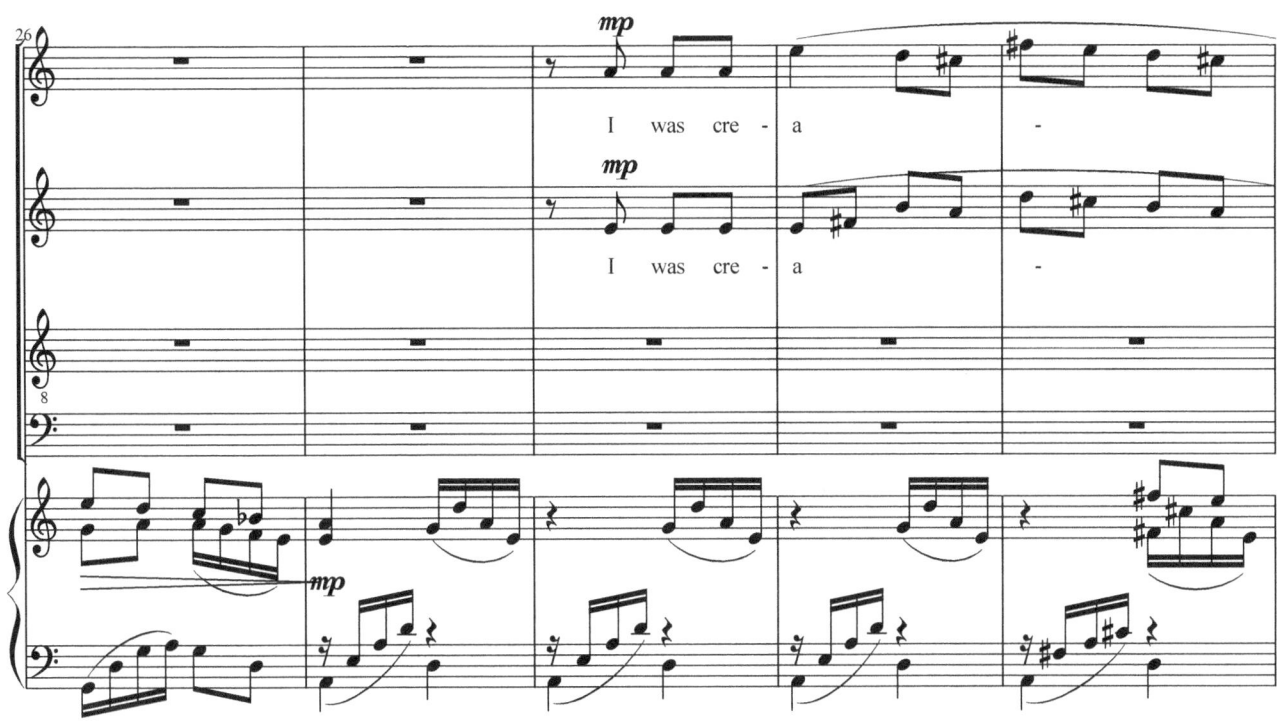

I was cre - a

I was cre - a

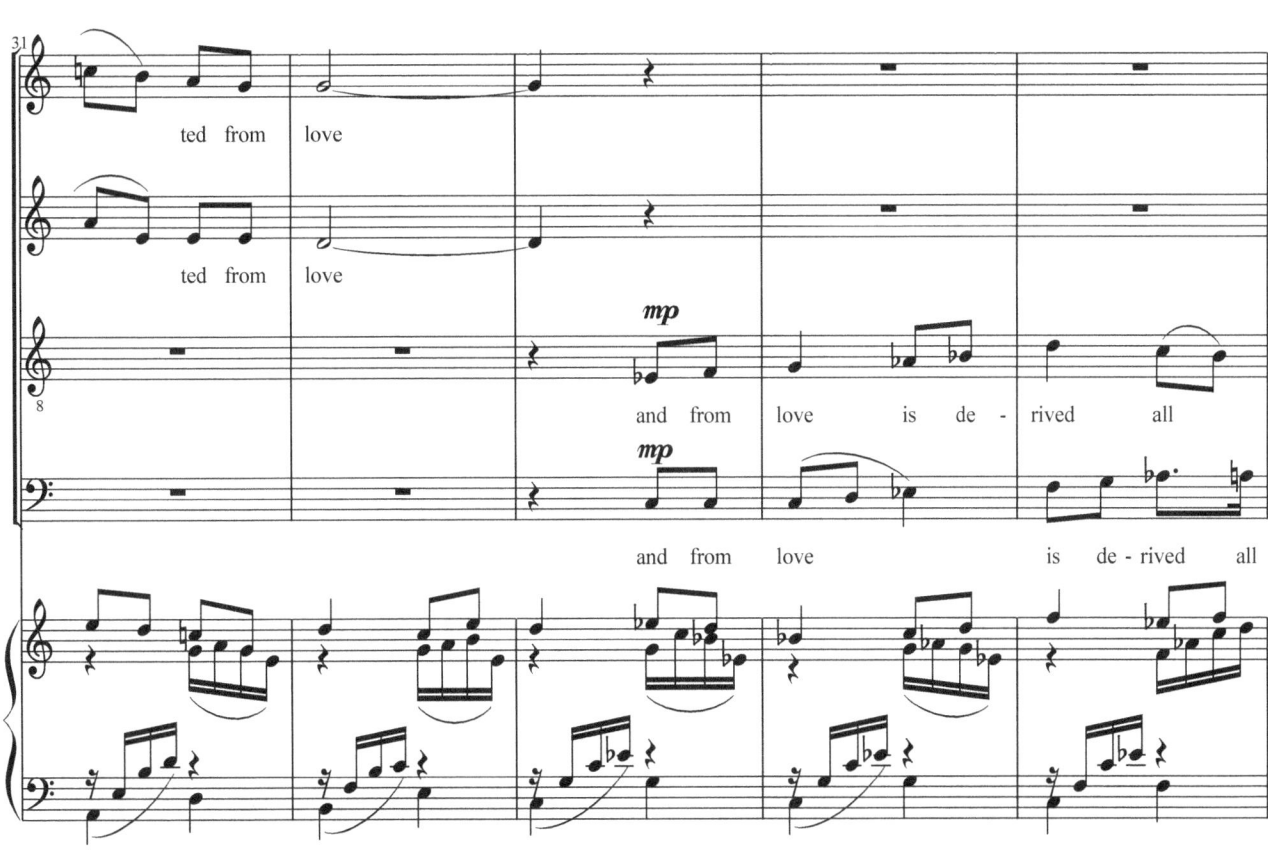

ted from love

ted from love

and from love is de - rived all

and from love is de - rived all

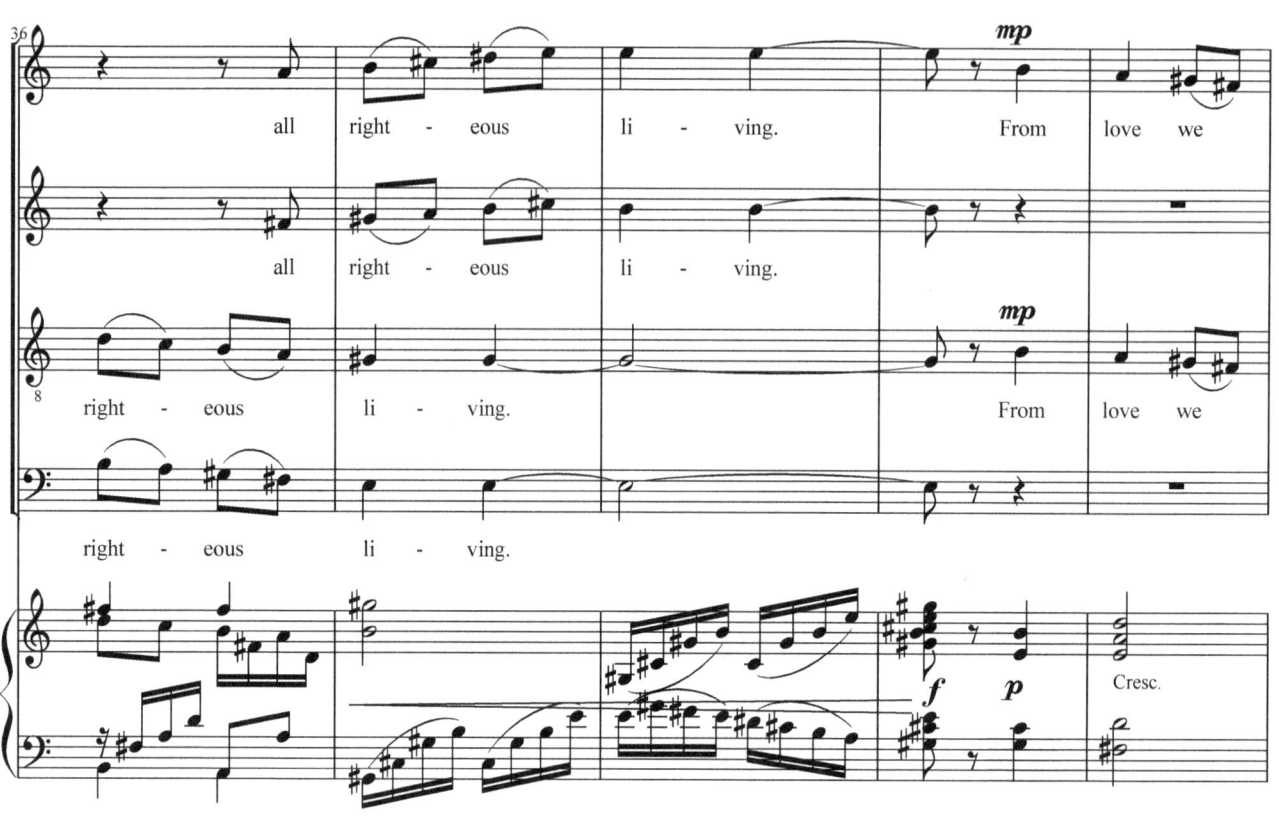

all right - eous li - ving. From love we

all right - eous li - ving.

right - eous li - ving. From love we

right - eous li - ving.

come; and to love we re - turn.

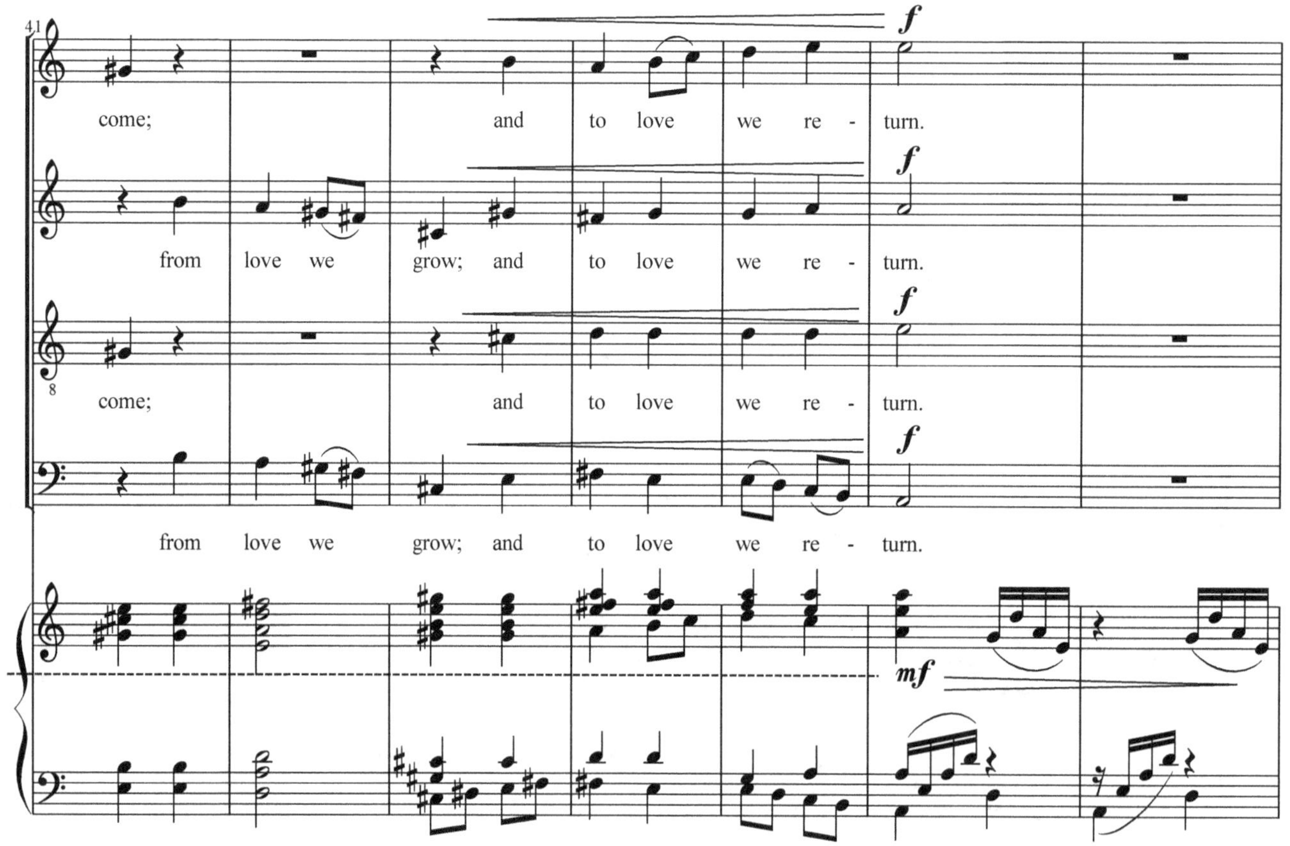

from love we grow; and to love we re - turn.

come; and to love we re - turn.

from love we grow; and to love we re - turn.

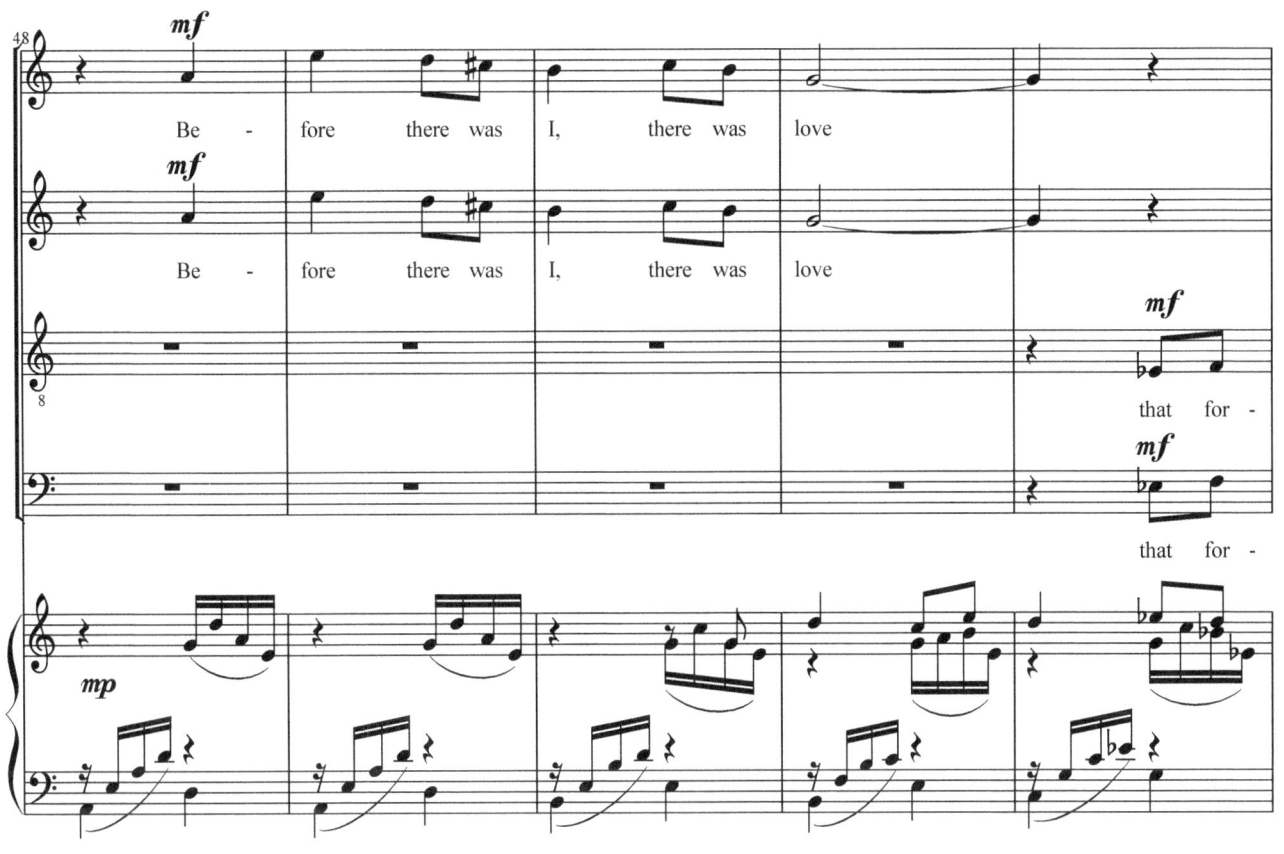

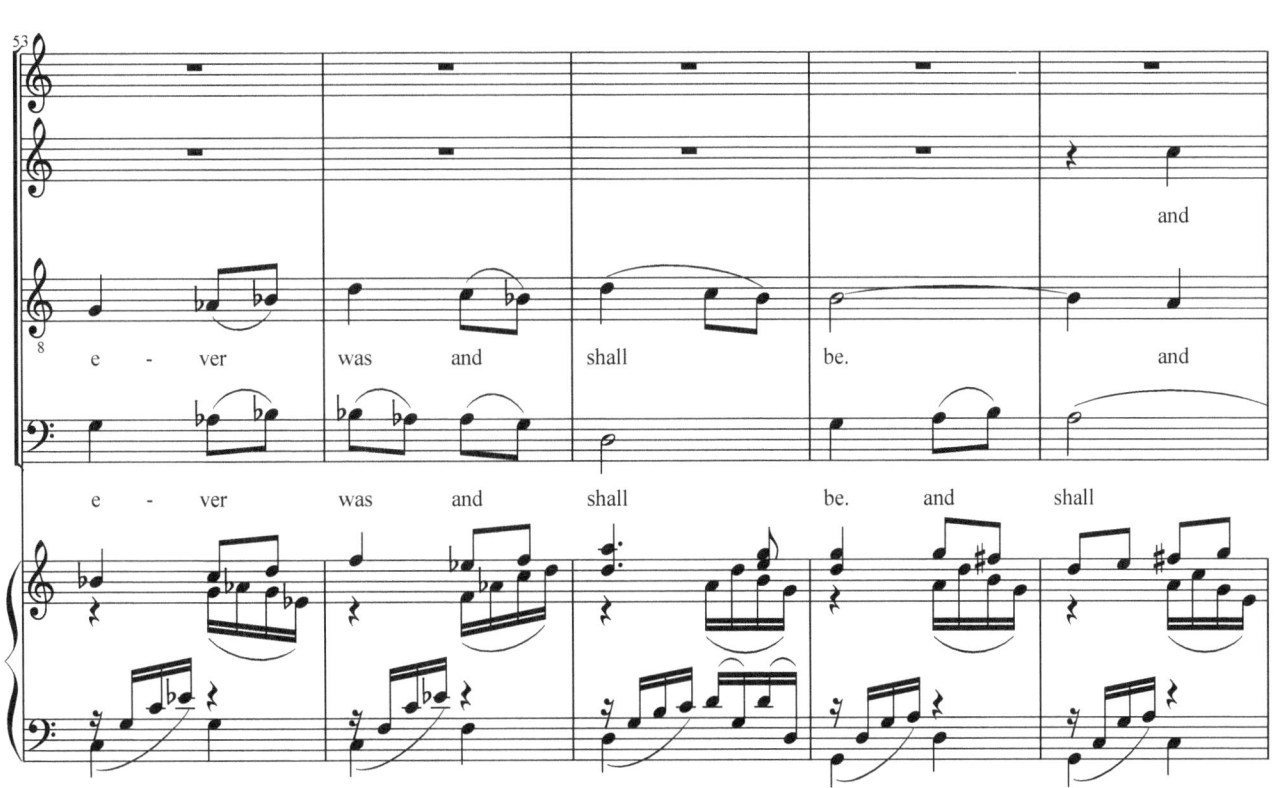

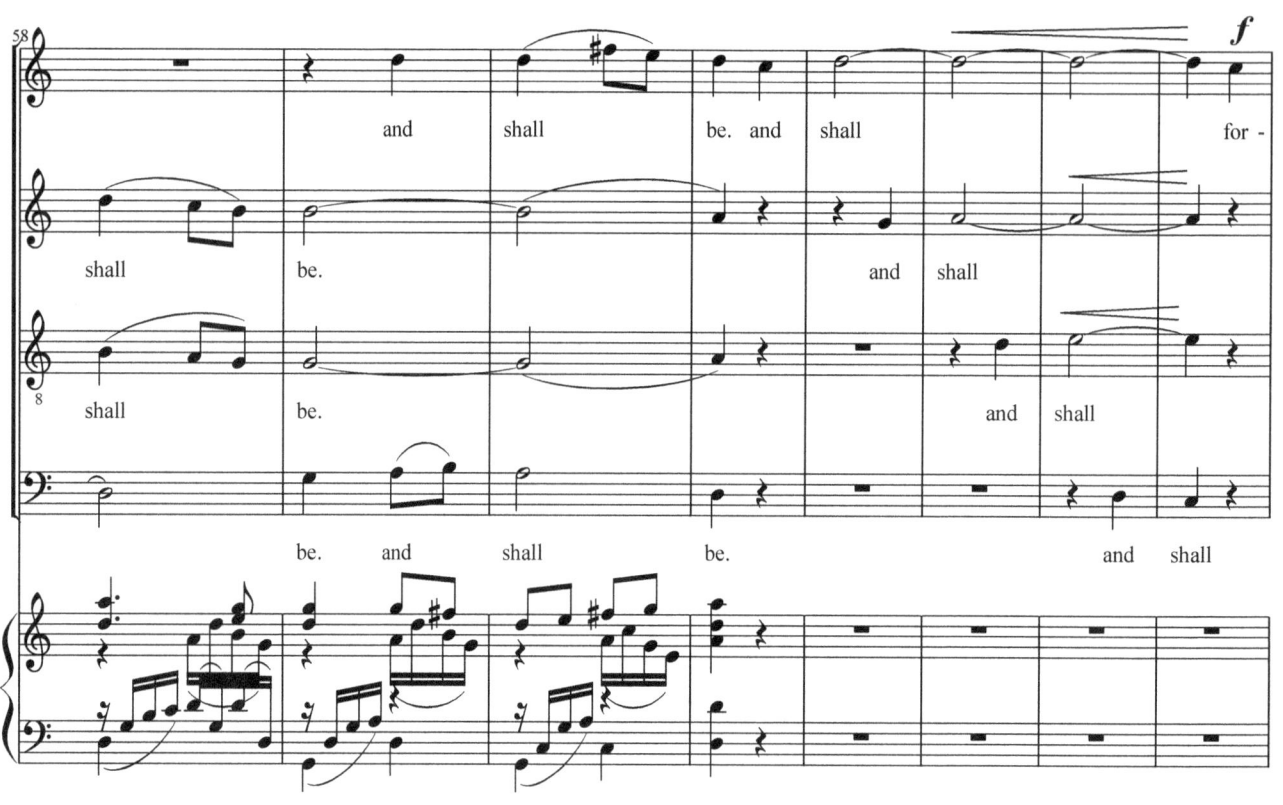

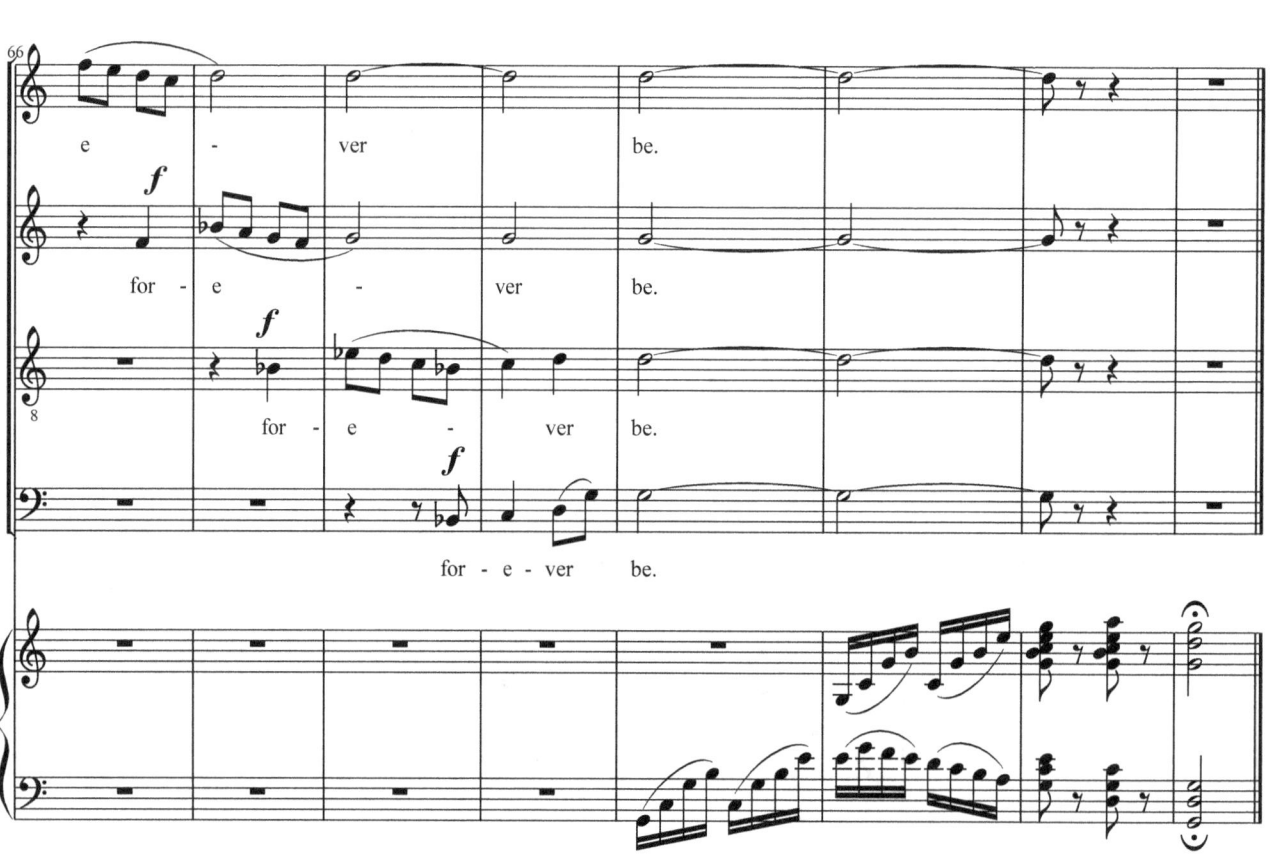

74

Seek Wisdom

from the Bible - Proverbs 2

from "Spiritual Songs"

Ken Langer

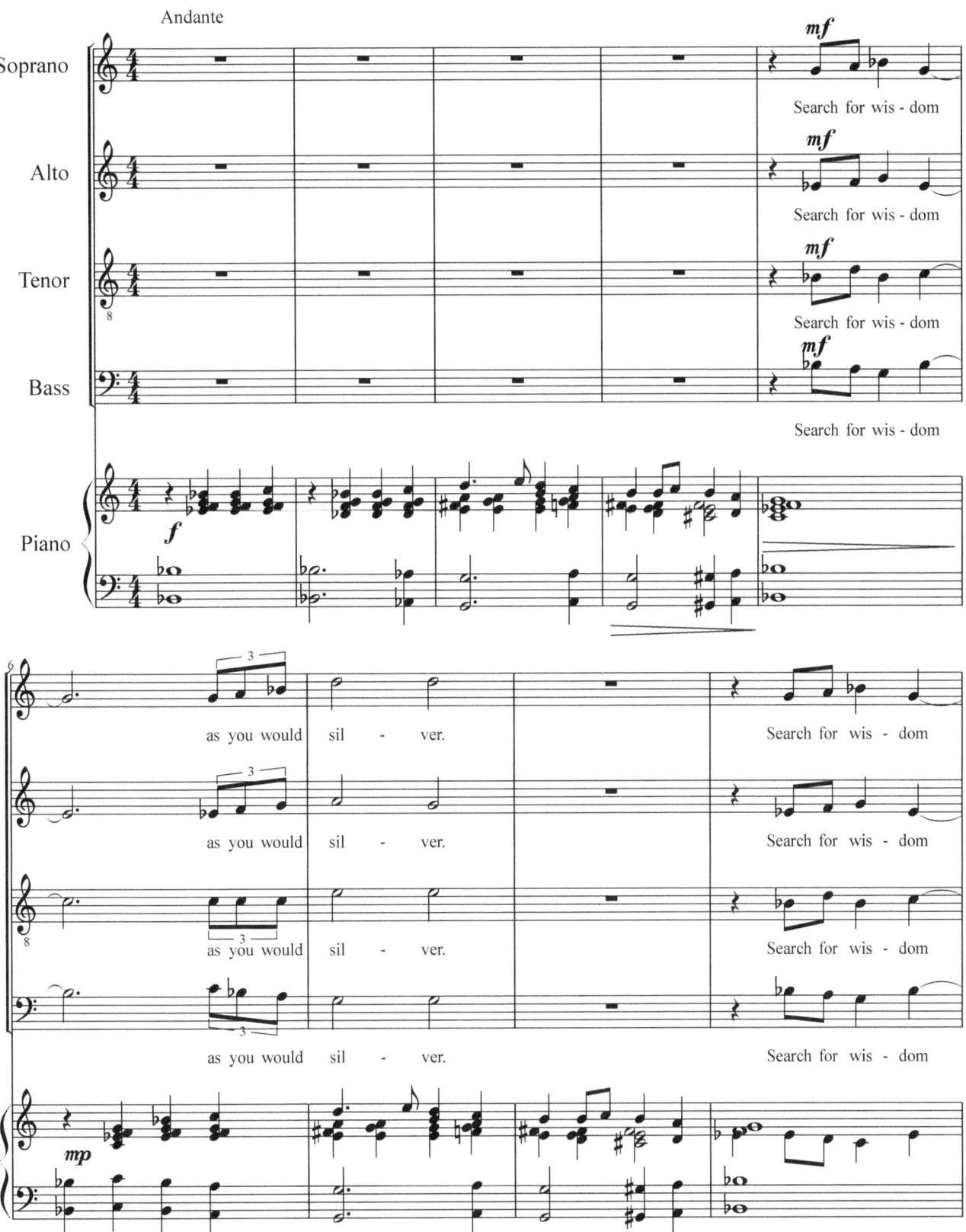

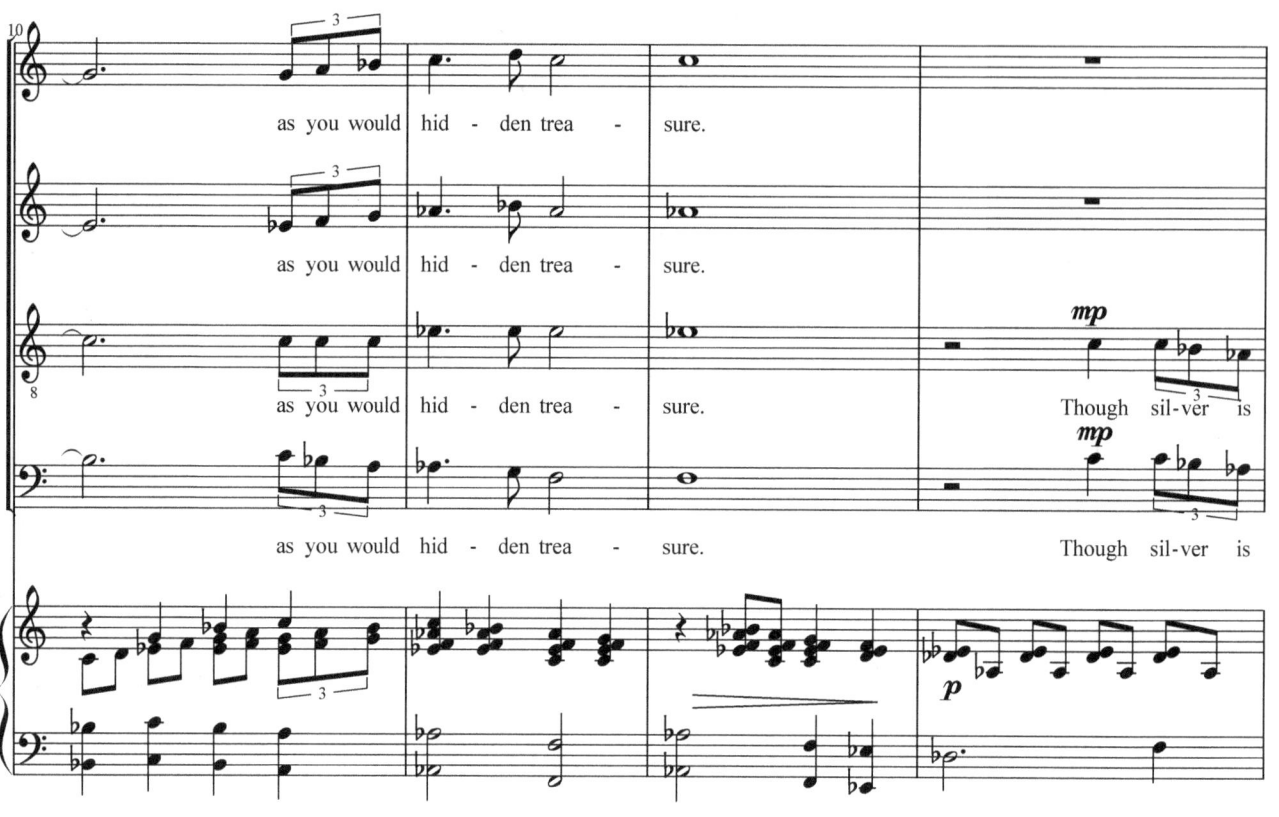

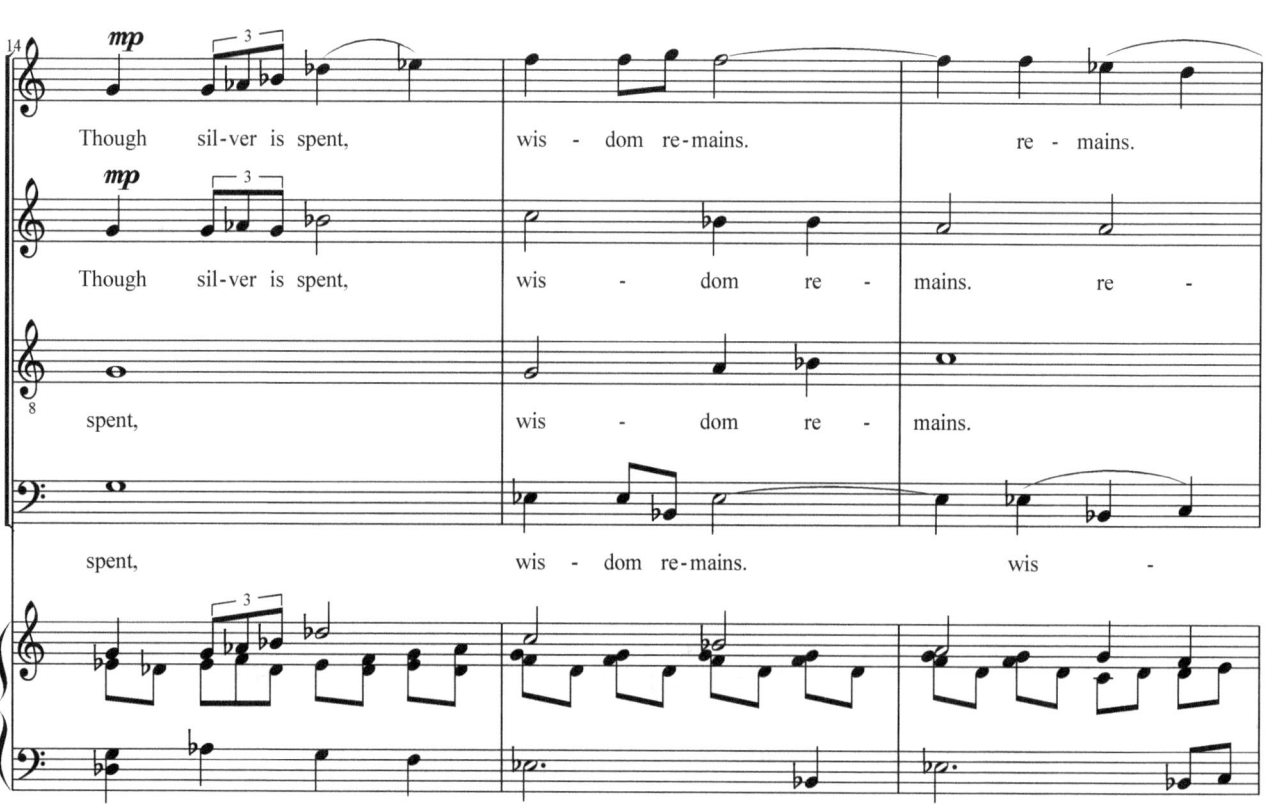

76

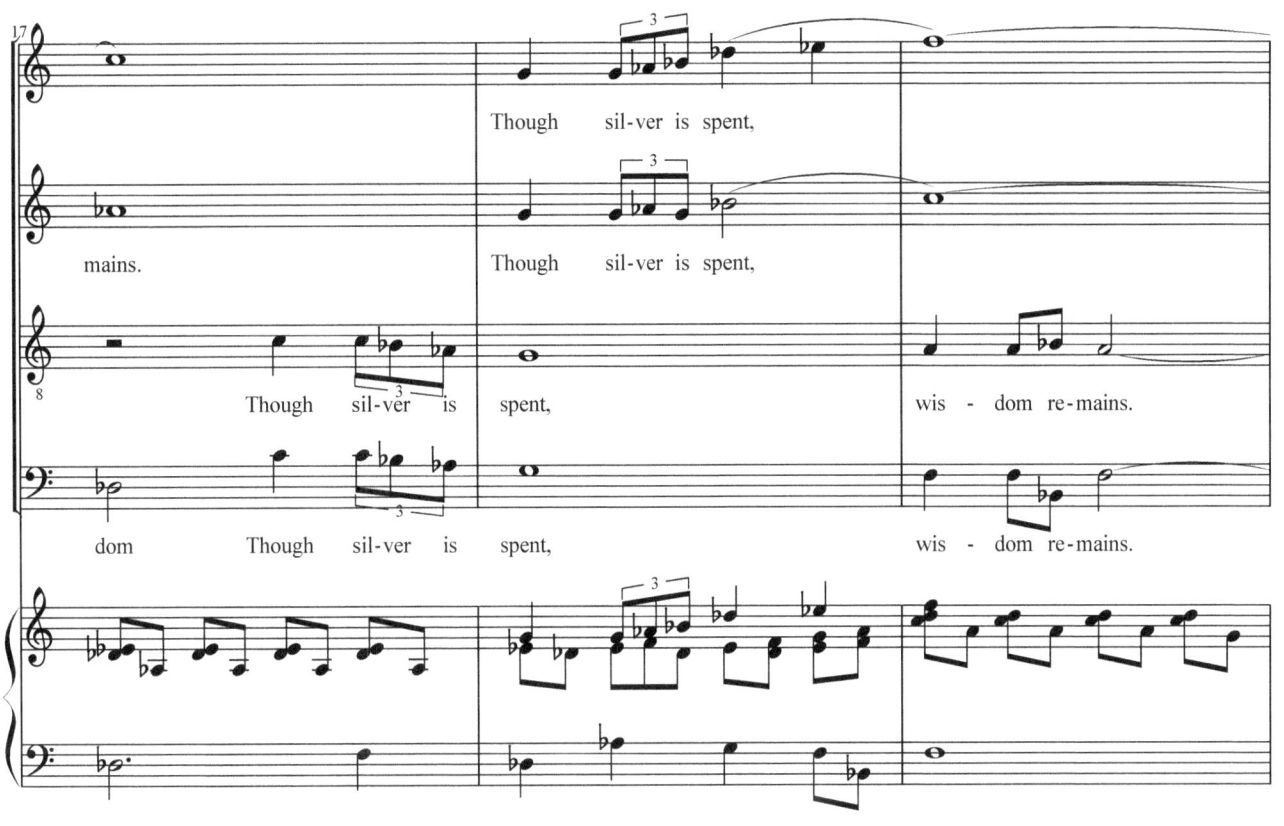

Though sil-ver is spent,

mains. Though sil-ver is spent,

Though sil-ver is spent, wis - dom re-mains.

dom Though sil-ver is spent, wis-dom re-mains.

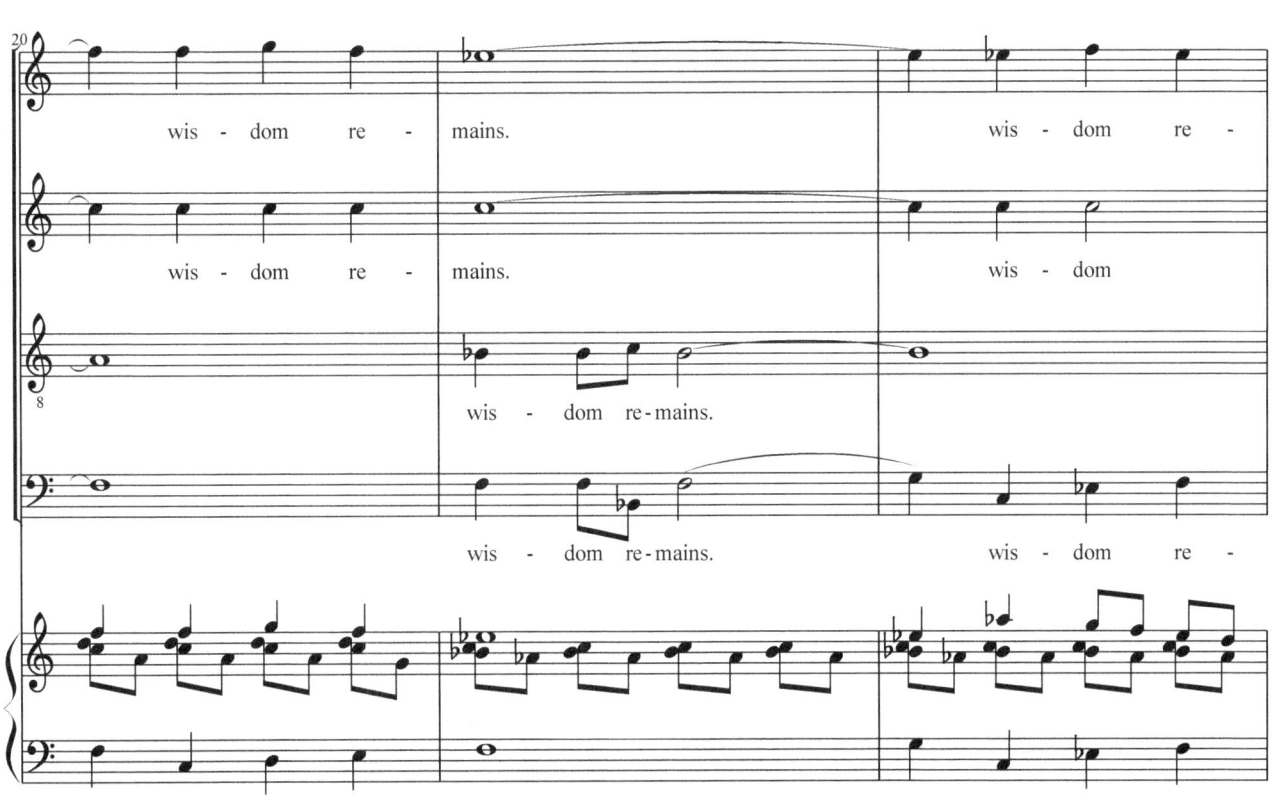

wis - dom re - mains. wis - dom re -

wis - dom re - mains. wis - dom

wis - dom re-mains.

wis - dom re-mains. wis - dom re -

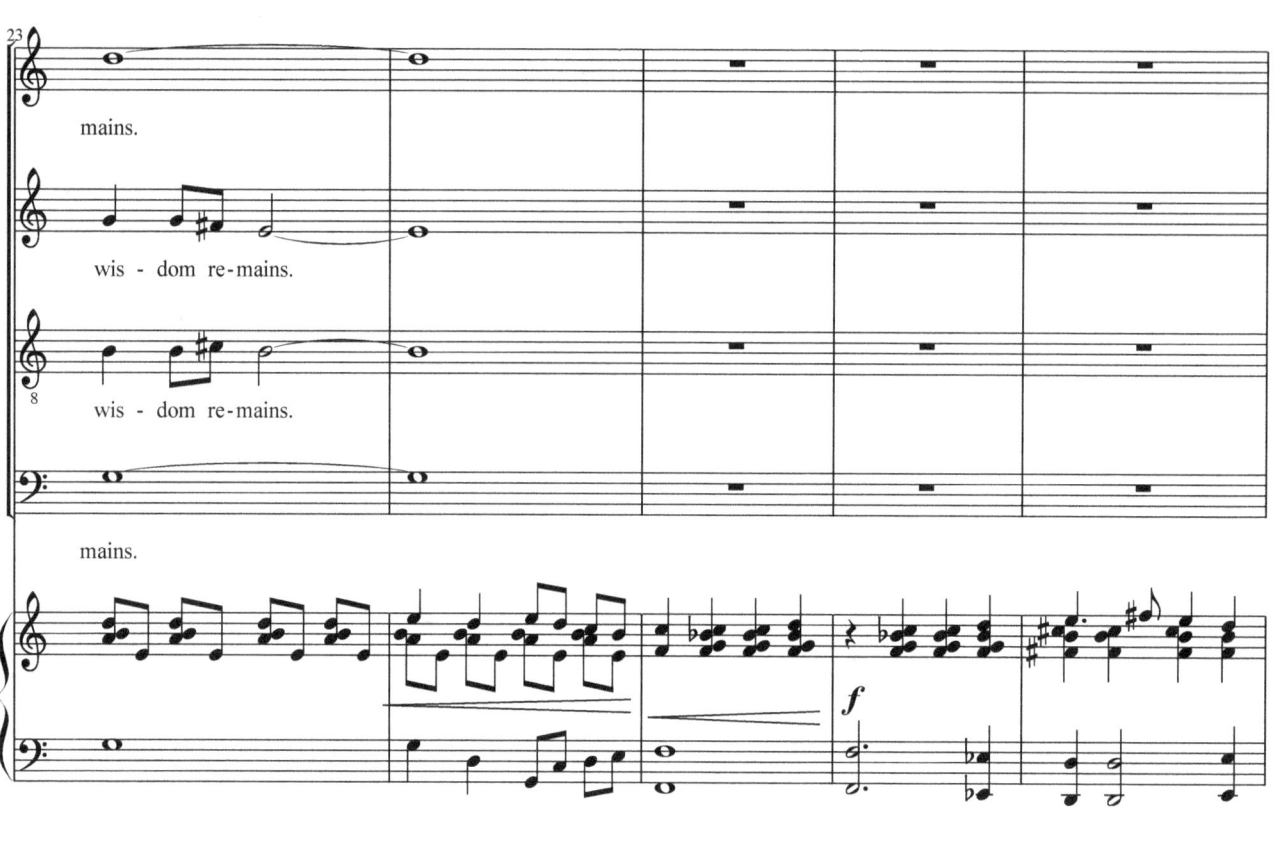

mains.

wis - dom re - mains.

wis - dom re - mains.

mains.

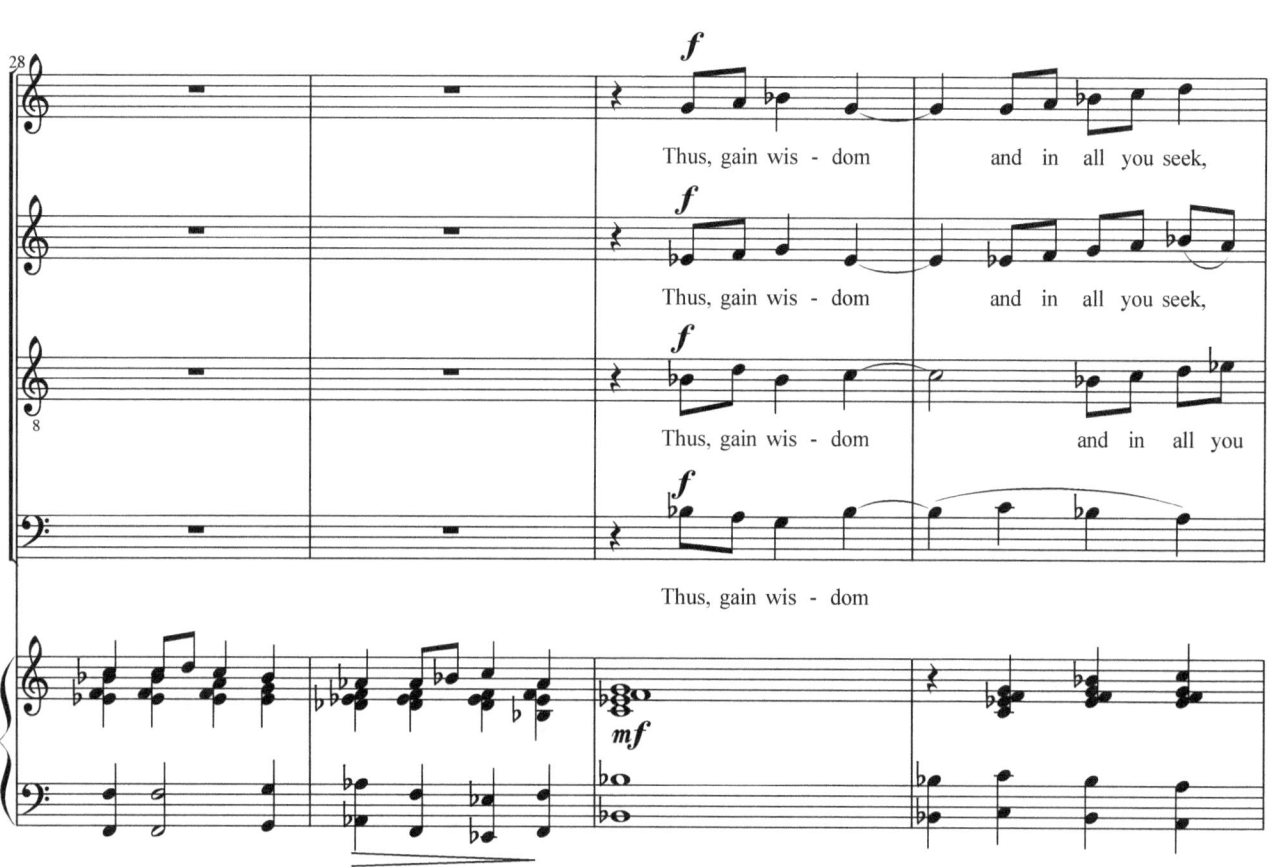

Thus, gain wis - dom and in all you seek,

Thus, gain wis - dom and in all you seek,

Thus, gain wis - dom and in all you

Thus, gain wis - dom

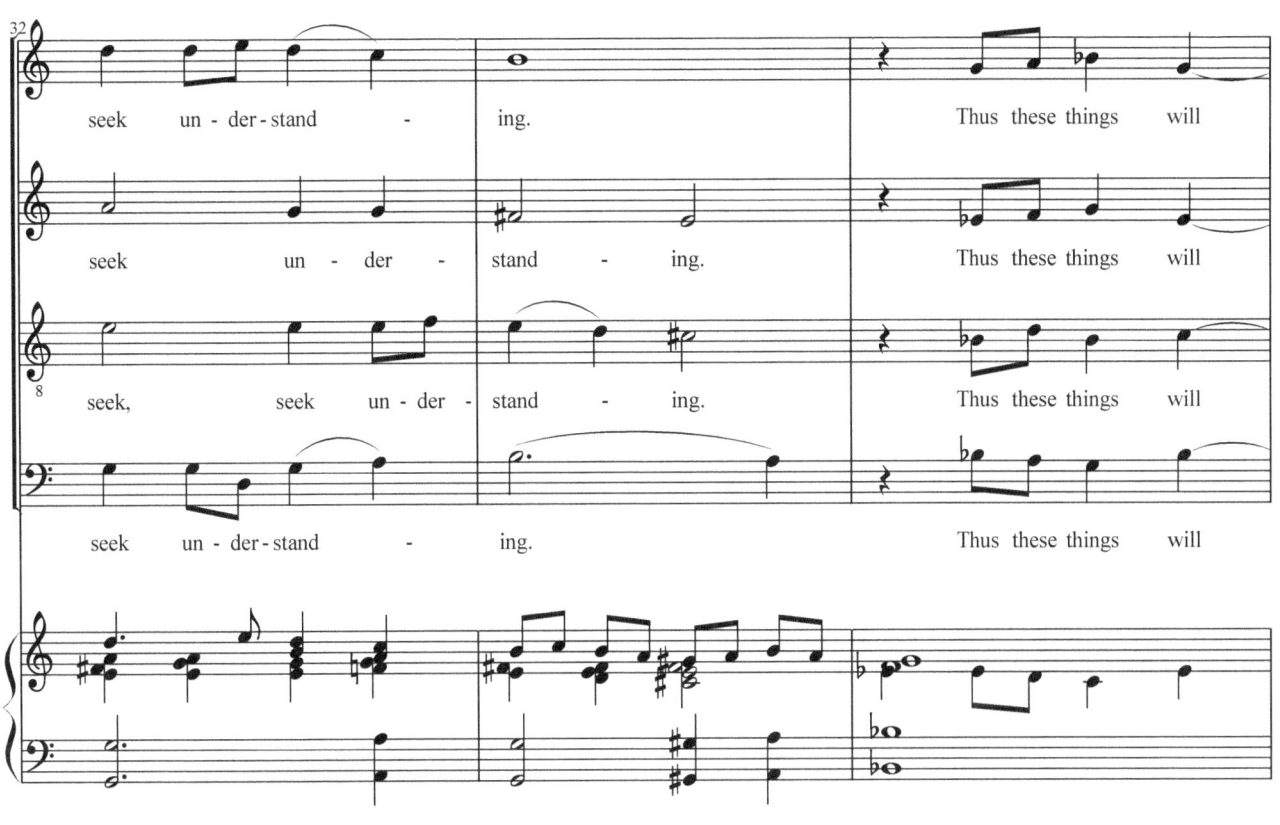

seek un-der-stand - ing. Thus these things will
seek un - der - stand - ing. Thus these things will
seek, seek un - der - stand - ing. Thus these things will
seek un - der-stand - ing. Thus these things will

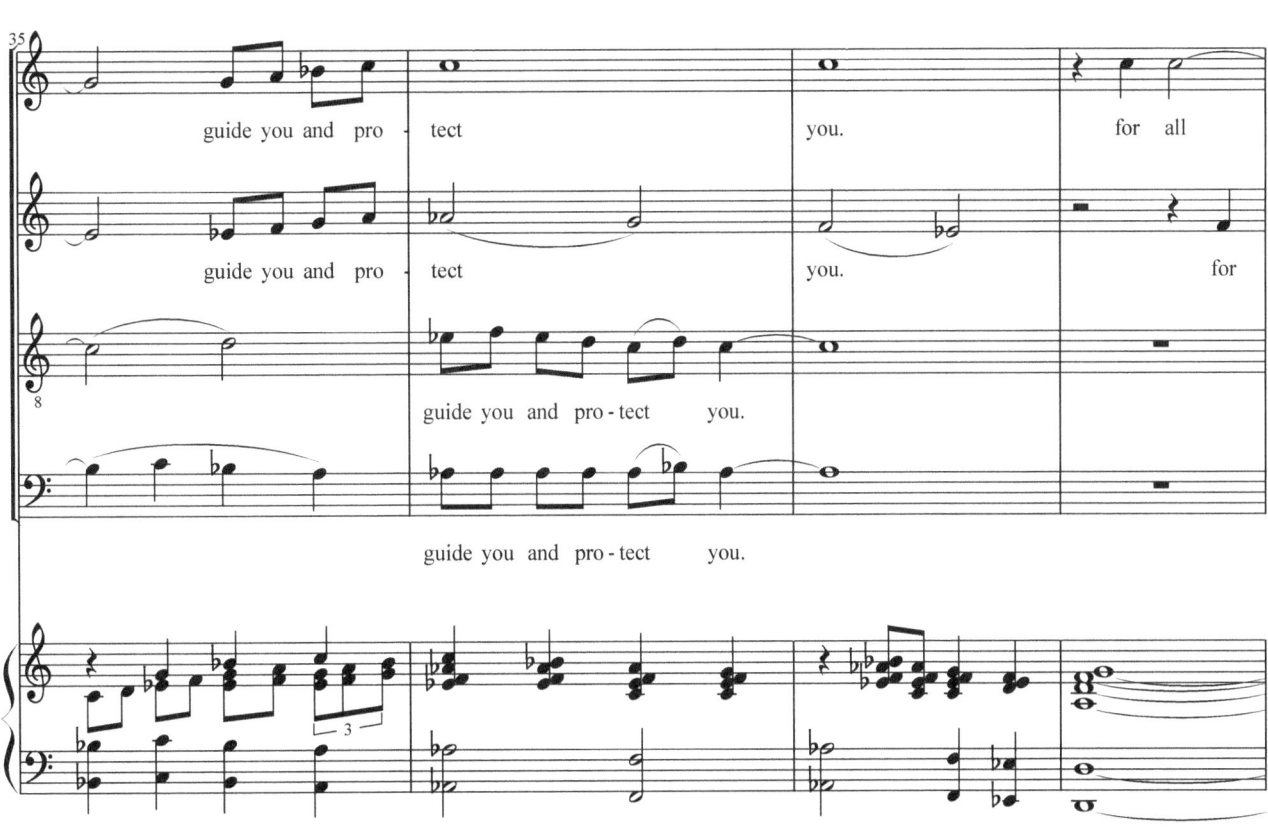

guide you and pro tect you. for all
guide you and pro tect you. for
guide you and pro - tect you.
guide you and pro - tect you.

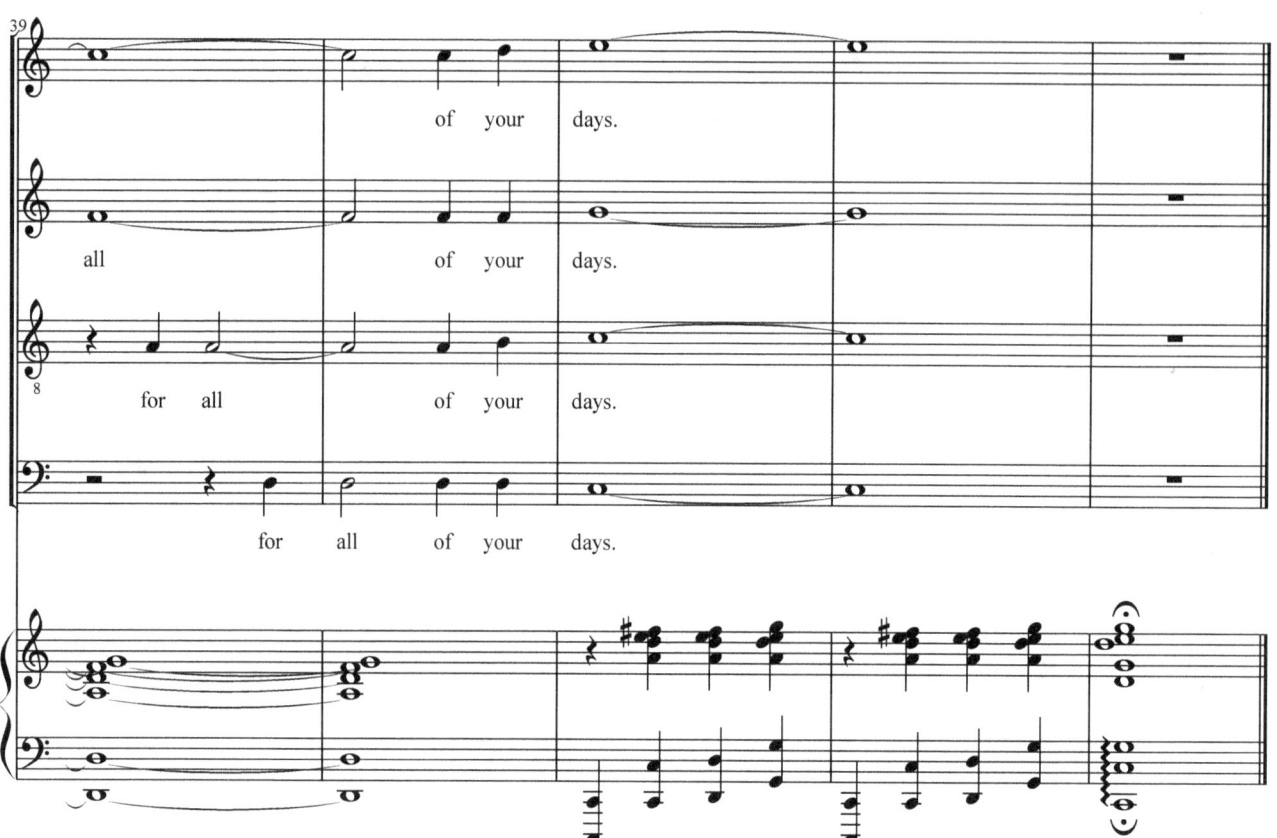

of your days.

all of your days.

for all of your days.

for all of your days.

Surrender
from "Spiritual Songs"

from the Koran - 91:1

Ken Langer

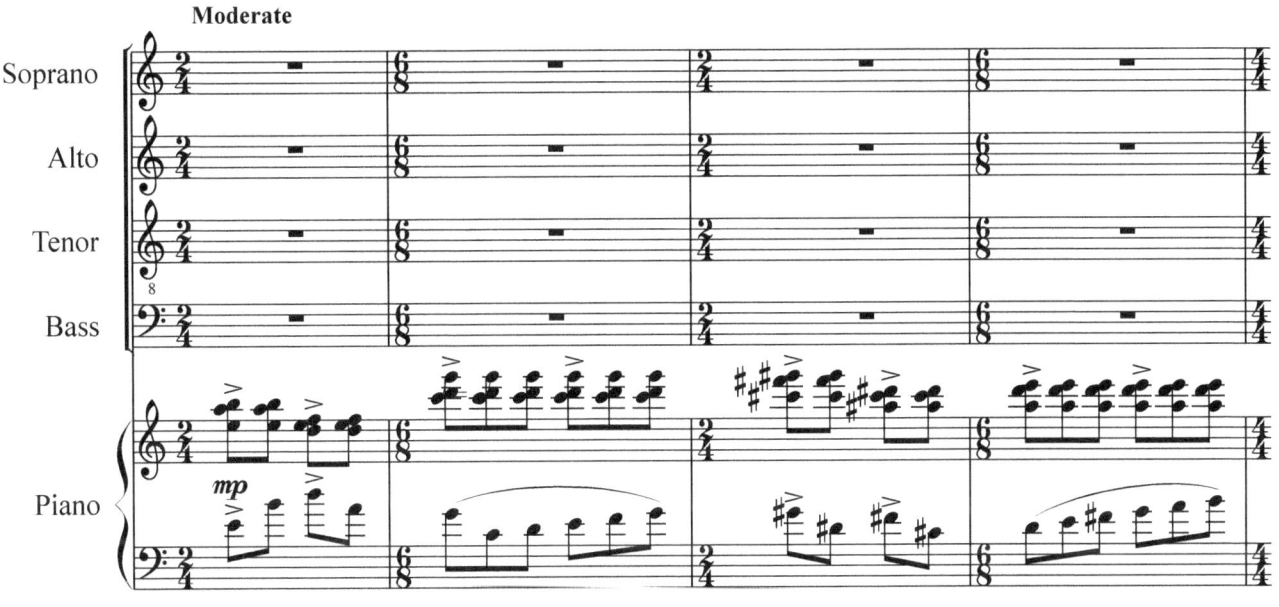

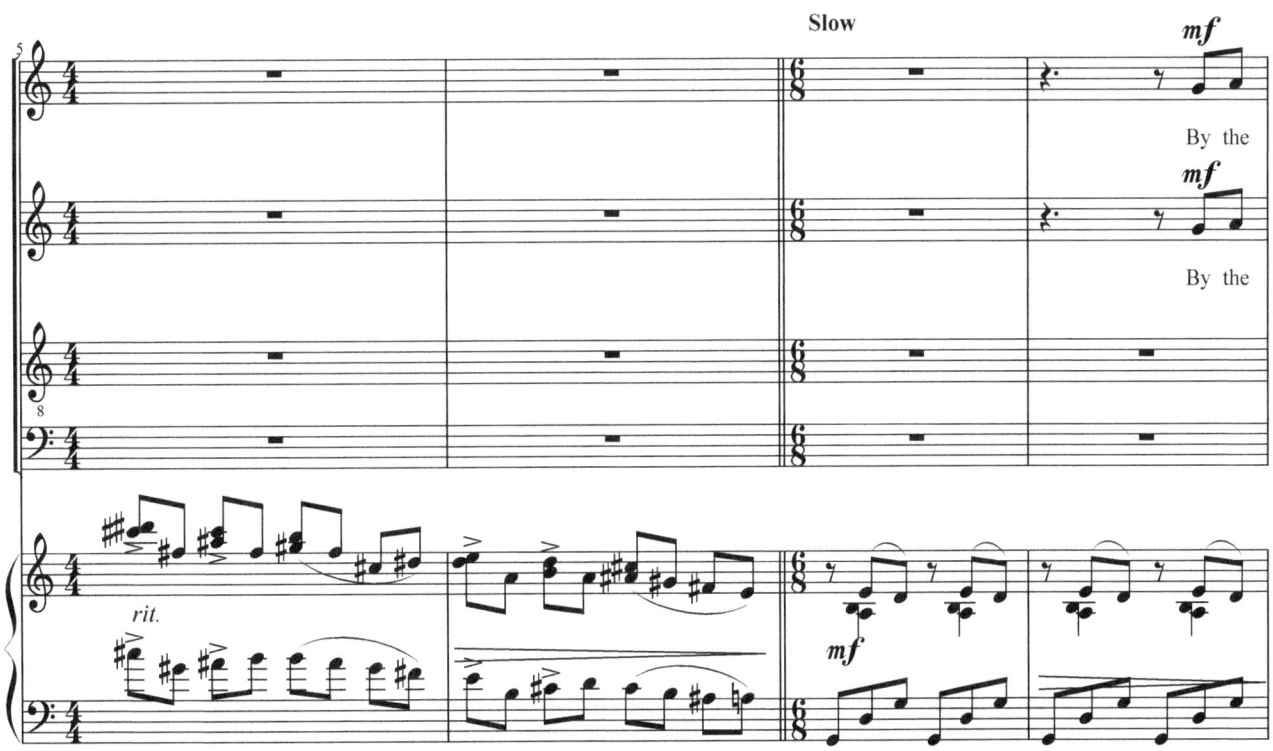

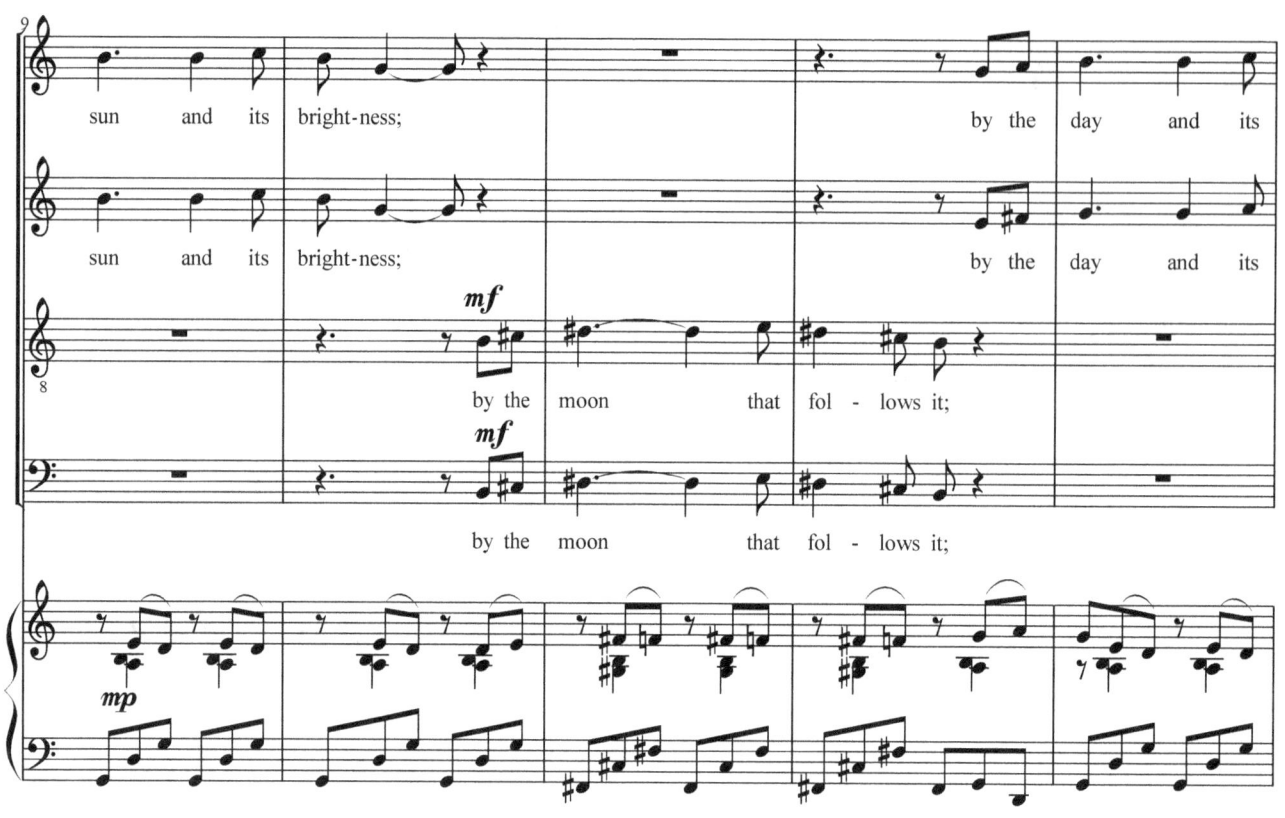

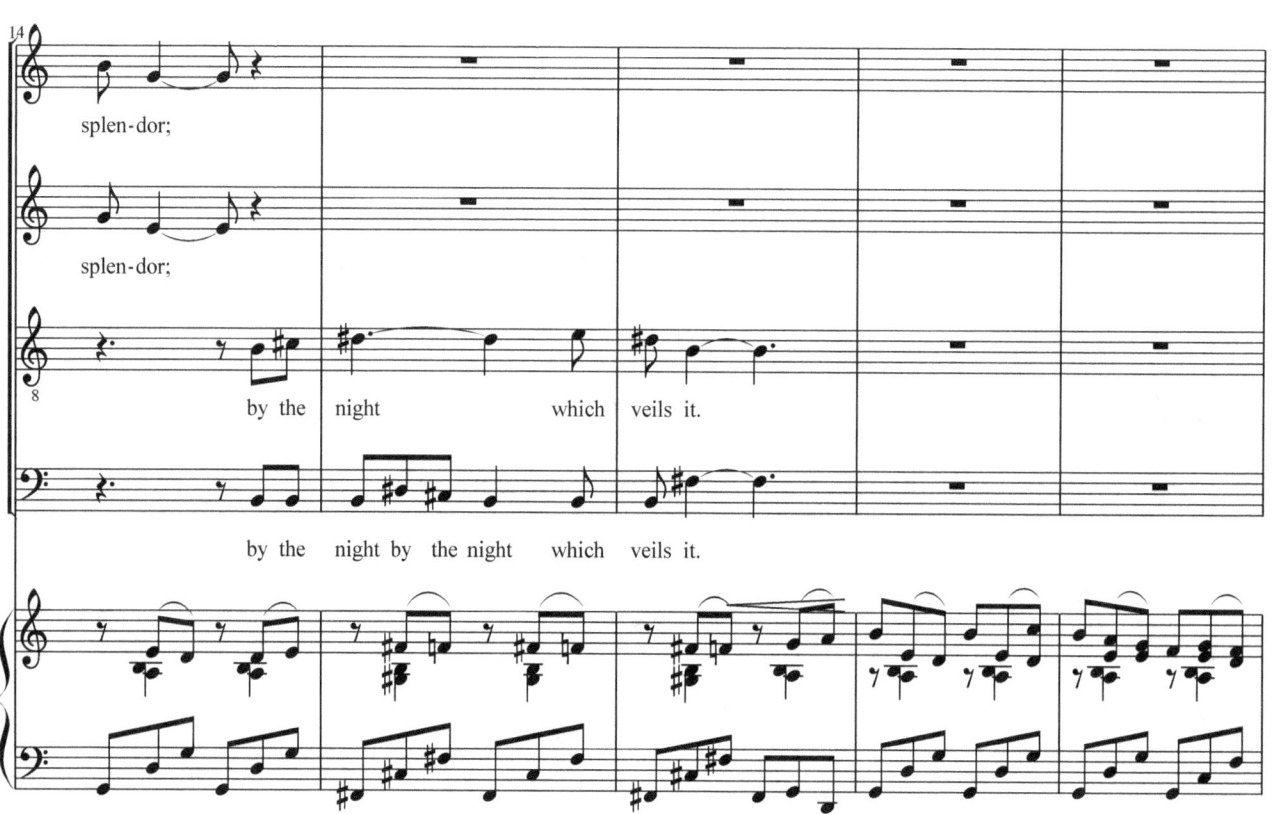

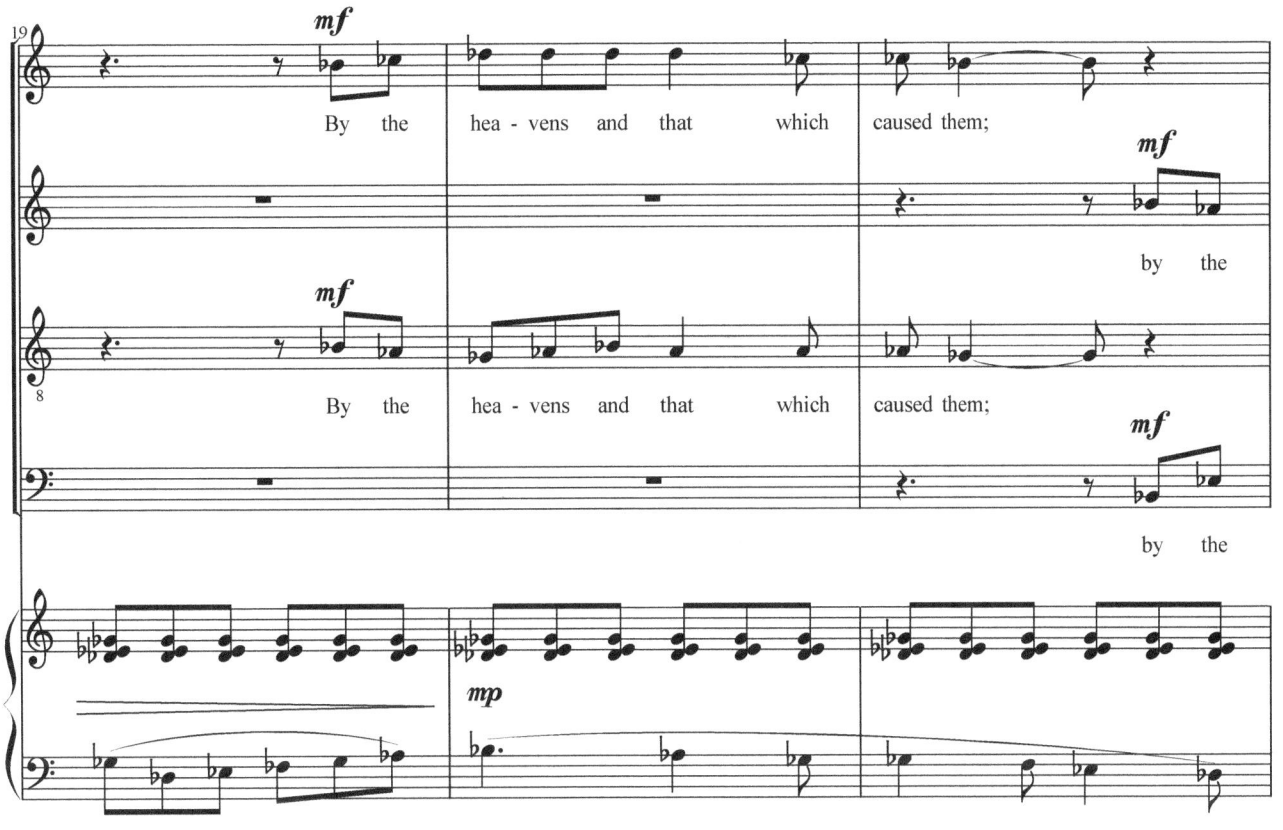

By the hea - vens and that which caused them;

by the

By the hea - vens and that which caused them;

by the

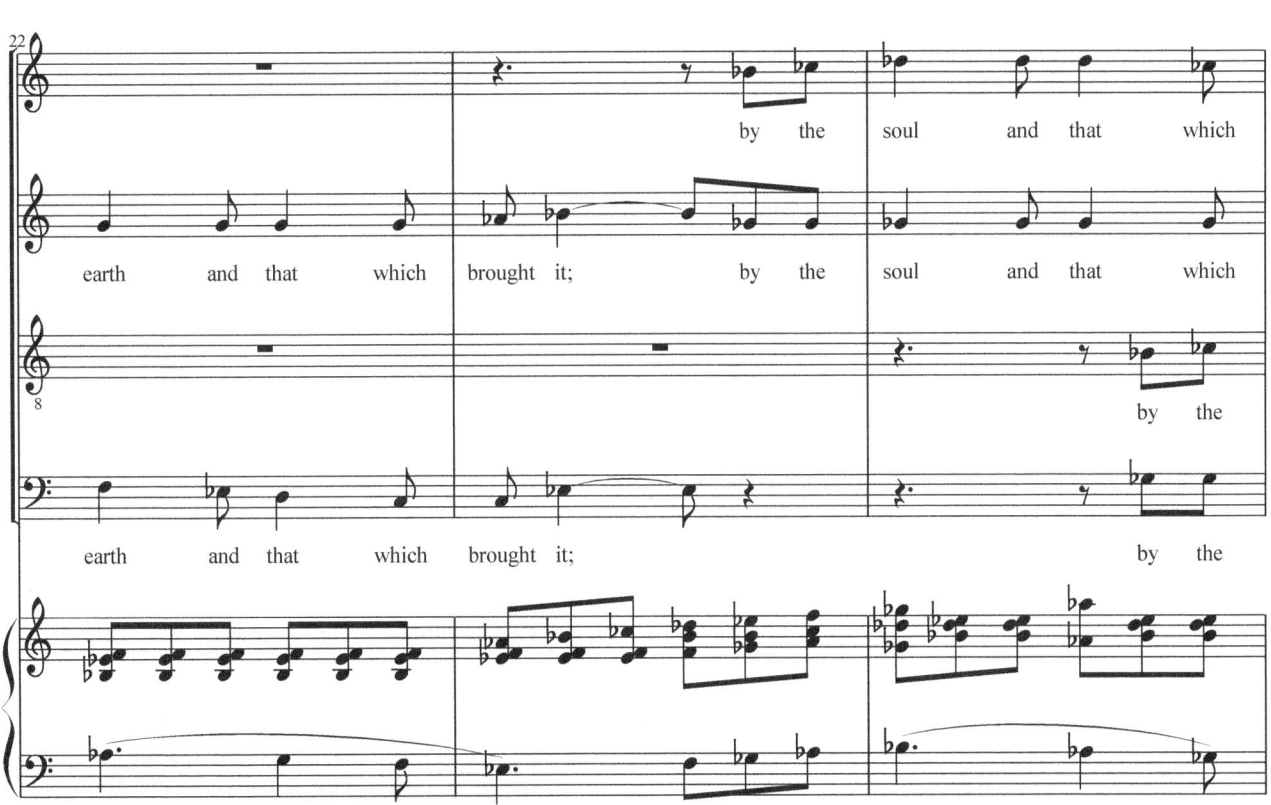

by the soul and that which

earth and that which brought it; by the soul and that which

by the

earth and that which brought it; by the

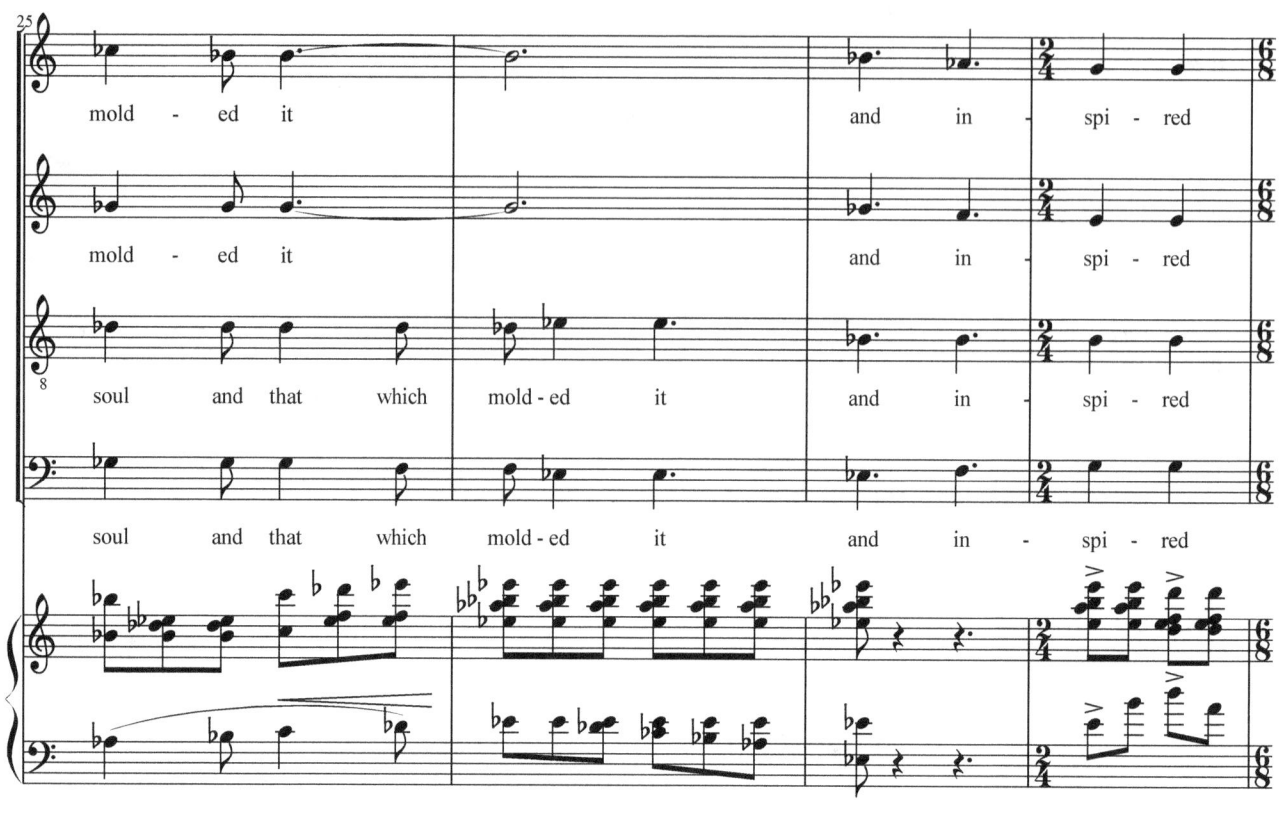

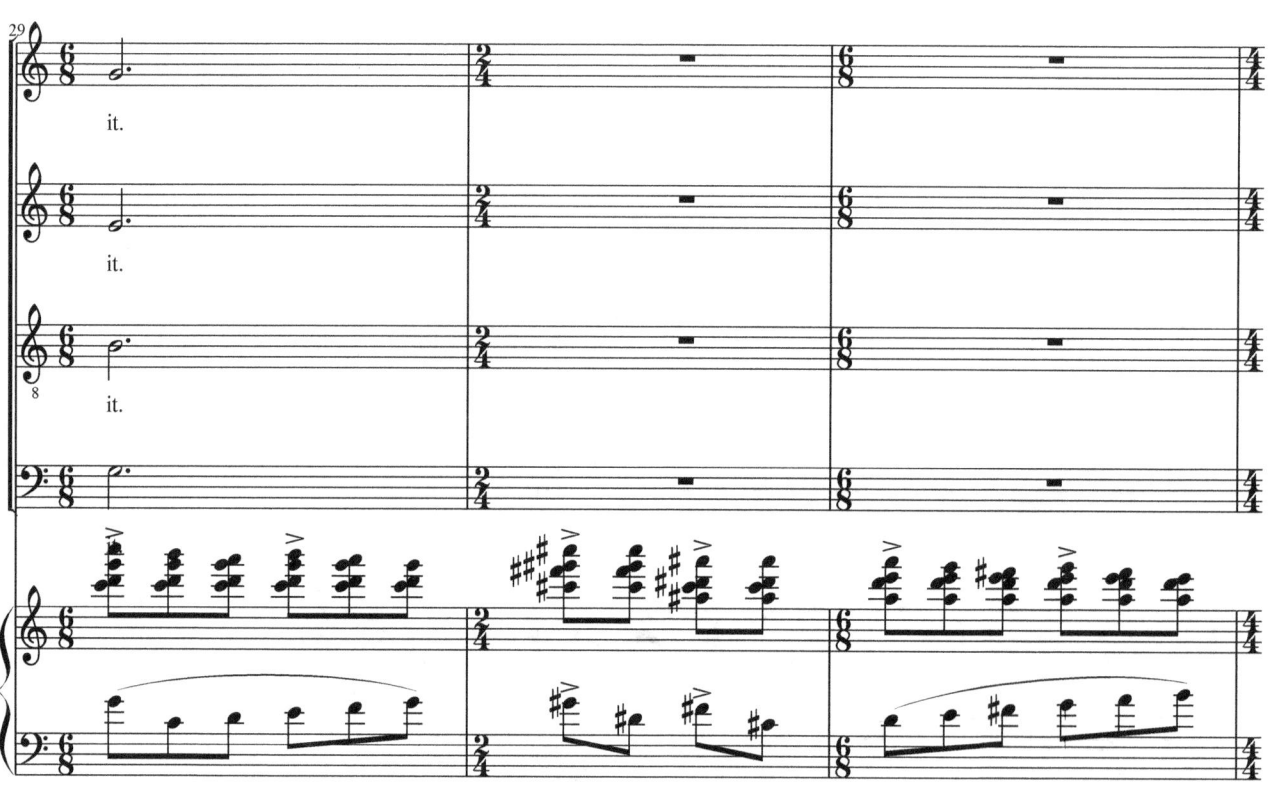

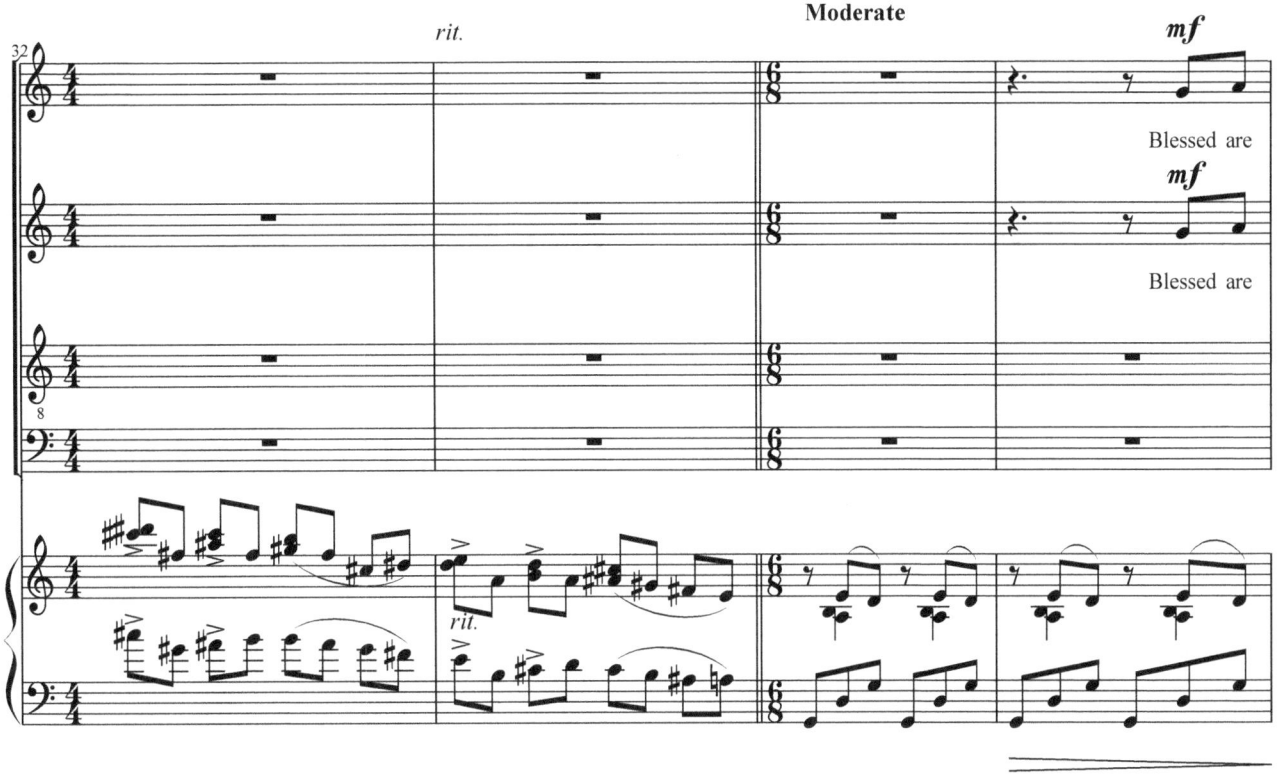

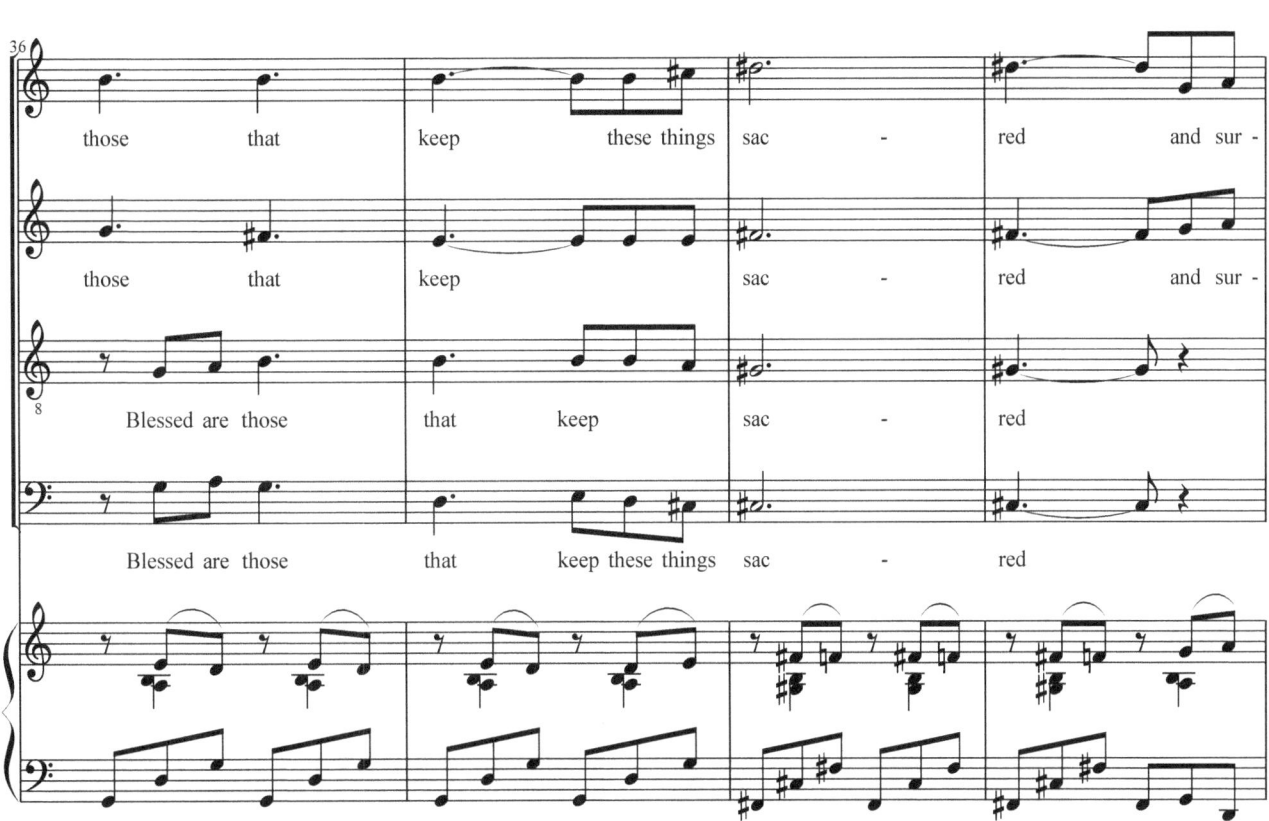

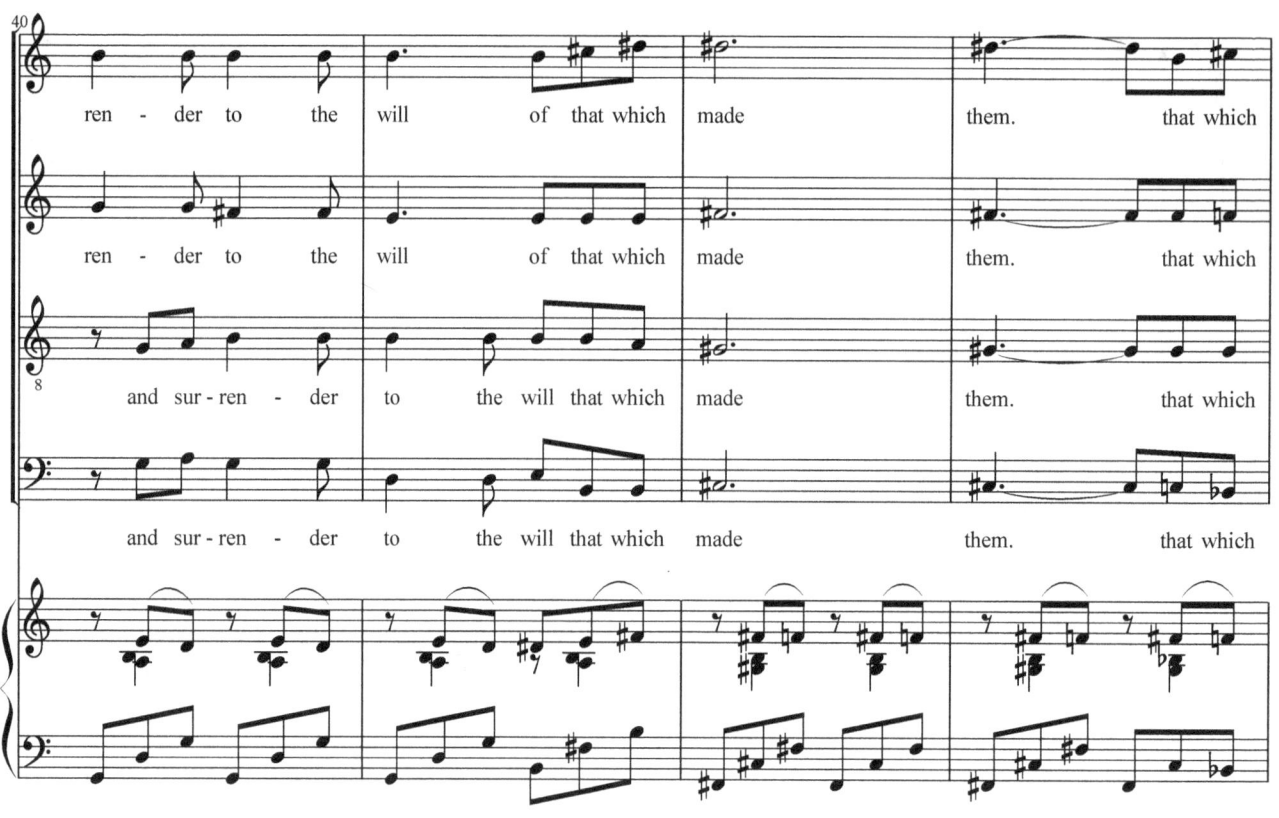

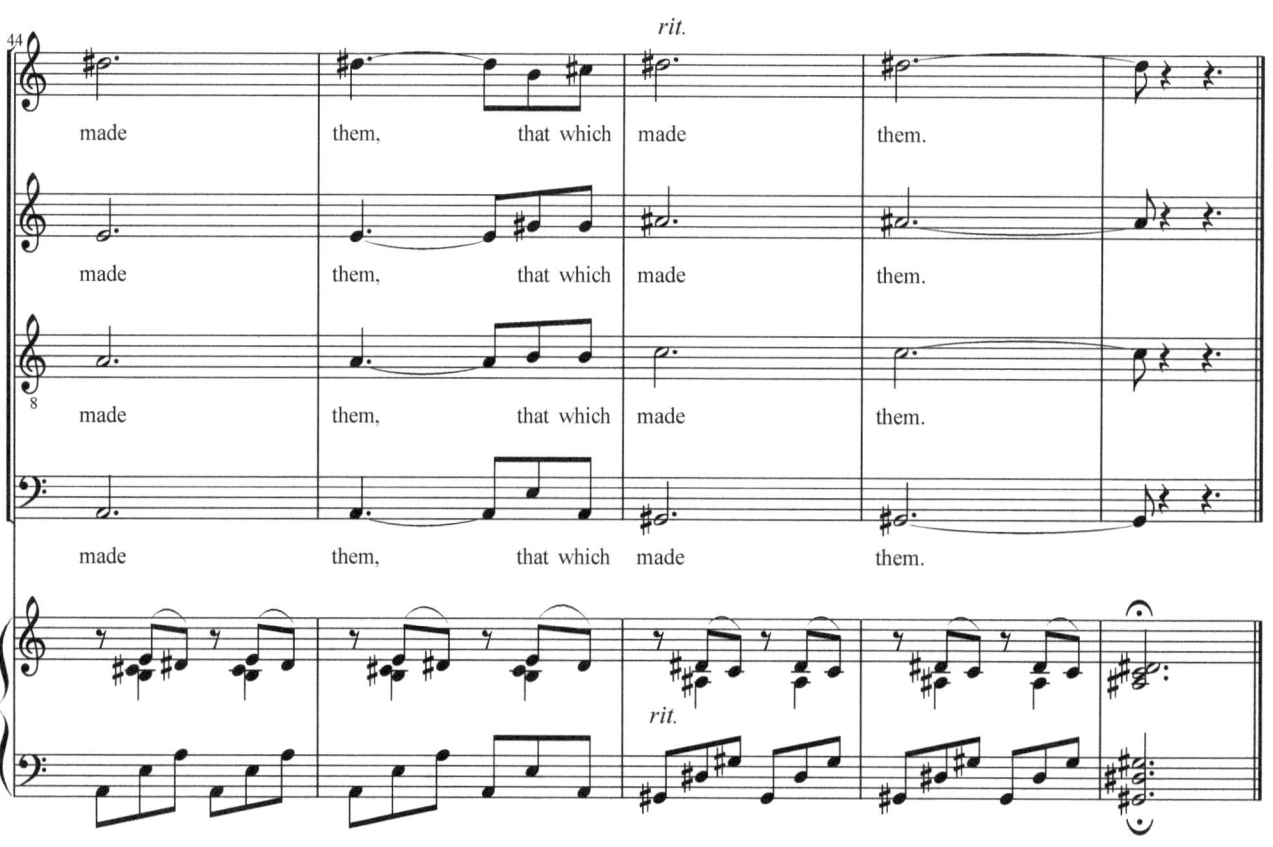

To Just Be

from the Tao Te Ching #37

from "Spiritual Songs"

Ken Langer

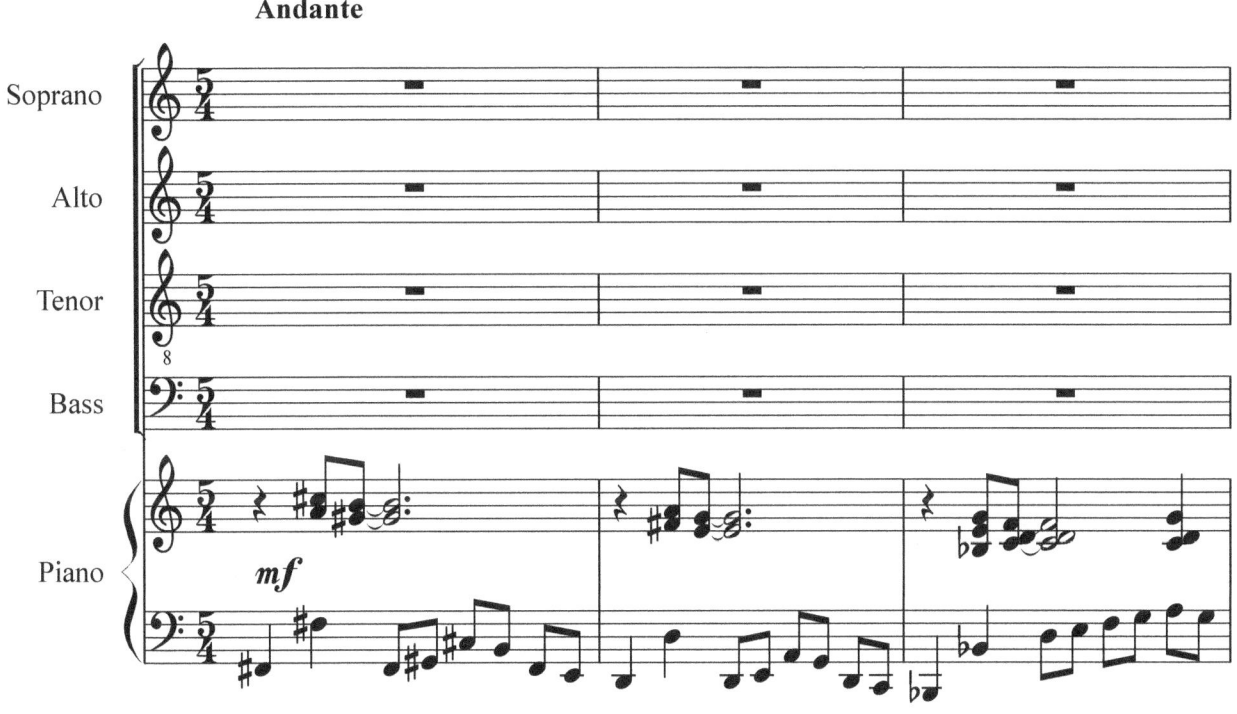

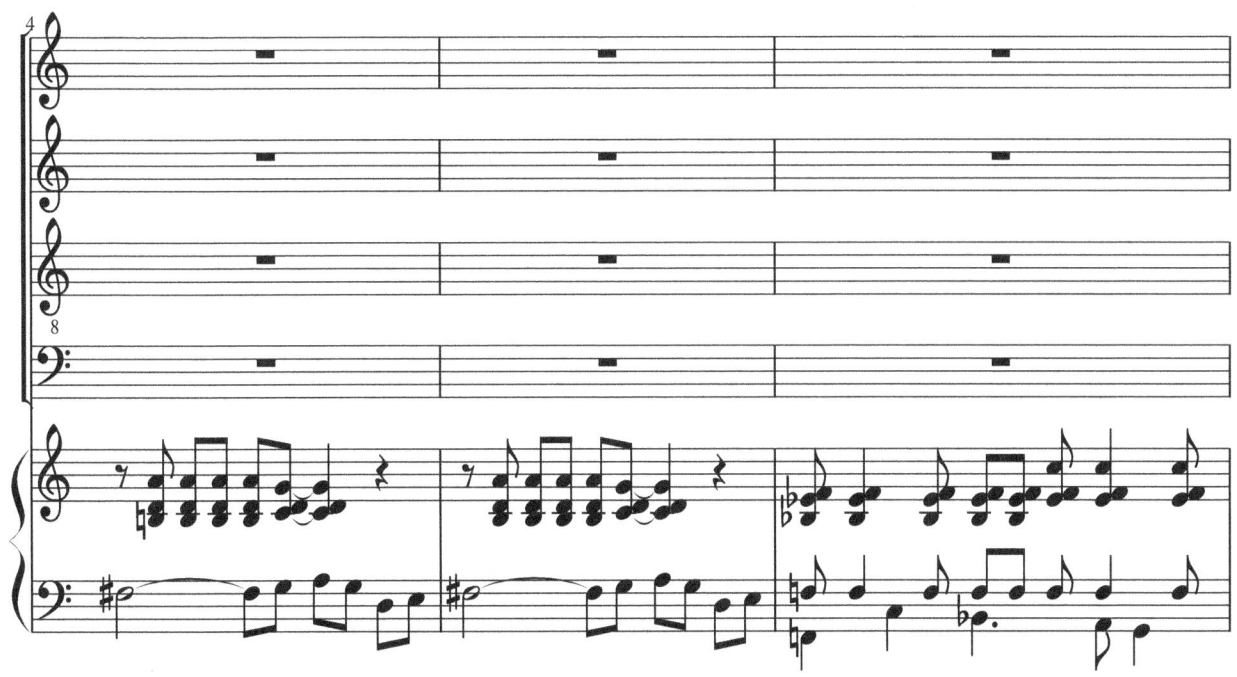

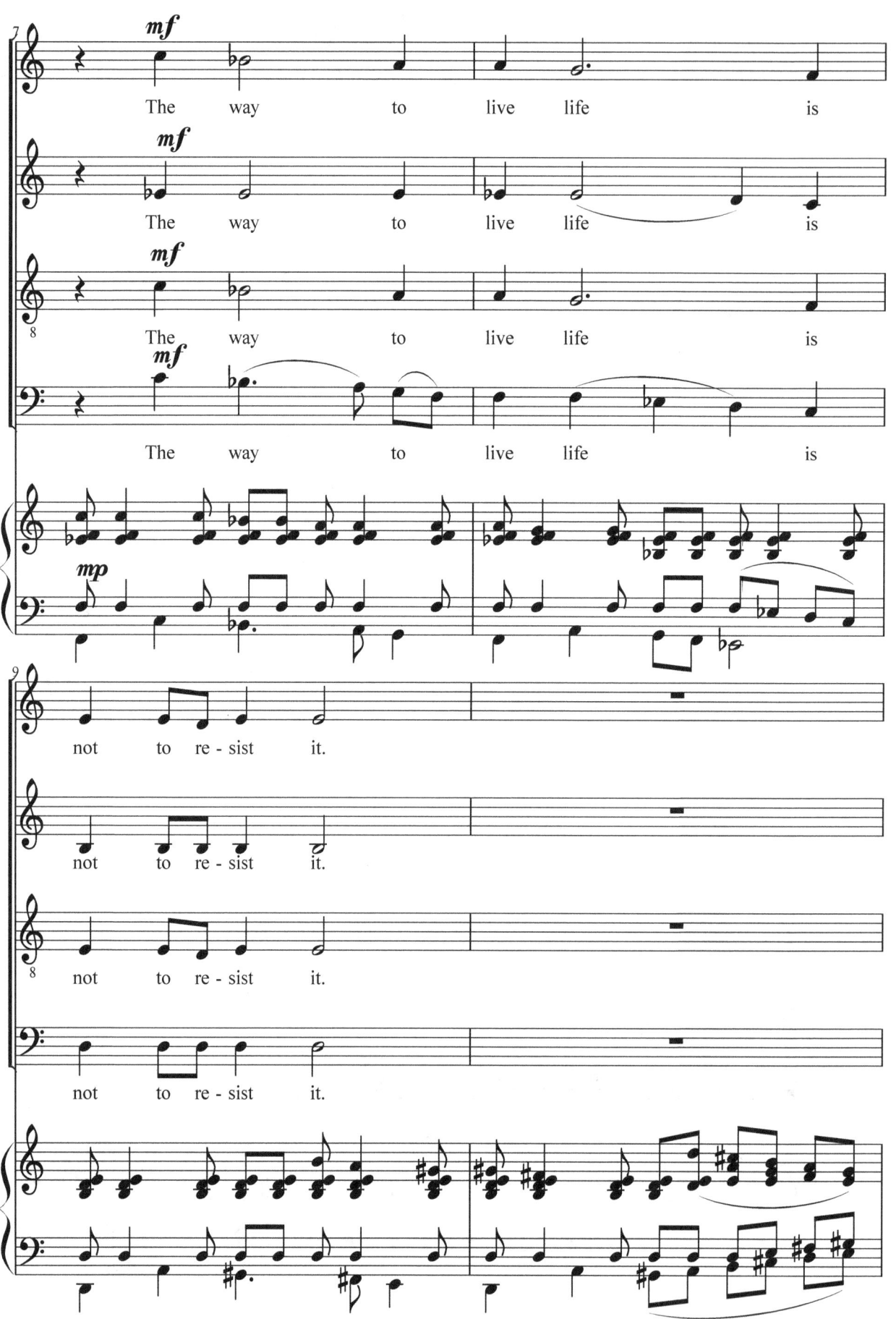

The way to live life is
The way to live life is
The way to live life is
The way to live life is

not to re-sist it.
not to re-sist it.
not to re-sist it.
not to re-sist it.

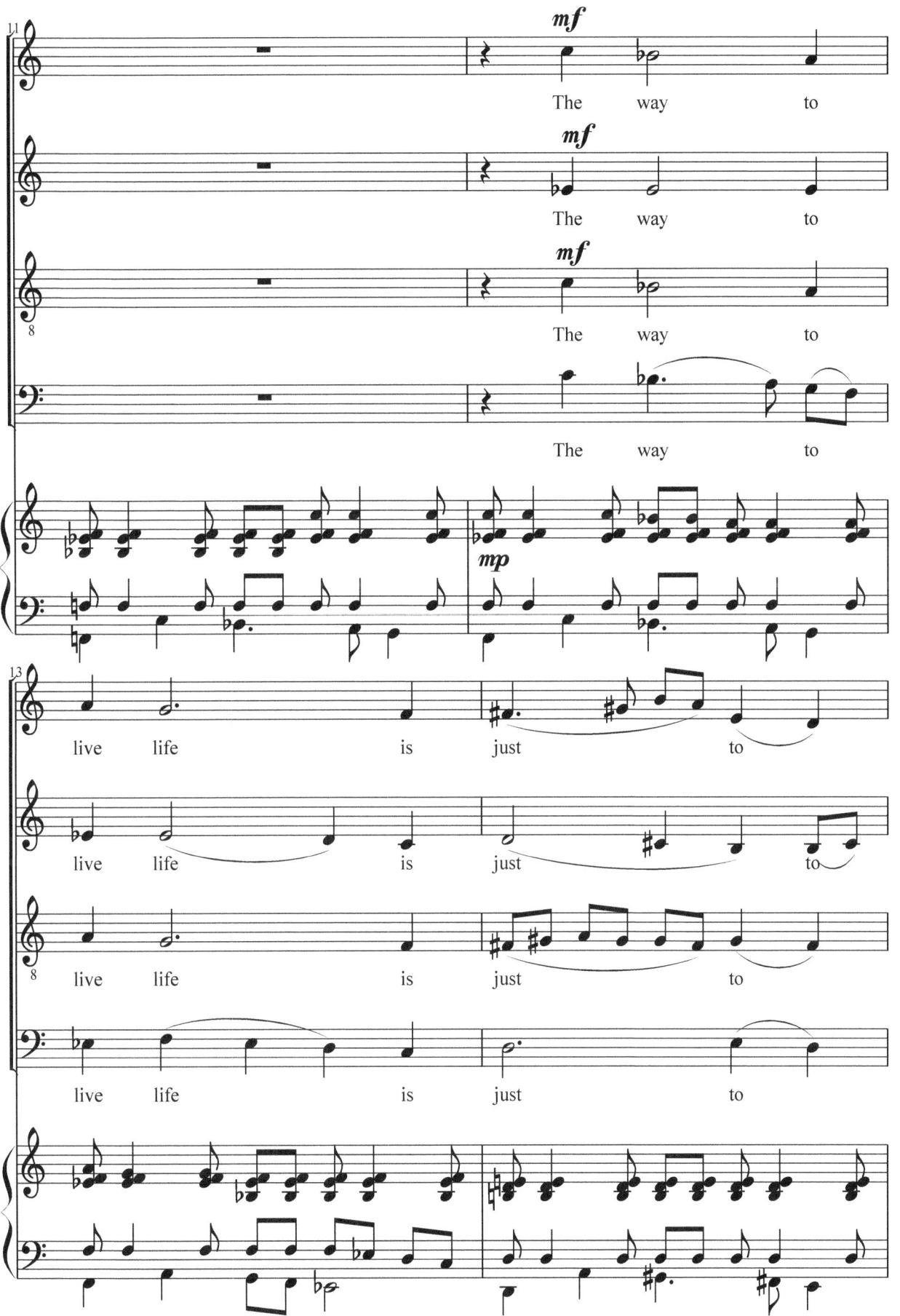

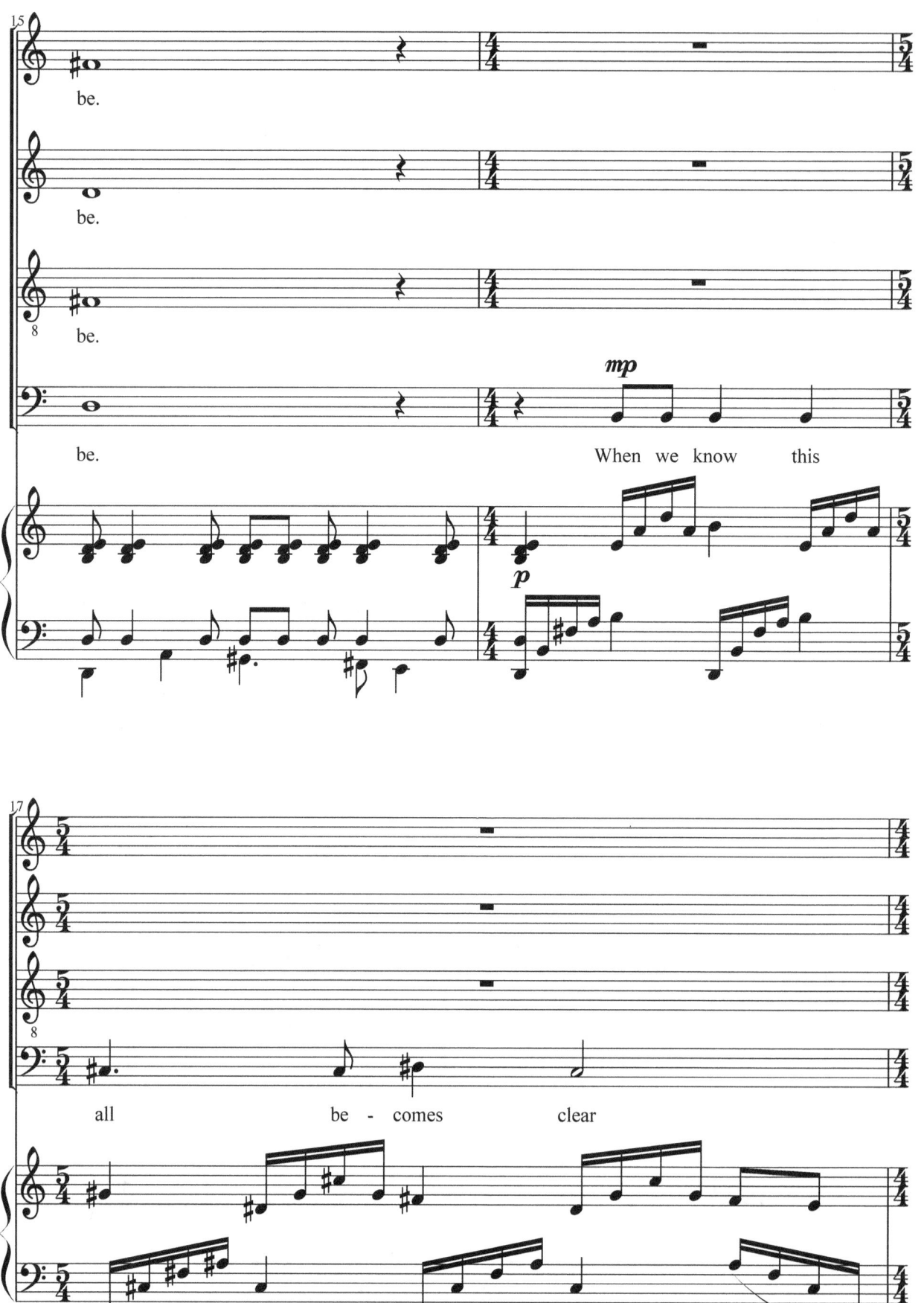

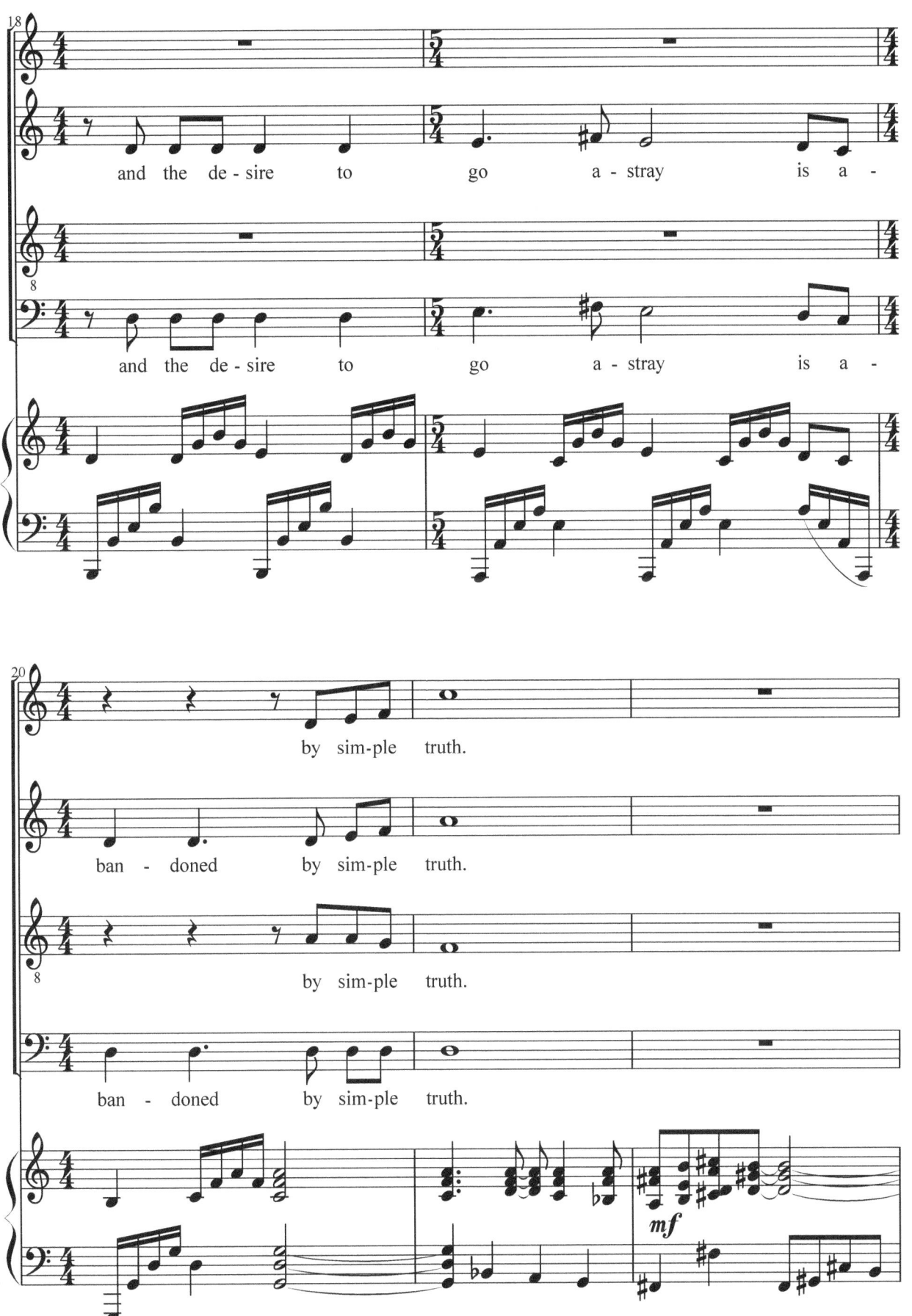

and the de - sire to go a - stray is a -

and the de - sire to go a - stray is a -

by sim-ple truth.

ban - doned by sim-ple truth.

by sim-ple truth.

ban - doned by sim-ple truth.

mf

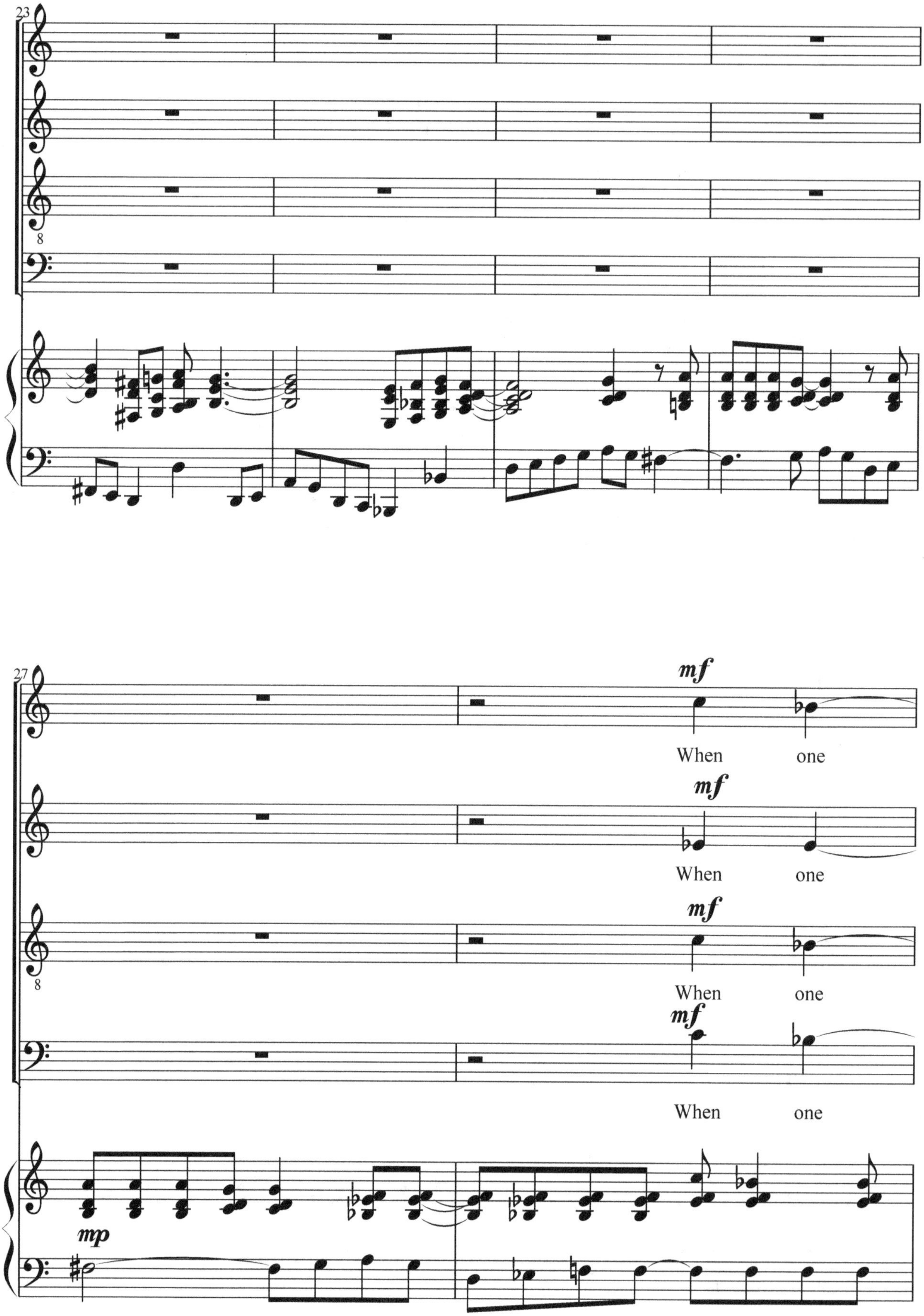

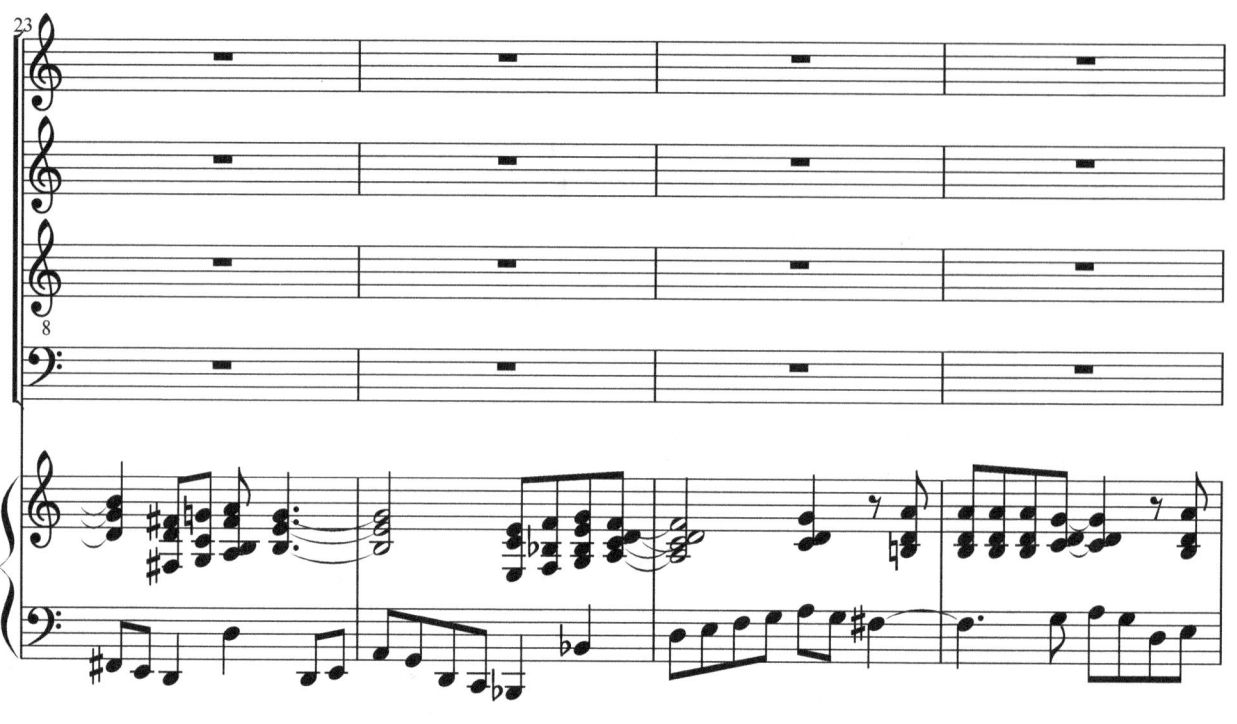

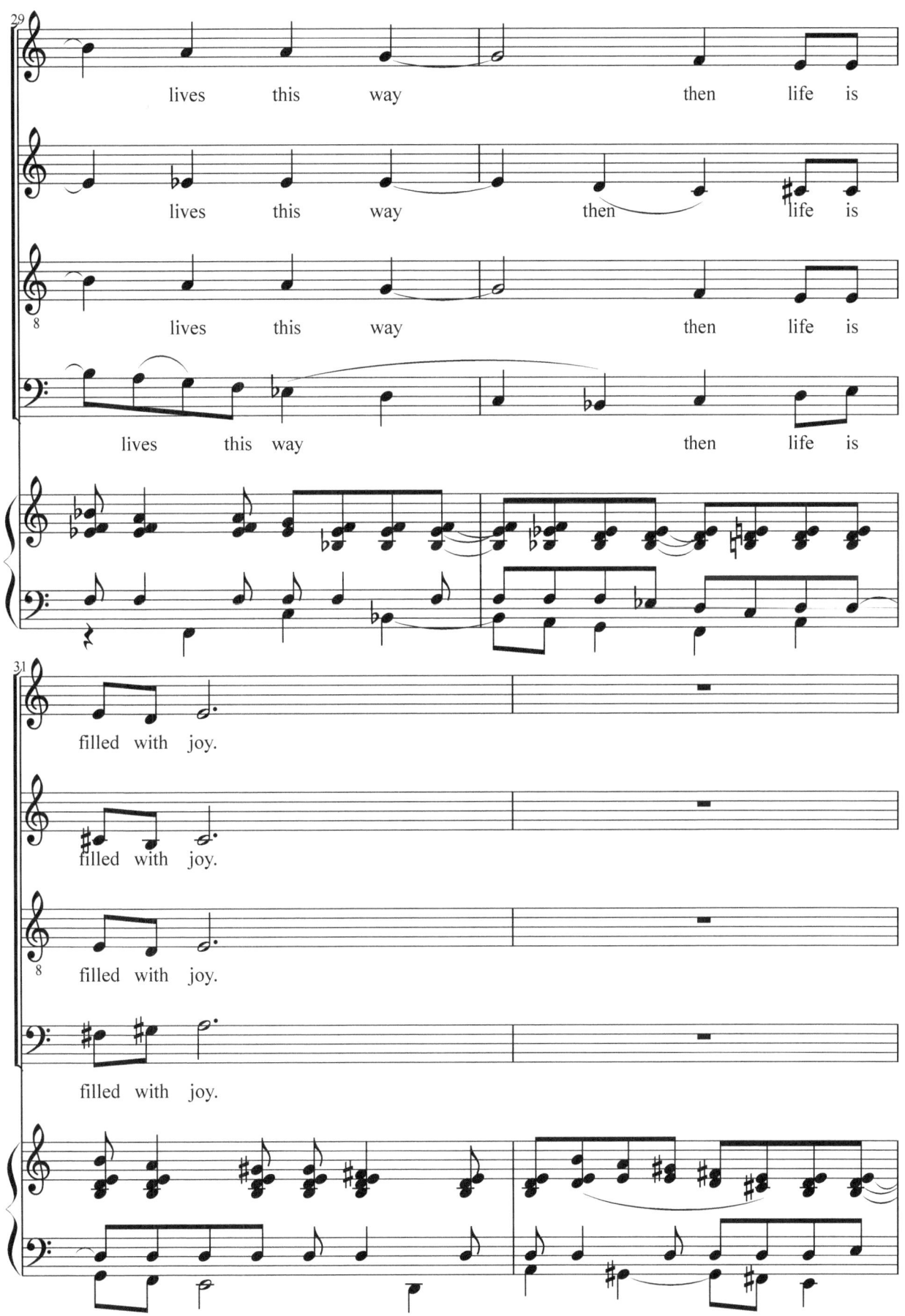

lives   this   way   then   life   is

lives   this   way   then   life   is

lives   this   way   then   life   is

lives   this   way   then   life   is

filled with   joy.

filled with   joy.

filled with   joy.

filled with   joy.

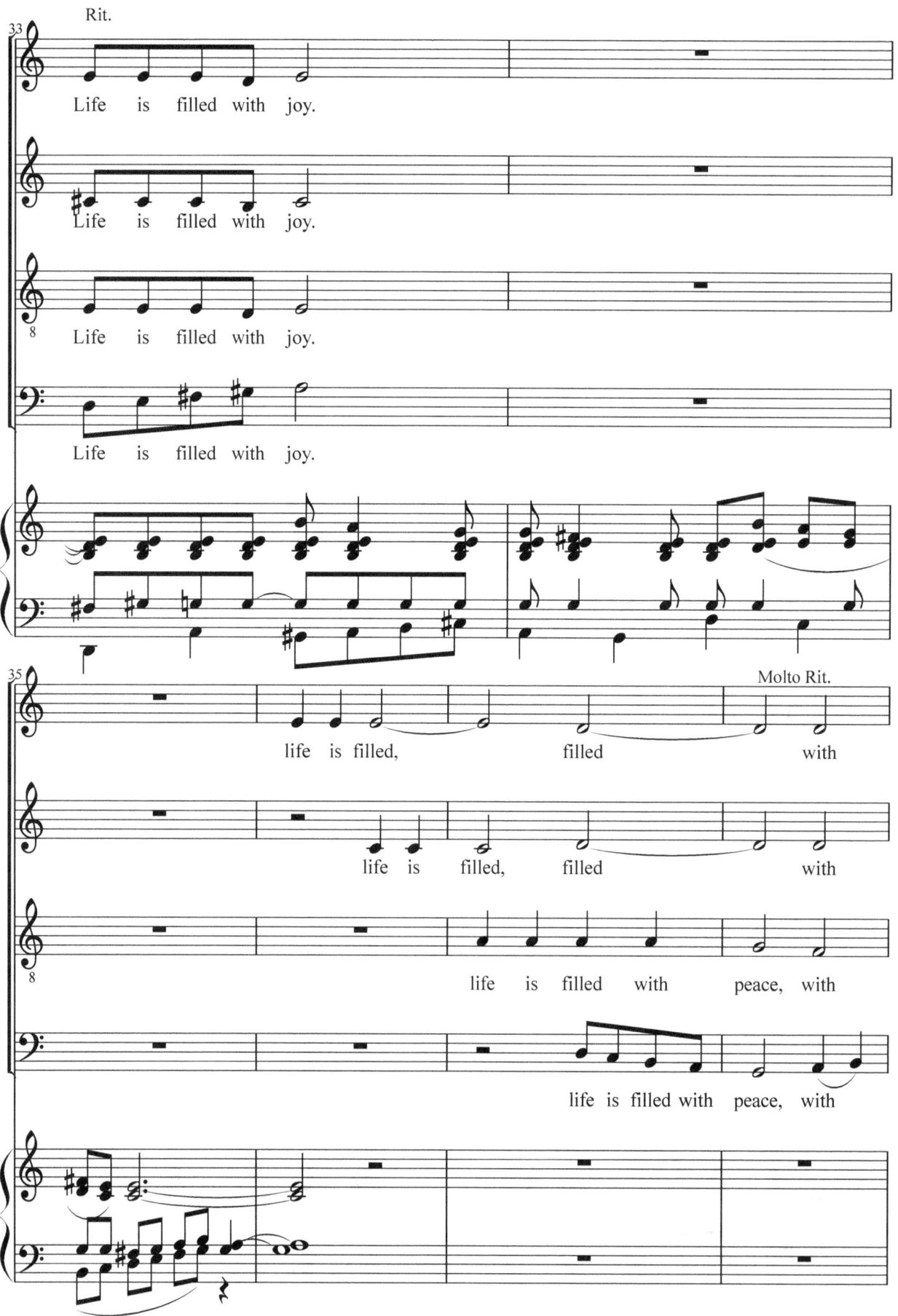

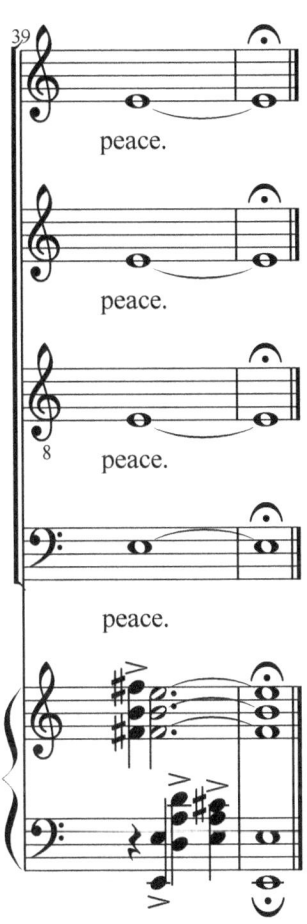

peace.

peace.

peace.

peace.

The Virtuous Person

The Analects of Confucius -xv.6

from "Spiritual Songs"

Ken Langer

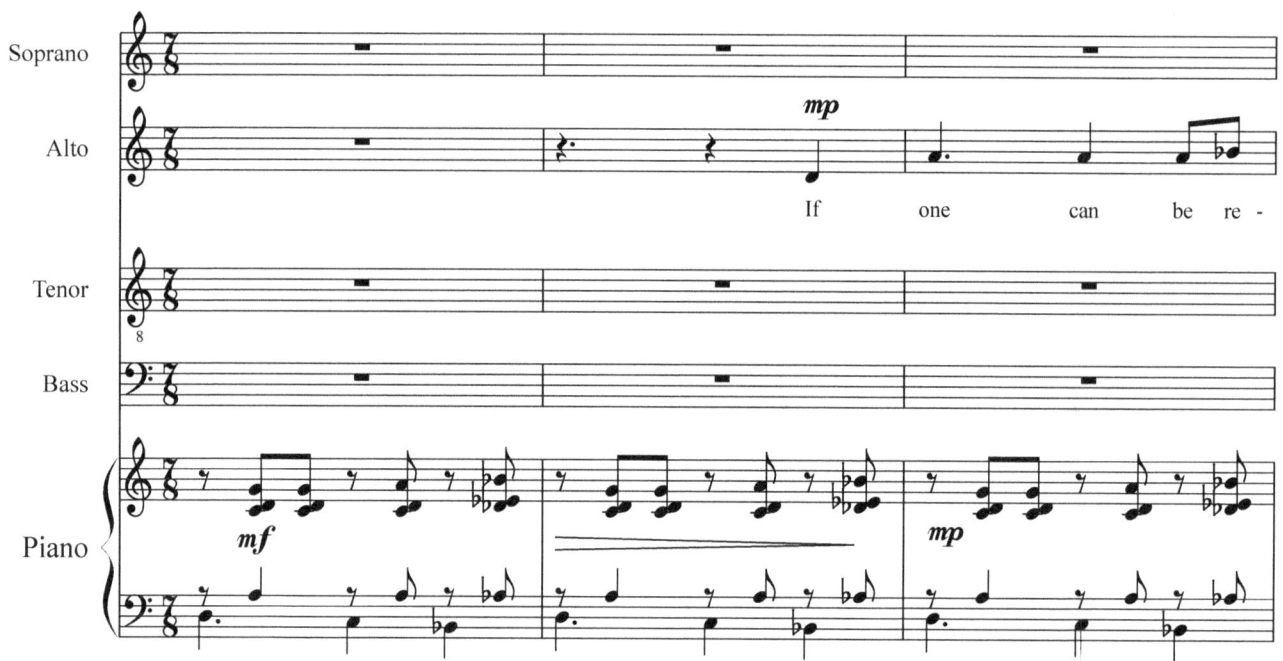

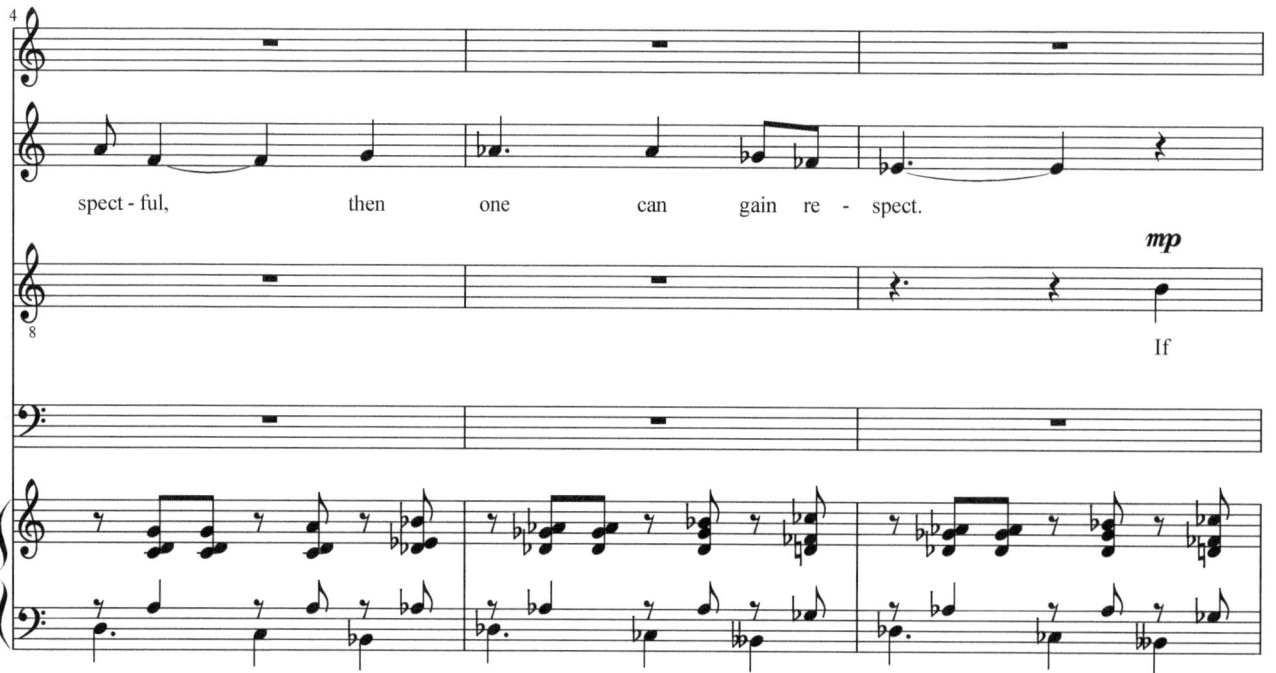

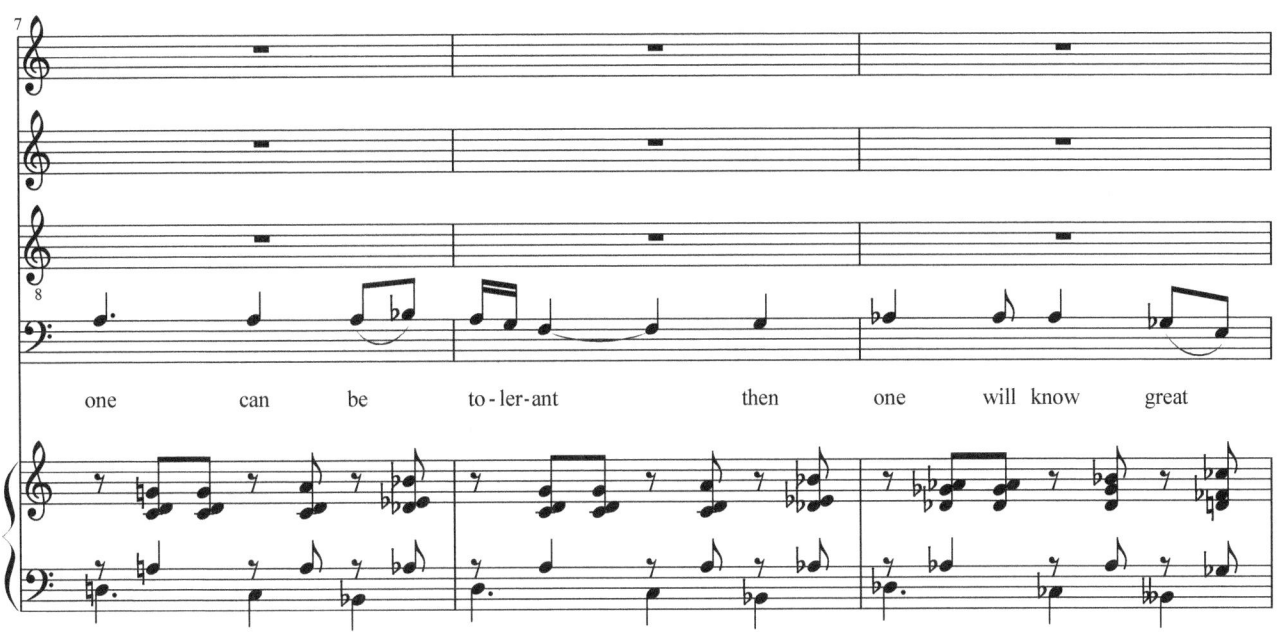

one can be to-ler-ant then one will know great

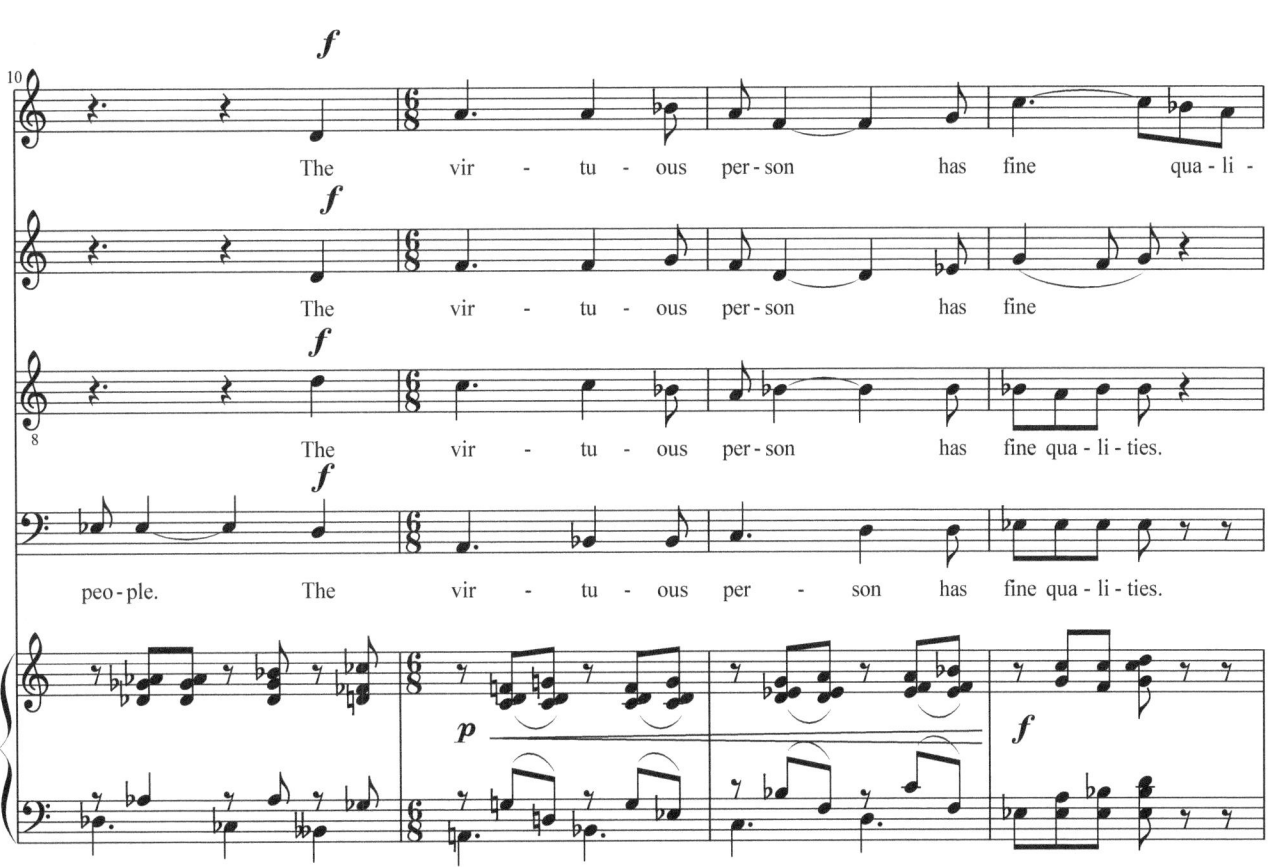

The vir-tu-ous per-son has fine qua-li-

The vir-tu-ous per-son has fine

The vir-tu-ous per-son has fine qua-li-ties.

peo-ple. The vir-tu-ous per-son has fine qua-li-ties.

97

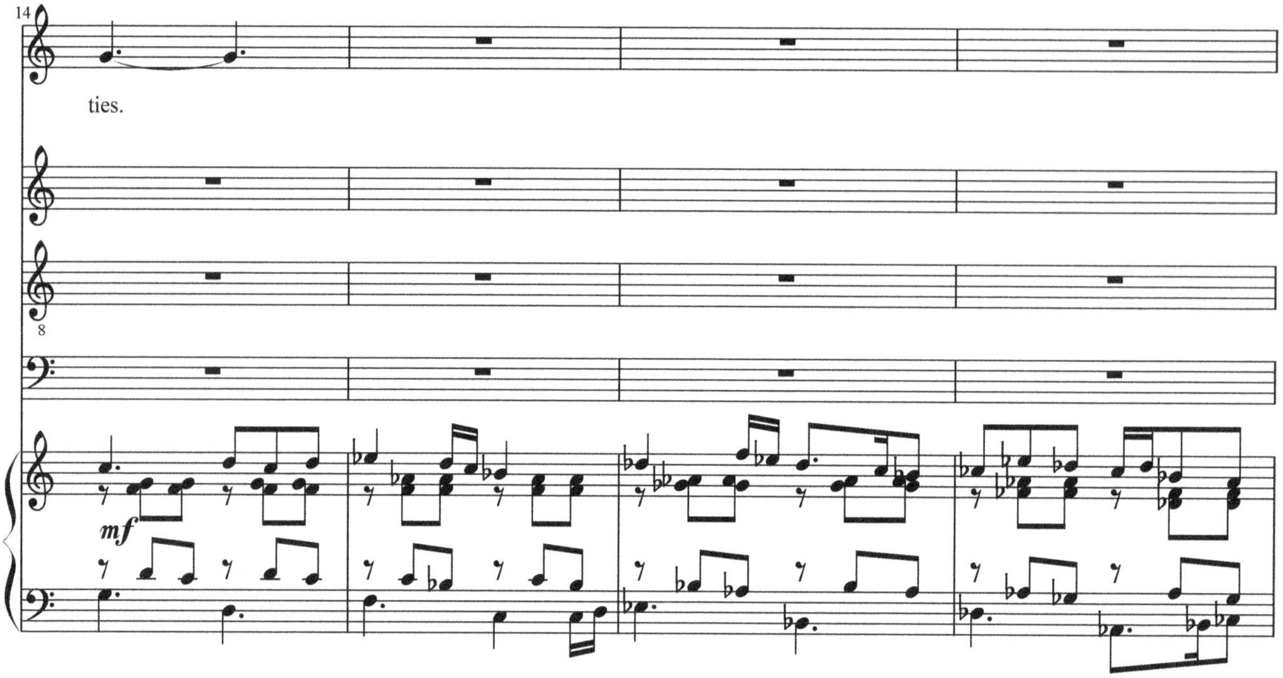

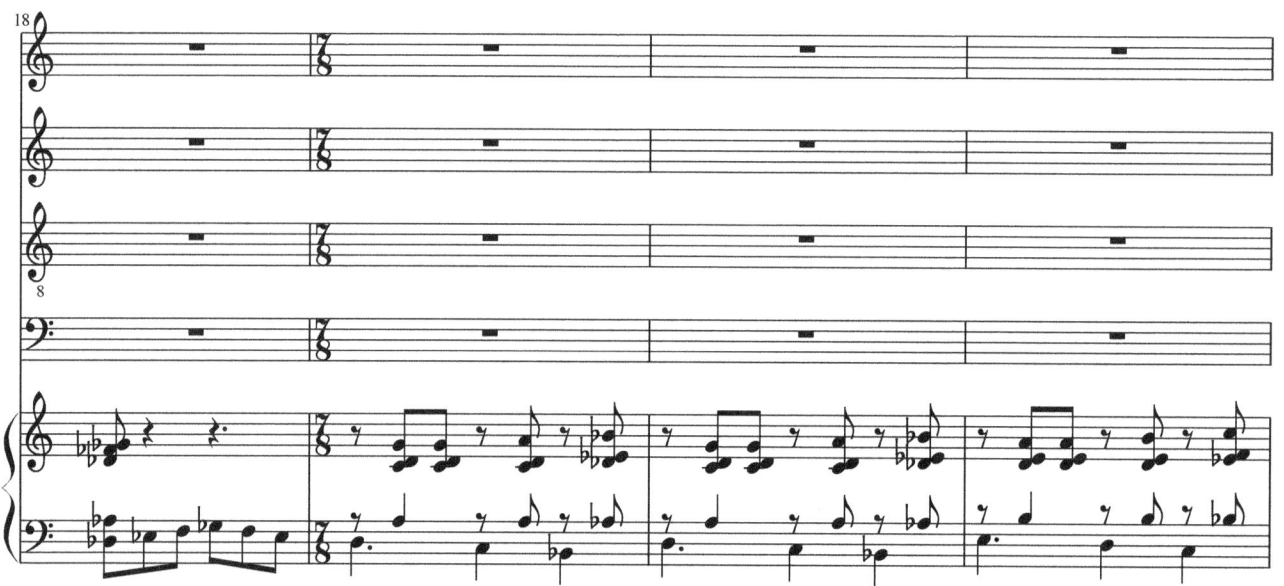

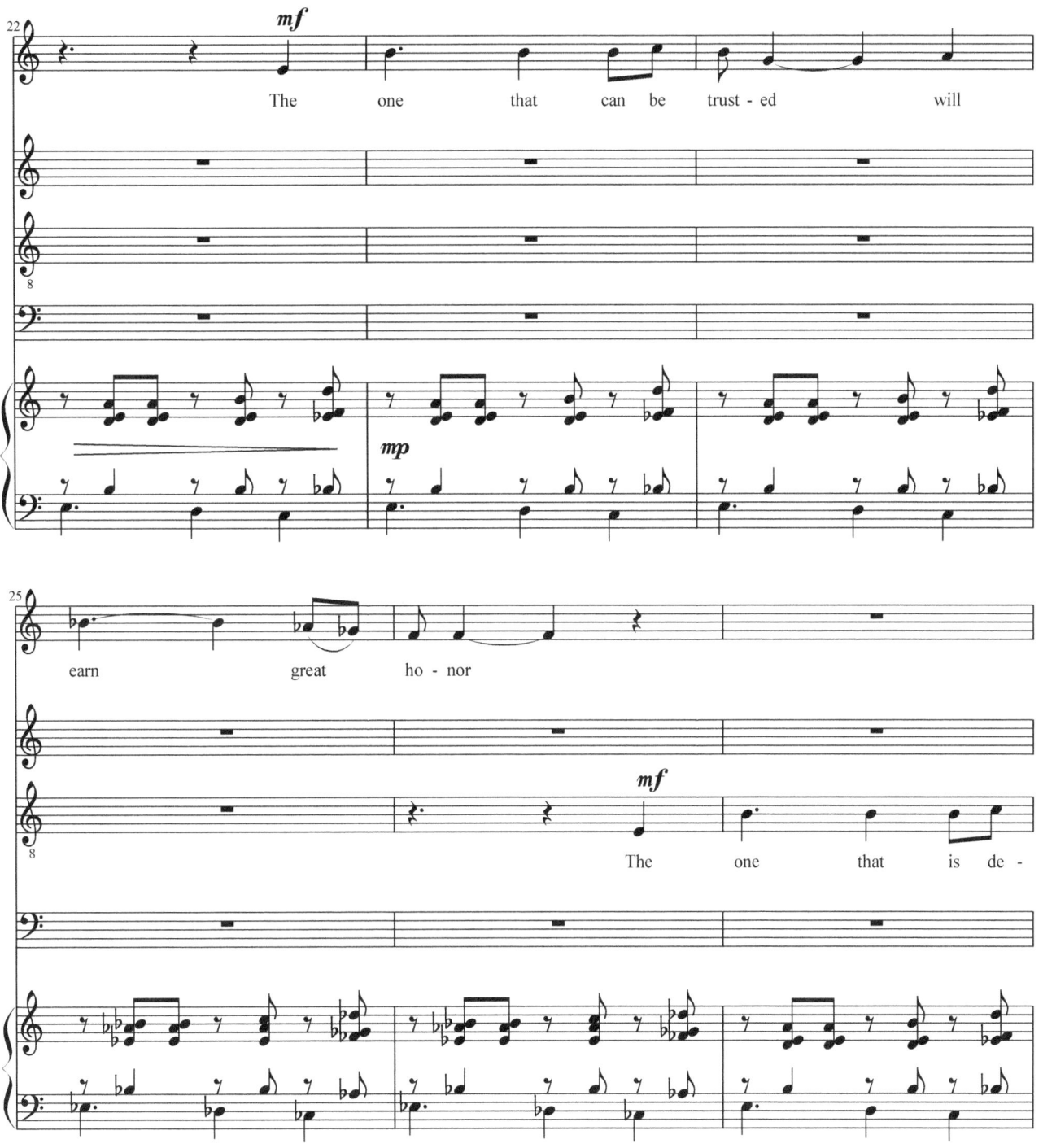

Lyrics:
The one that can be trust-ed will earn great ho-nor The one that is de-

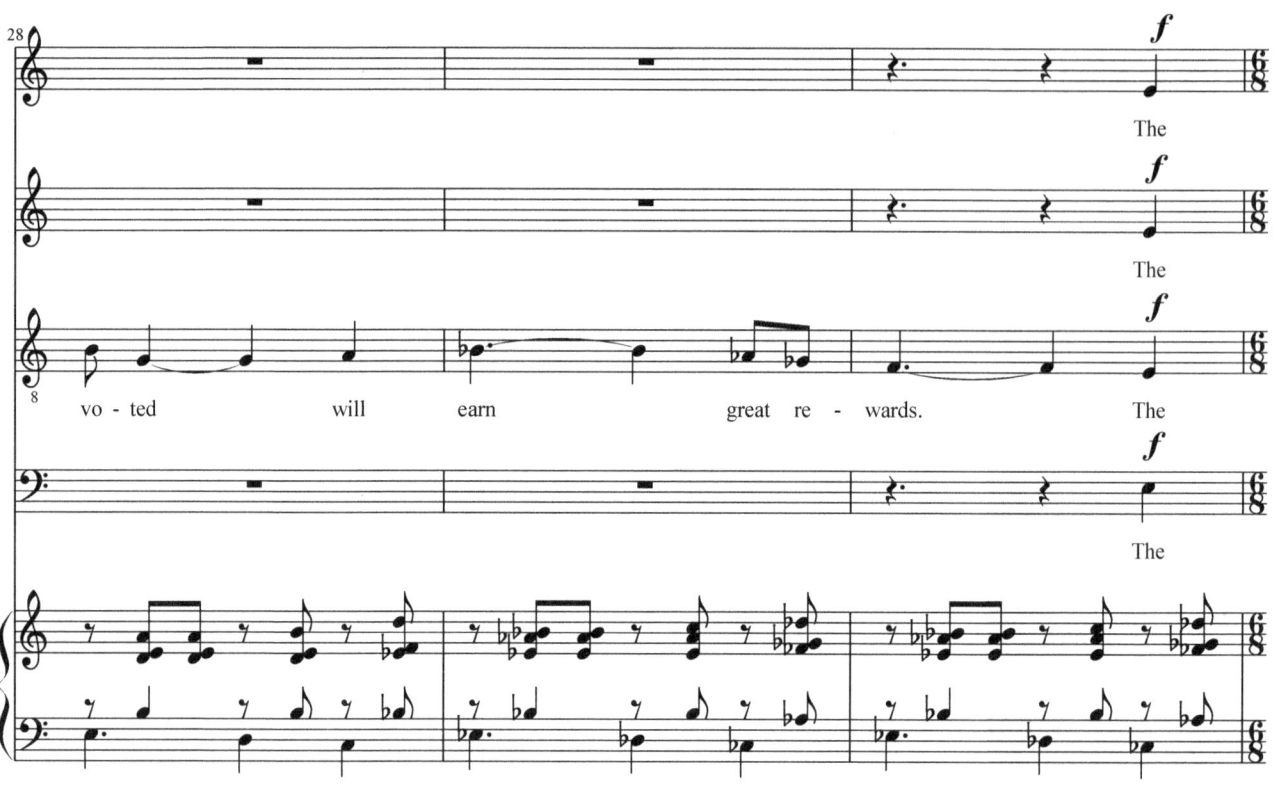

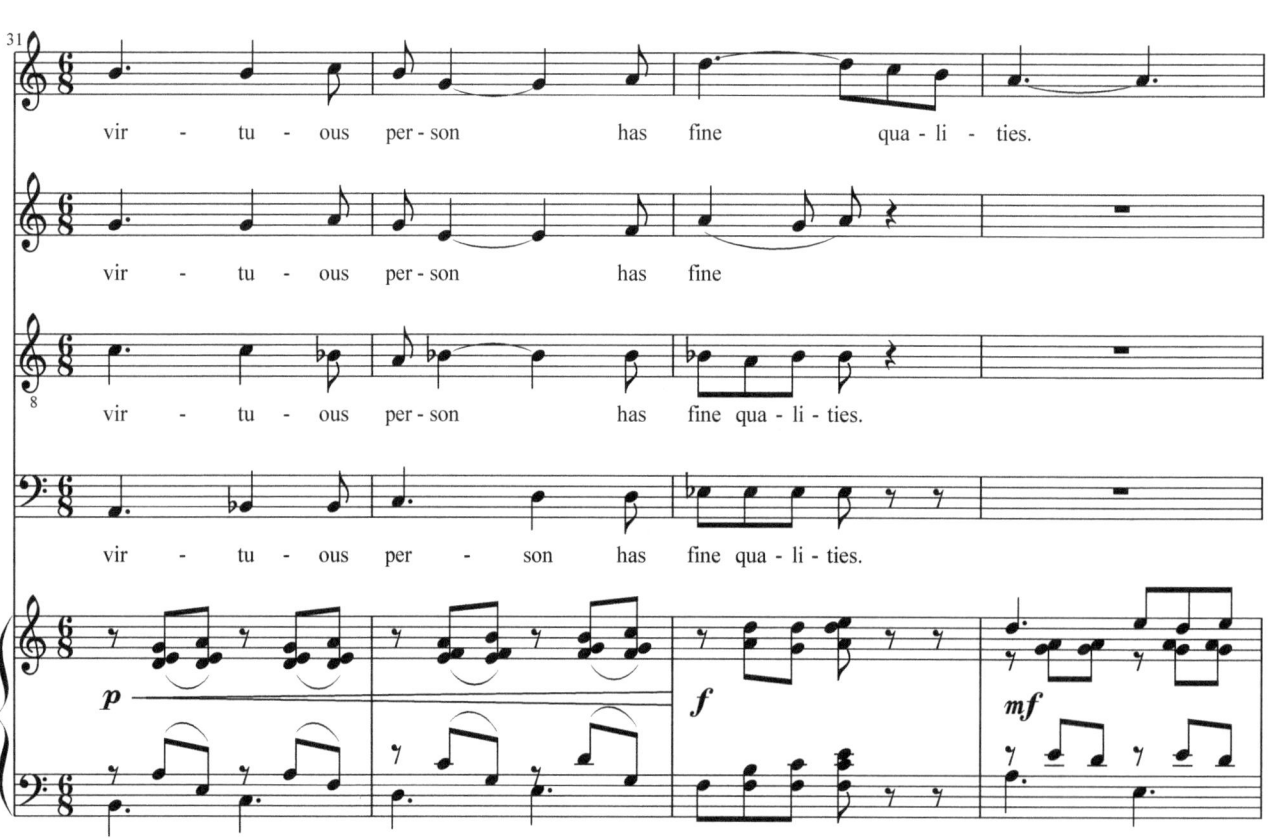

100

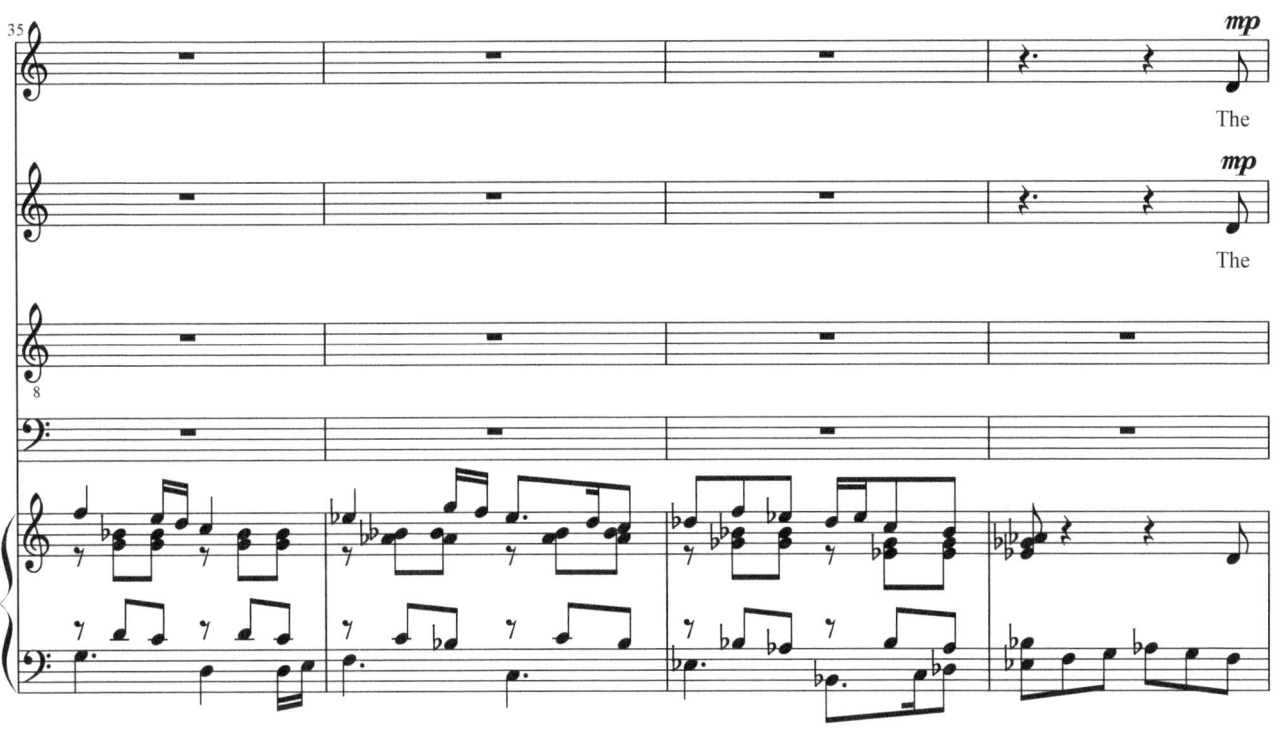

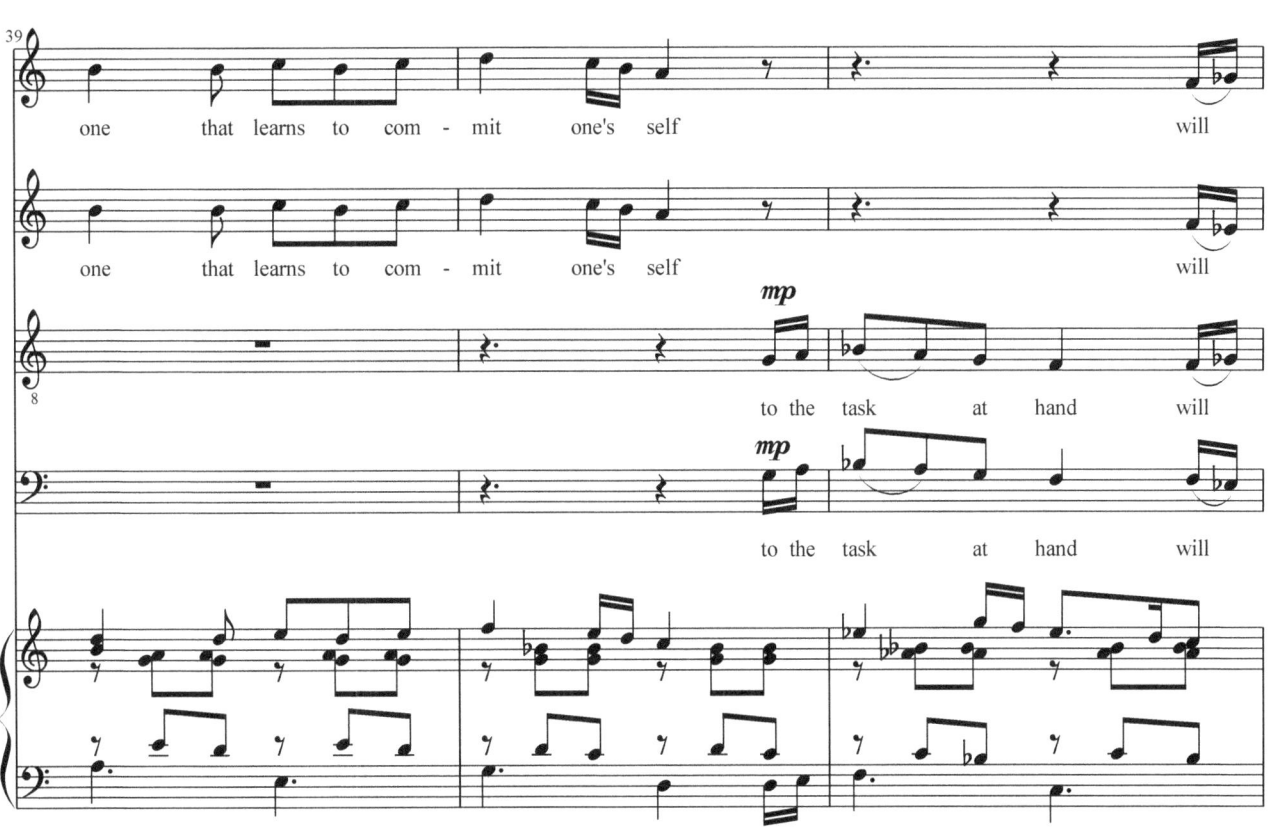

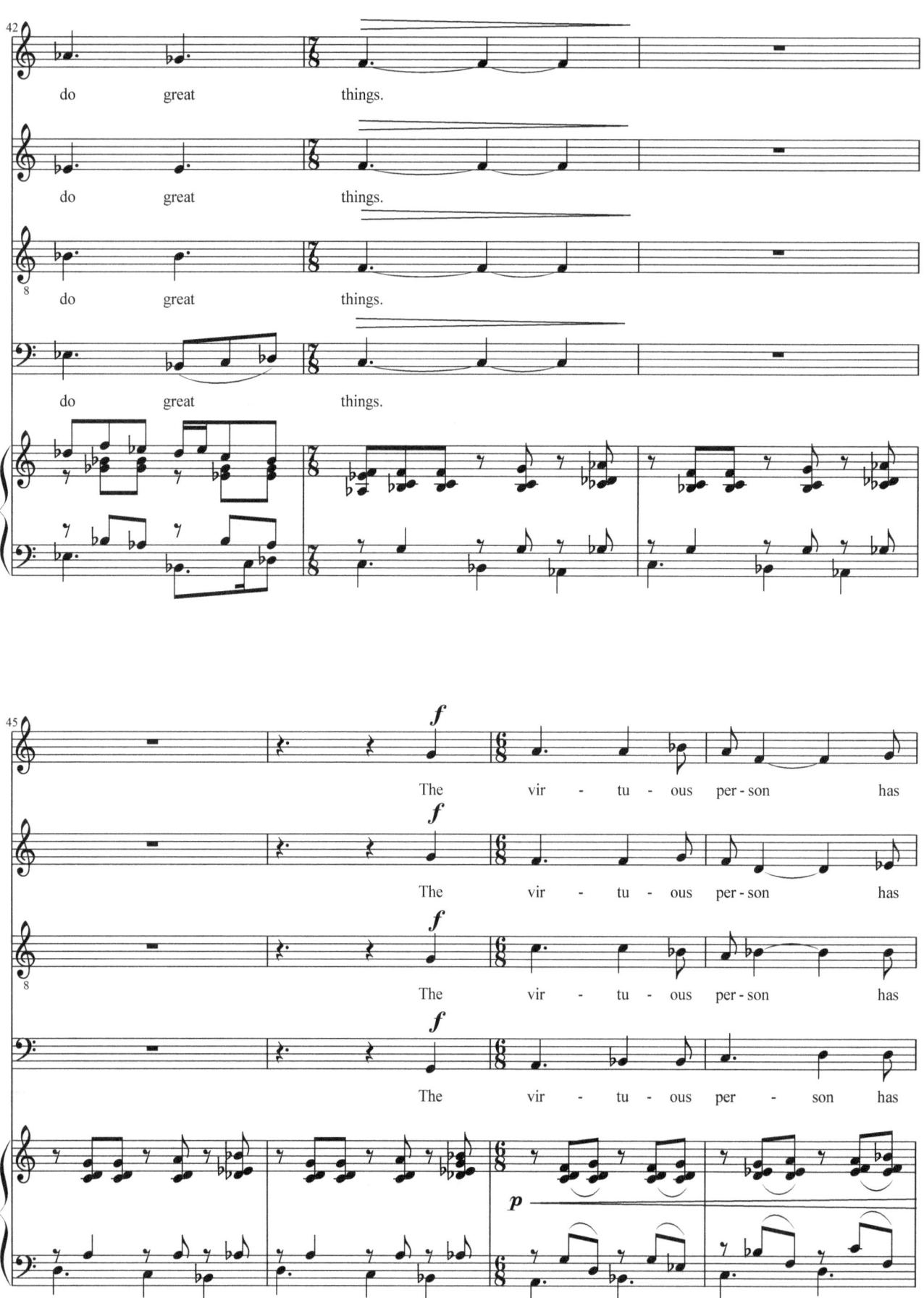

do great things.

do great things.

do great things.

do great things.

f

The vir - tu - ous per - son has

f

The vir - tu - ous per - son has

f

The vir - tu - ous per - son has

f

The vir - tu - ous per - son has

p

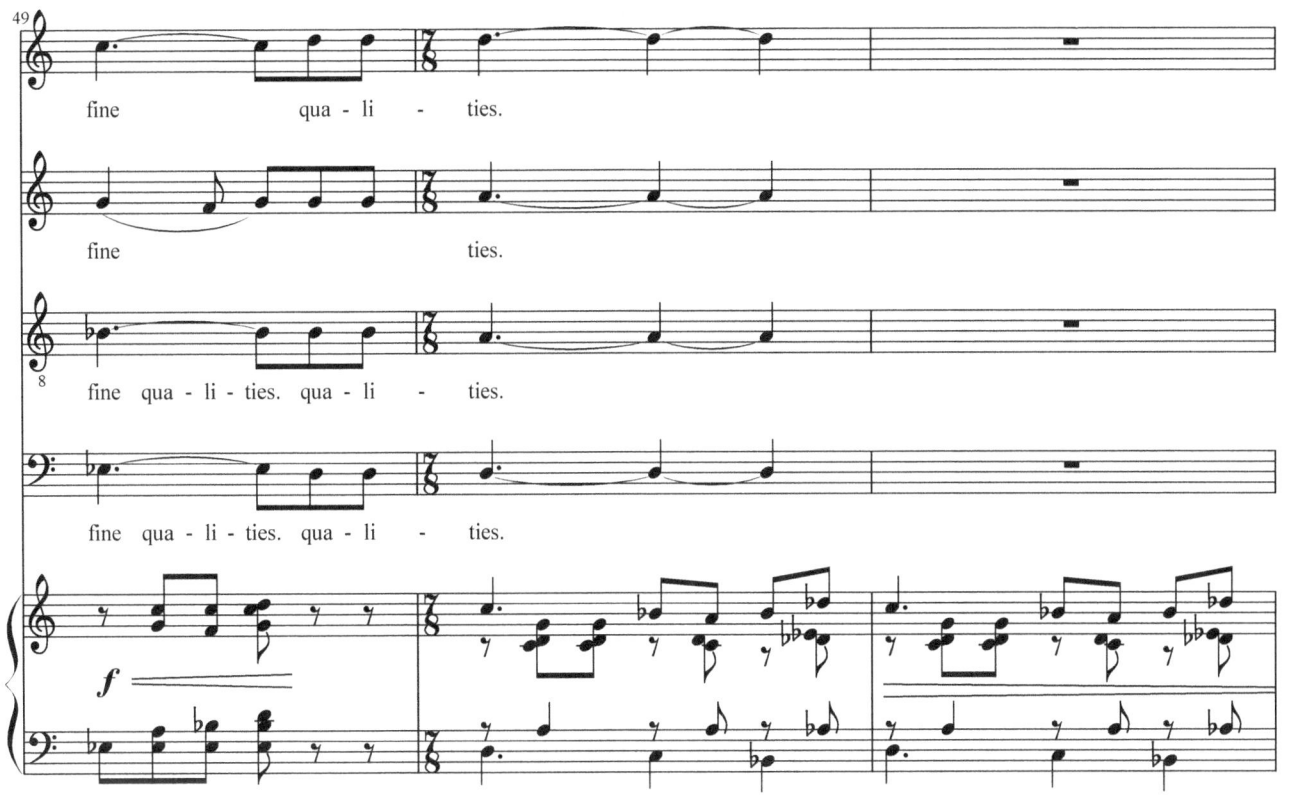

fine qua-li - ties.

fine ties.

fine qua - li - ties. qua - li - ties.

fine qua - li - ties. qua - li - ties.

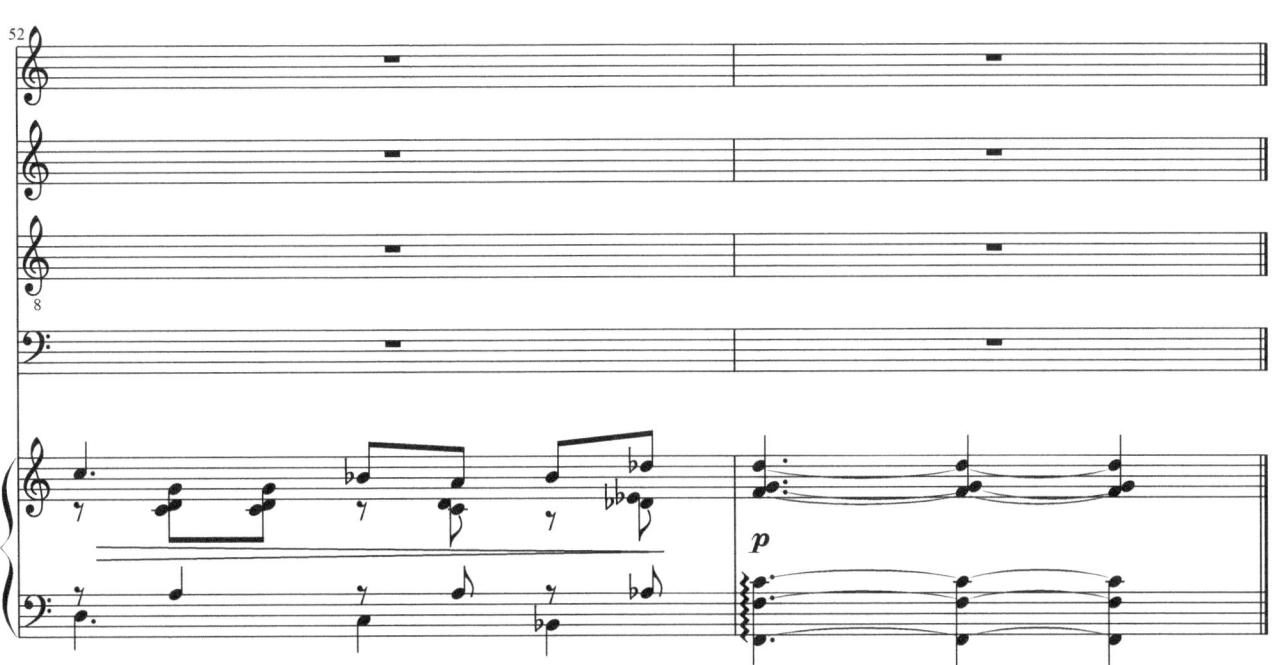

You Are That

(from The Bhagavad Gita)

from "Spiritual Songs"

Ken Langer

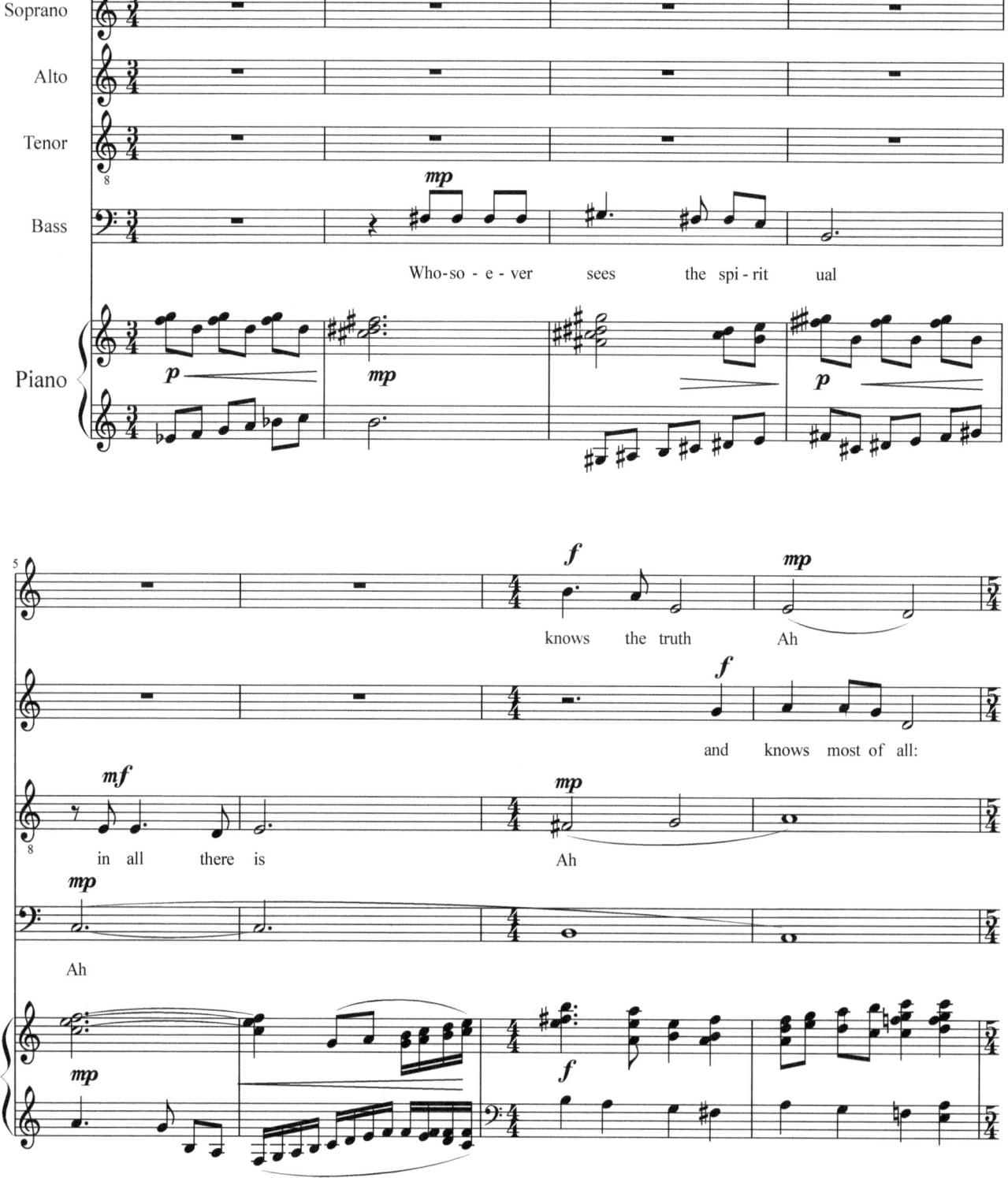

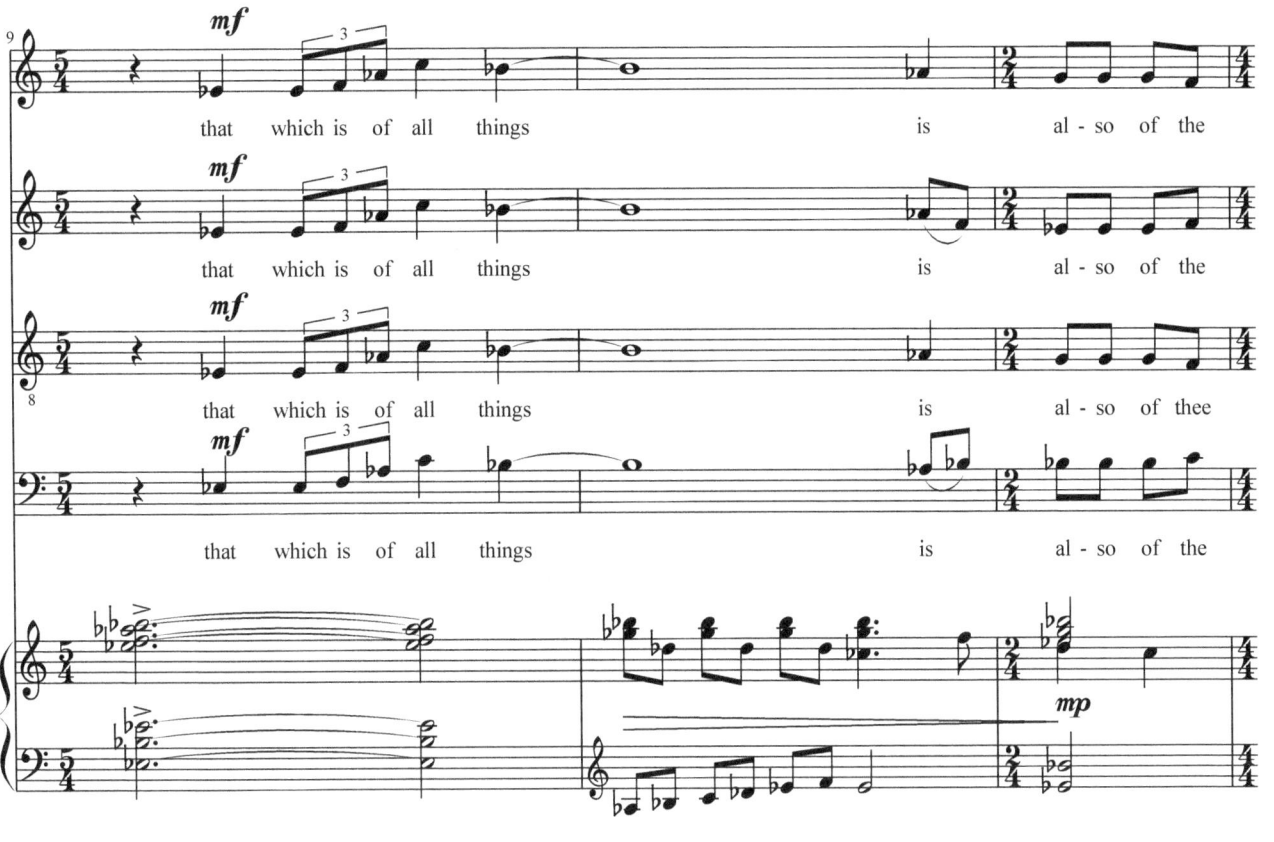

that which is of all things   is   al - so of the

that which is of all things   is   al - so of the

that which is of all things   is   al - so of thee

that which is of all things   is   al - so of the

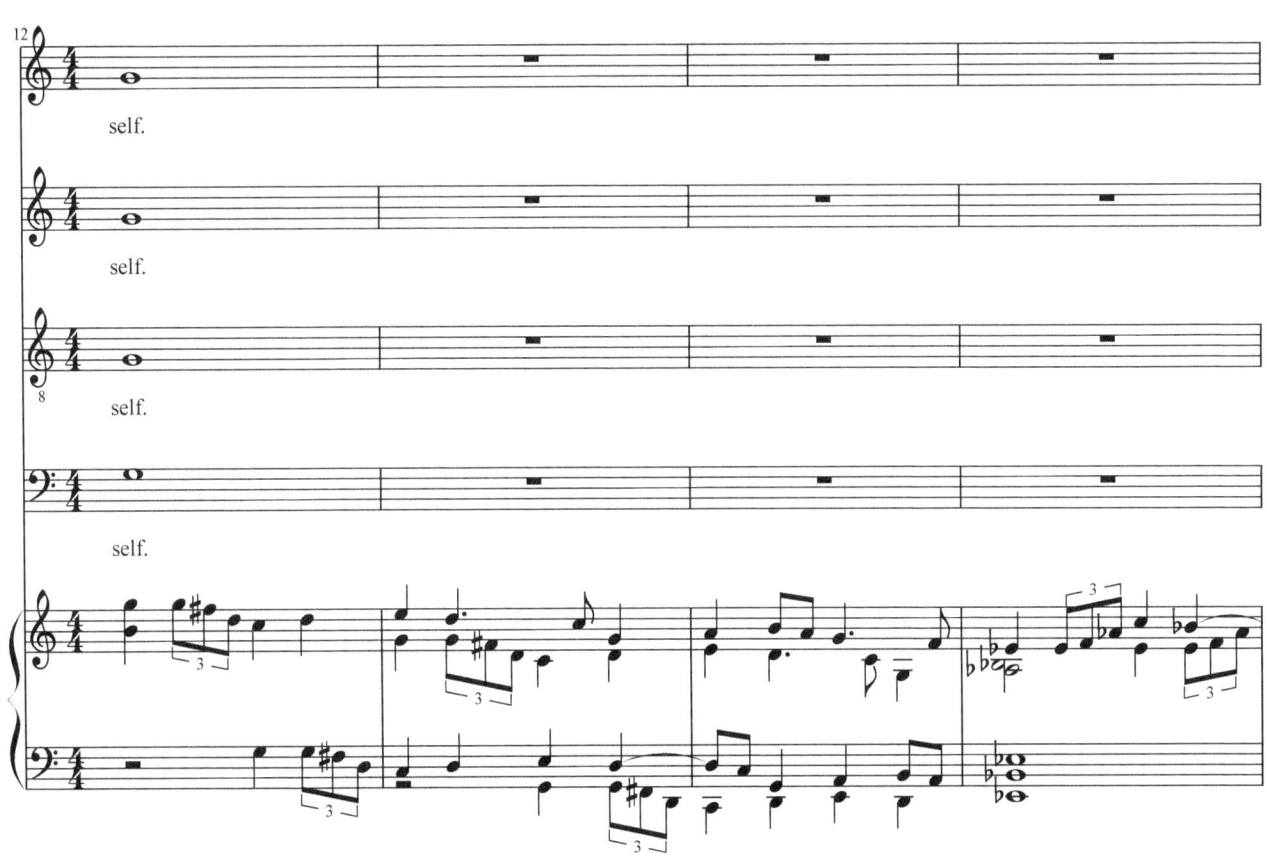

self.

self.

self.

self.

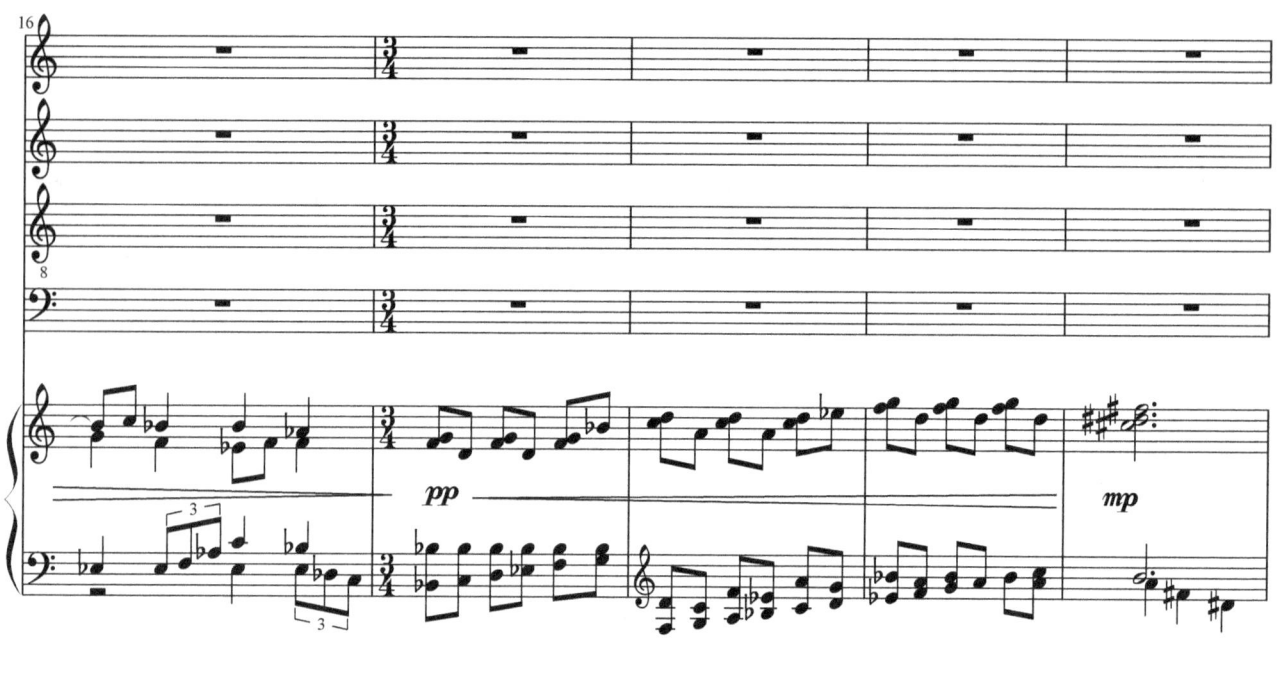

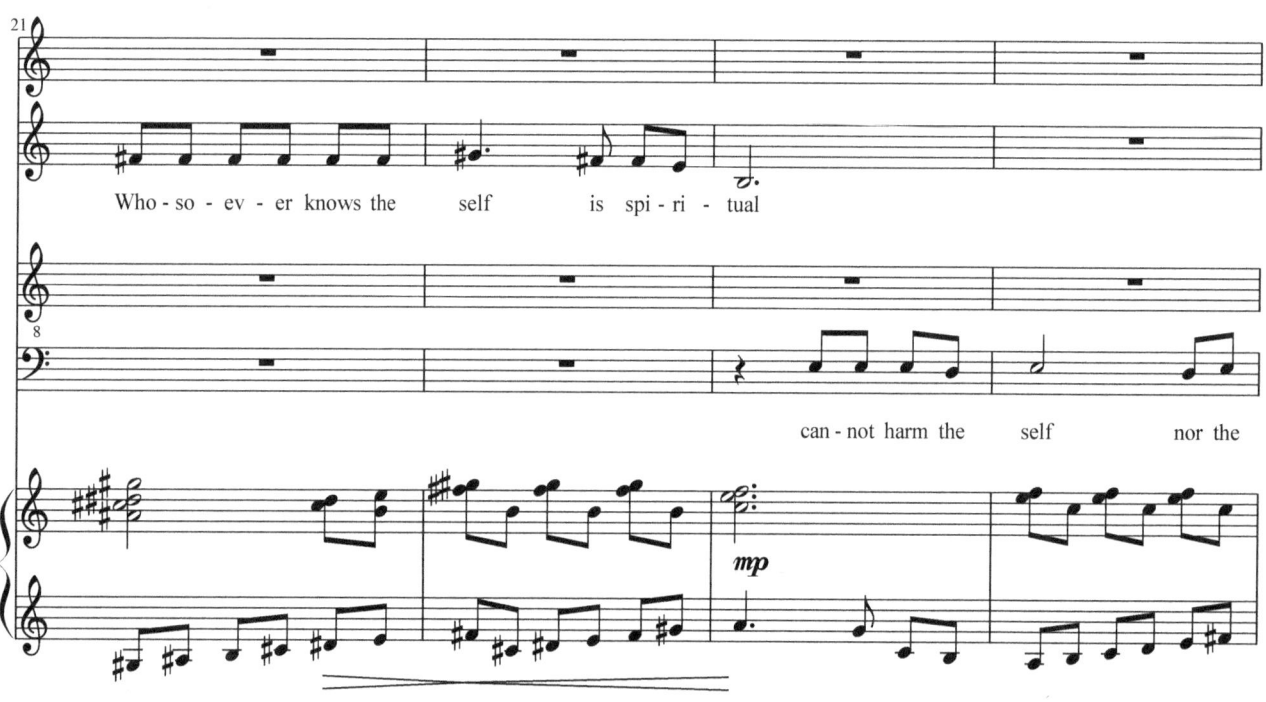

Who - so - ev - er knows the self is spi - ri - tual

can - not harm the self nor the

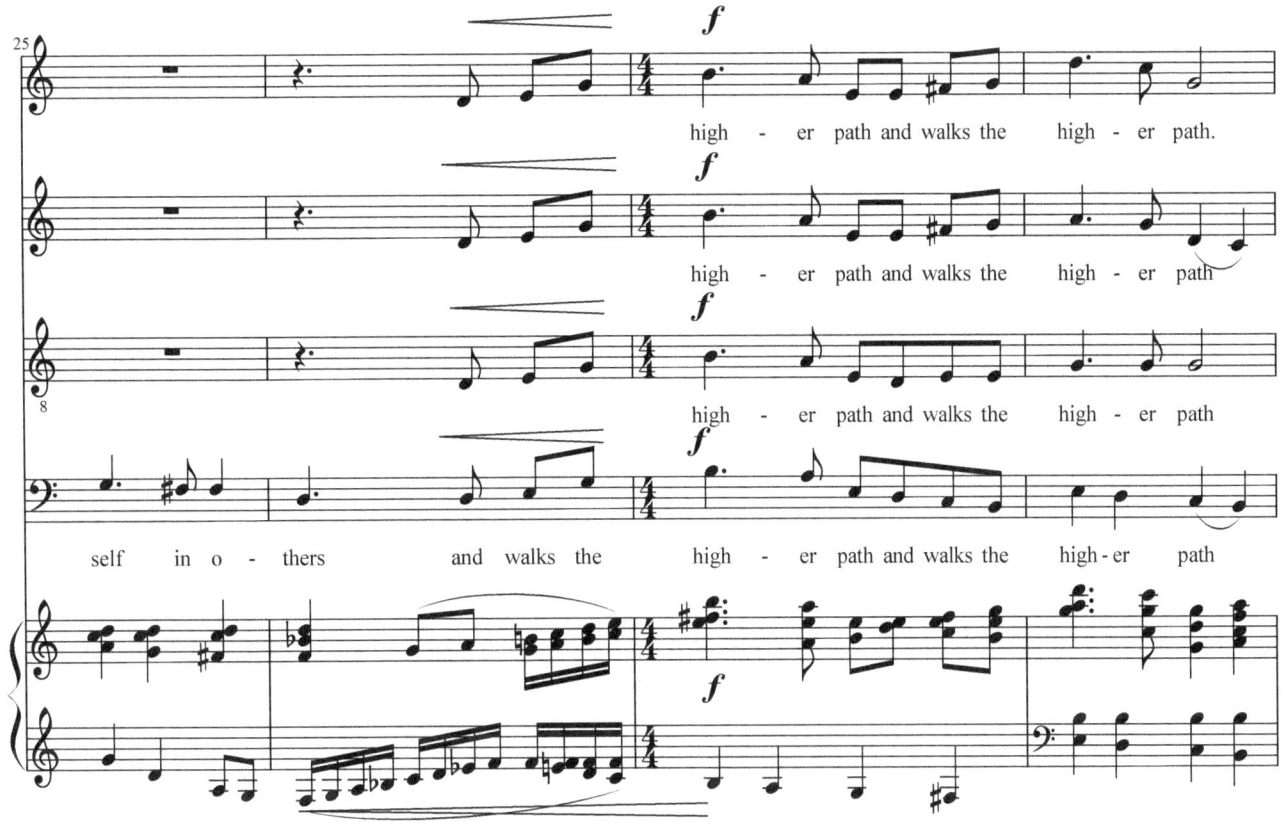

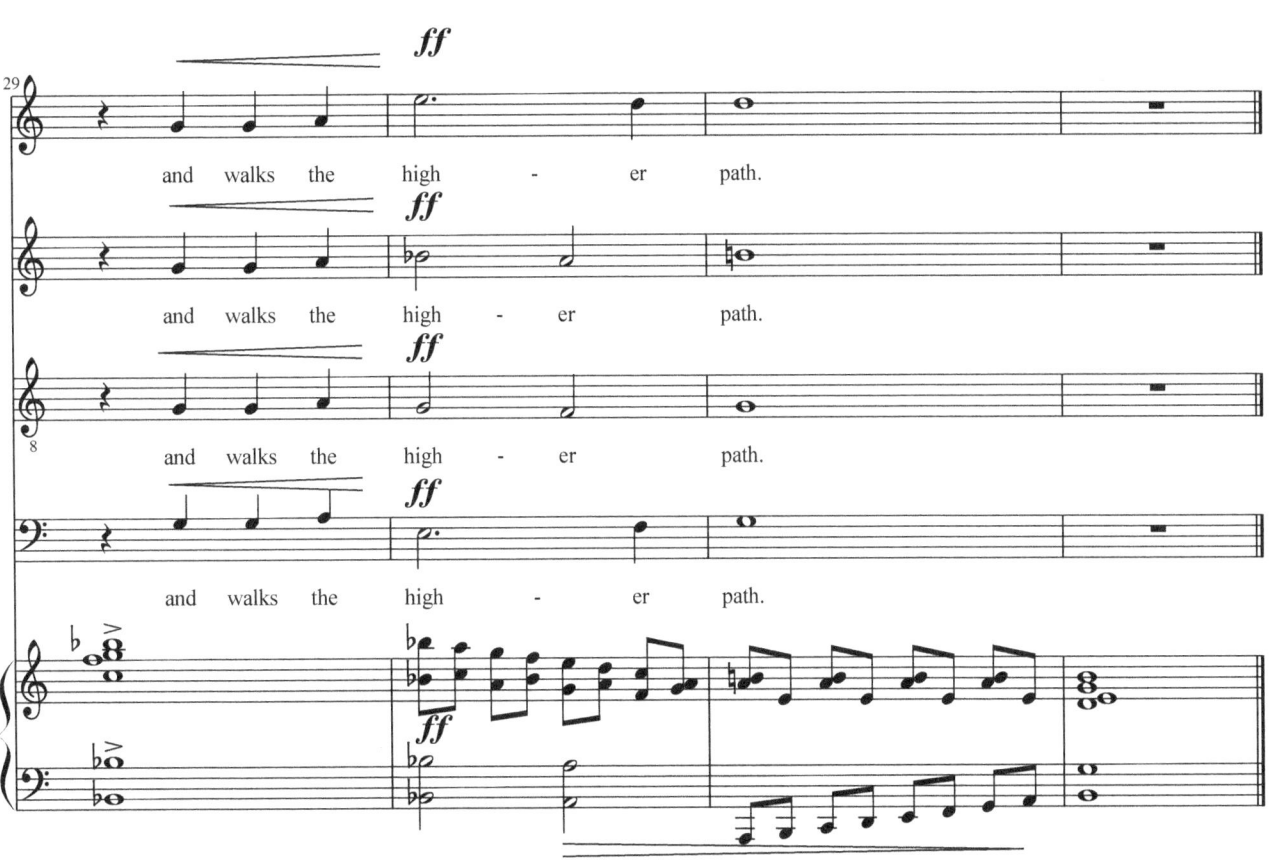

About The Composer

Dr. Kenneth Langer was born in the Pittsburgh area in 1959. He began playing trumpet in the 5th grade and decided in high school to make music his career.

Dr. Langer earned a Bachelor's Degree in Music Education at James Madison University in Harrisonburg, Virginia; a Master's of Music Degree at Radford University in Radford, Virginia; and a Ph.D. In Music Theory and Composition at Kent State University in Kent, Ohio. Since that time, he has taught music at several small colleges.

He has also been the full-time Director of Music and Arts at the Eno River Unitarian-Universalist Fellowship in Durham, North Carolina and the Assistant Conductor and Resident Composer at the Montpelier Unitarian-Universalist Church in Montpelier, Vermont.

During his twenty years of writing over 150 original works of music for various genres including brass, chorus, strings, orchestra, wind ensemble, and woodwinds; he has received numerous awards for his compositions including being named Vermont's Composer of the Year in the year 2000 and winning placement in several international composition contests. He has commercially published well over 30 compositions.

Dr. Langer currently lives in the Boston area with his family where he works as the Head of the Music Program at Northern Essex Community College in Haverhill, Massachusetts.

Publishers

Music For Brass

Nichols Music Company (Ensemble Publications)
P.O. Box 32 Ithaca, NY 14851-0032
www.enspub.com

Solid Brass Music
P.O. Box 2277 Rome GA, 30164
www.solidbrassmusic.com

Cimarron Music Press
15 Corrina Lane Salem CT 06420s
www.cimarronmusic.com

Wehr's Music House
www.wehrs-music-house.com

Music For Chorus

Yelton Rhodes Music
1236 N. Sweetzer Avenue #5 West Hollywood CA 90069
www.yrmusic.com